The Editor

DEBORAH LUTZ is the Thruston B. Morton Endowed Chair of English at the University of Louisville. Her books include *The Brontë Cabinet: Three Lives in Nine Objects* and *Relics of Death in Victorian Literature and Culture.* She is editor of the Fourth Norton Critical Edition of Charlotte Brontë's *Jane Eyre.*

A NORTON CRITICAL EDITION

Robert Louis Stevenson

STRANGE CASE OF DR. JEKYLL AND MR. HYDE

AN AUTHORITATIVE TEXT
CONTEXTS
CRITICISM

SECOND EDITION

Edited by

DEBORAH LUTZ
UNIVERSITY OF LOUISVILLE

W. W. NORTON & COMPANY
Independent Publishers Since 1923

W. W. Norton & Company has been independent since its founding in 1923, when William Warder Norton and Mary D. Herter Norton first published lectures delivered at the People's Institute, the adult education division of New York City's Cooper Union. The firm soon expanded its program beyond the Institute, publishing books by celebrated academics from America and abroad. By midcentury, the two major pillars of Norton's publishing program—trade books and college texts—were firmly established. In the 1950s, the Norton family transferred control of the company to its employees, and today—with a staff of five hundred and hundreds of trade, college, and professional titles published each year—W. W. Norton & Company stands as the largest and oldest publishing house owned wholly by its employees.

Manufacturing by Maple Press
Book design by Antonina Krass
Production manager: Stephen Sajdak

Library of Congress Cataloging-in-Publication Data

Names: Stevenson, Robert Louis, 1850–1894, author. | Lutz, Deborah, editor.
Title: Strange case of Dr. Jekyll and Mr. Hyde : an authoritative text,
    contexts, criticism / Robert Louis Stevenson ; edited by Deborah Lutz,
    University of Louisville.
Description: Second edition. | New York, N.Y. : W. W. Norton & Company,
    2020. | Series: A Norton critical edition | Includes bibliographical references.
Identifiers: LCCN 2020016854 | ISBN 9780393679212 (paperback)
Subjects: LCSH: Stevenson, Robert Louis, 1850–1894. Strange case of
    Dr. Jekyll and Mr. Hyde. | GSAFD: Gothic fiction.
Classification: LCC PR5485.A2 L56 2020 | DDC 823/.8—dc23
LC record available at https://lccn.loc.gov/2020016854

ISBN: 978-0-393-67921-2 (pbk.)

W. W. Norton & Company, Inc., 500 Fifth Avenue, New York, N.Y. 10110
    www.wwnorton.com
W. W. Norton & Company Ltd., 15 Carlisle Street, London W1D 3BS

1 2 3 4 5 6 7 8 9 0

Contents

Criticism 113

Acknowledgments

I am indebted to previous editors of Stevenson's novella, especially Katherine Linehan, Jenni Calder, Martin Danahay, Roger Luckhurst, and Richard Drury. I am grateful to the staff at the Morgan Library, especially John Vincler and Maria Isabel Molestina-Kurlat; to Special Collections at Princeton's Firestone Library; to the friendly librarians at the Beinecke at Yale for bringing out many bits of Stevensoniana to show me. At the University of Louisville, I thank my research assistants Kelly Carty and Carter Reid Elsea; the Thruston B. Morton endowment, which made travel to see the manuscripts possible; and Glynis Ridley, the chair of the English Department. For providing comments on an early version of the introduction, I thank Susan Ryan, Ellen Rosenman, Mary Jean Corbett, and Nancy Henry. At W. W. Norton, my warm thanks go to Carol Bemis, Thea Goodrich, and Rachel Goodman for their generous assistance. This book is dedicated to Wayne Koestenbaum for his abundance and his early and continued influence on my work.

A Note on the Text

The text used for this Norton Critical Edition is that of the first British edition, published on January 9, 1886 by Longmans, Green, and Co., for which Robert Louis Stevenson read and corrected the page proofs. A few obvious misprints have been silently corrected, and the punctuation of the quotations has been Americanized.

Illustrations

Introduction

Robert Louis Stevenson believed in the usefulness of dreams. He was proven right when he awoke one night, in 1885, with the idea for his Jekyll and Hyde tale. It came as a great gift. "I was very hard up for money, and I felt I had to do something. I thought and thought, and tried hard to find a subject to write about. At night I dreamed the story, not precisely as it is written . . . all I dreamed about Dr. Jekyll was that one man was being pressed into a cabinet, when he swallowed a drug and changed into another being."[1] His wife, Fanny, roused him from this nightmare, and he said angrily, "Why did you wake me? I was dreaming a fine boguey tale."[2] No wonder the story has a fever-dream atmosphere, clutching one like a nightmare up to the end. Stevenson himself felt this way about the best sort of reading. After finishing Fyodor Dostoevsky's *Crime and Punishment*, he wrote to one friend, "it is not reading a book, it is having a brain fever, to read it," and to another, "it was like having an illness . . . it is a room, a house of life, into which they [the reader] themselves enter, and are tortured or purified."[3]

Sleep had always been a problem for Stevenson. A "professional sickist," as he called himself, he suffered from serious illness throughout his life, especially from a lung condition that brought on severe hemorrhaging.[4] Insomnia struck often, and we have many descriptions of him writing in bed. As a child, fevers led to "terrible long nights, that I lay awake, troubled continually with a hacking, exhausting cough, and praying for sleep or morning from the bottom of my shaken little body."[5] Given various drugs to sleep, Stevenson would later graduate to stronger ones like morphine. (In this light, the character Jekyll, a doctor who invents a drug to help him

1. Quoted in J. A. Hammerton, *Stevensoniana: An Anecdotal Life and Appreciation of Robert Louis Stevenson* (J. Grant, 1907), pp. 84–85.
2. Graham Balfour, *The Life of Robert Louis Stevenson* (Scribner's, 1901), vol. 2, pp. 15–17. See the excerpt in the Composition section of this Norton Critical Edition.
3. *The Letters of Robert Louis Stevenson*, ed. Bradford A. Booth and Ernest Mehew (Yale UP, 1995), vol. 5, pp. 151, 221.
4. Quoted in Claire Harman, *Myself and the Other Fellow: A Life of Robert Louis Stevenson* (Harper Collins, 2005), p. 207.
5. Stevenson, "Memoirs of Himself," *Collected Works*, Vailima Edition (Scribner's, 1923), vol. 26, pp. 215–16.

escape from himself, is addicted.)[6] Stevenson's childhood night terrors had a religious flavor, probably because his nurse, Alison Cun-
ningham, impressed on him her Calvinistic belief in mortal sin and
eternal damnation. She told him lurid stories of the devil, and he
read about Satan in popular Scottish folklore, learning that one
must continually strive against him lest he find an entrance. Even
though Stevenson lost his faith as an adult, he lends *Strange Case of
Dr. Jekyll and Mr. Hyde* a flavor of these early dreams of the devil,
with Dr. Jekyll creating a separate self to act on his transgressive
passions and to carry the sin. Many readers of Stevenson's time saw
Jekyll's doppelgänger, called Mr. Hyde, as a figure for the devil, and
preachers used the popular story in their sermons as a moral warning: degradation and ruin came from acting on one's unholy desires.

When Stevenson had his dream about Jekyll, he was in one of the
most stable periods of a life that, after childhood, had a rootless,
shambolic quality. Born into an established Scottish family in
Edinburgh, Stevenson was expected to follow the family trade and
become an engineer—his grandfather, father, and uncles built
lighthouses—but fairly early on he took up a bohemian existence.
He rebelled against his family's solid bourgeois ideals, spending
time with prostitutes, wearing velvet jackets and his hair long.
When living in France in his twenties in an artists' colony, he met
an American woman, ten years his senior, named Fanny Osbourne.
With two children and provisionally separated from her husband,
Fanny studied to be an artist. When Stevenson eventually married
her after her divorce, they settled down briefly in 1884 in a house
his family bought for them in Bournemouth, on the southern coast
of England. They called it Skerryvore, after a family-built lighthouse. He had already published *Treasure Island* in 1881 as a serial
in a boys' magazine, but it wouldn't make him famous (and bring in
much-needed money) until after it came out in book form, at the
end of 1883. The one-legged Long John Silver, with his parrot on
his shoulder and his rum drinking, was worlds away from the
sophisticated professional men in the late-Victorian London of
Jekyll and Hyde, published in January 1886. Yet the characters
shared in Stevenson's wanderlust, whether on a ship looking for
buried treasure or in a modern city, walking the streets at night
spoiling for adventure.

During the three years he and Fanny spent at Skerryvore, Stevenson had many writing projects on the boil at once, including *Kidnapped,* another boys' tale first published serially. Cultivating his
great talent for friendship, he formed a lifelong bond with the writer

6. See, for instance, Thomas L. Reed, *The Transforming Draught: Jekyll and Hyde, Robert
Louis Stevenson and the Victorian Alcohol Debate* (McFarland, 2006).

Cover of first British paper-covered edition, January 1886. (Note the publisher's pen-and-ink alteration of the date, from 1885 to 1886.) Courtesy of the Harry Elkins Widener Collection, Houghton Library of the Harvard College Library. HEW 10.10.21.

Henry James, despite an inauspicious beginning six years earlier, when James had found Stevenson "a shirt-collarless bohemian and a great deal (in an inoffensive way) of a *poseur*."[7] Just before Stevenson began writing *Jekyll and Hyde*, the artist John Singer Sargent painted him pacing in the Skerryvore dining room, Fanny sitting in a chair in a diaphanous dress and scarf. Men who gathered round him found his attractions almost mesmeric. Stevenson possessed, said one, "more than any man I ever met, the power of making other men fall in love with him."[8] There is no proof that Stevenson ever had sex with men, and his relationship with Fanny remained close, if complicated. But his biographer Claire Harman notes that his dress and gestures echoed those of "Uranians" or "inverts"—that is, homosexuals.[9] A homosocialism permeates *Jekyll and Hyde*, as it does many of his stories. In a world of bachelor men and their close circle of male clubs, women are excluded entirely. This was never exactly Stevenson's own way, but his intimacy with his male friends remained a grounding center of his identity. After *Jekyll and Hyde* was published, some of Stevenson's gay contemporaries found it alarming. One way of reading Jekyll's unspecified desires, so overwhelming that he must act on them, but so shameful that he turns himself into a different person to do it, could include sex with other men.[1] Stevenson's friend John Addington Symonds, who struggled to suppress his own homosexual urges—longings considered sinful, degrading, and against nature to most of his contemporaries—wrote Stevenson that the story appalled him. It "touches one too closely," he said, "most of us at some epoch of our lives have been upon the verge of developing a Mr. Hyde."[2]

Much like his friend Symonds, who traveled widely and wrote about different cultures, Stevenson had a hard time staying put. At Skerryvore he felt like "a weevil in a biscuit," trapped in a too-calm surfeit.[3] Despite his chronic illness, restlessness was in his nature. Many of his books were travelogues, such as *Travels with a Donkey in the Cévennes, An Inland Voyage, The Amateur Emigrant,* and *The South Seas: A Record of Three Cruises.* He went on walking tours, canoe trips, and sea adventures on schooners, yachts, and other vessels. He lived in a miniature Swiss chalet in France, a cabin in the Adirondack Mountains in New York, a bunkhouse in an abandoned

7. Henry James, *The Letters of Henry James,* ed. Leon Edel (Harvard UP, 1975), vol. 2, p. 225.
8. Andrew Lang, *Adventures Among Books* (Longmans, Green, and Co., 1905), p. 51.
9. Harman, *Myself and the Other Fellow,* p. 213.
1. See, for instance, Elaine Showalter, *Sexual Anarchy: Gender and Culture at the Fin de Siècle* (Viking, 1990), chapter 6, excerpted in the Criticism section of this volume.
2. *The Letters of John Addington Symonds,* ed. Herbert M. Schueller and Robert L. Peters (Wayne State UP, 1969), vol. 3, p. 121.
3. *Letters,* vol. 5, p. 37.

John Singer Sargent's *Portrait of Robert Louis Stevenson and His Wife Fanny* (oil on canvas, 1885). Ian Dagnall/Alamy Stock Photo. Stevenson wrote of it in a letter to a friend, "It is, I think, excellent but it is too eccentric to be exhibited. . . . All this is touched in lovely, with that witty touch of Sargent's; but of course, it looks dam queer as a whole."[4]

silver mining camp on Mount Saint Helena in California, the village dwelling of a subchief in Tahiti, and a ramshackle house on an island in Samoa. One wonders: was he chasing something? Or did he feel pursued? Perhaps this need to be always on the hunt for new experiences grew from his heightened awareness of impending mortality. In a long letter to a friend, in part about the death of Stevenson's tutor, Fleeming Jenkin, of blood poisoning, he wrote that he didn't believe in the "immortality business," because

> the world would indeed be too good to be true; but we were put here to do what service we can, for honour and not for hire; the sods cover us, and the worm that never dies, the conscience, sleeps well at last: these are the wages, besides what we receive so lavishly day by day; and they are enough for a man who knows his own frailty and sees all things in the proportion of reality. . . . Happinesses are but his wayside campings; his

4. Quoted in Jenni Calder, *Robert Louis Stevenson: A Life Study* (Oxford UP, 1980), p. 22.

> soul is in the journey: he was born for the struggle and only
> tastes his life in effort and on the condition that he is opposed.[5]

Keeping his spirits high, facing the death always shadowing him
with a cheerful fatalism, Stevenson threw himself into the fray,
despite his broken-down body.

His stories hold this agitated, fretful quality. Pursuits fuel plots,
usually one man chasing after another, although the search for treasure or the truth structure a number of tales, most famously *Treasure Island*. In *Jekyll and Hyde*, the central character and detective
figure, Mr. Utterson, hunts down Hyde on the night streets of London in order to find out his (and Jekyll's) secret. Utterson, a respectable lawyer, thinks to himself at a critical juncture, "If he be
Mr. Hyde . . . I shall be Mr. Seek" (13).[6] This restlessness also
characterized his writing life. He often started working on books,
sometimes in collaboration with male friends, and only occasionally
had the patience to see them through to the end. Once the initial
idea was put down, he felt urged to move on. His surviving notebooks, journals, and papers have a harum-scarum quality, with doodles in the margins, missing pages, and a large number of unfinished
pieces. Even the now-precious manuscript of *Jekyll and Hyde* exists
only in incomplete drafts, possibly because of the author's disorga-
nized heedlessness. Much of the magic of the book's plot, split into
sections and never sticking with one narrator, comes from this
unsettling (and unsettled) quality. Starting from Utterson's point of
view, the story ends without it. The final unveiling of Jekyll's secrets
comes in a letter written by Jekyll himself telling the "full statement
of the case." The tale feels incomplete, as if one isn't reading a book,
but instead looking through a stack of papers with pages missing.
Bits of writing and documents litter the story, telling fragments of
the truth. A partial accounting of these papers: a large envelope containing a will handwritten by Jekyll, a note from Jekyll instructing
Utterson about the order in which to read other papers, a "considerable packet sealed in several places" (38) containing "Dr. Lanyon's
Narrative" and "Henry Jekyll's Full Statement of the Case," Jekyll's
notebook detailing his experiments, instructions to chemists, and
numerous curious letters. Stevenson's "strange case" broadcasts
itself as a material piece of writing that is being read—by Utterson,
by others, by us. He pays attention to paper, handwriting, signa-
tures, and jottings in the margins of books. In the final analysis,
there is no omniscient narrator handing down a truth, but only a
collection of impressions and personal experiences.

---

5. Letter to Edmund Gosse, January 2, 1886. *Letters*, vol. 5, p. 172.
6. All citations are from this Norton Critical Edition.

First page of the manuscript Stevenson sent to his printers. The deliberate dropping of "The" from the title, making it *Strange Case*—as Stevenson wrote on the title page of the final draft—rather than *The Strange Case*, gives it the immediacy of a newspaper headline, as do a number of his section headings, such as "Remarkable Incident of Dr. Lanyon." The Morgan Library & Museum, New York, NY. MA 628. Purchased by Pierpont Morgan, 1909. Photo: The Morgan Library & Museum / Art Resource, NY.

Transforming

Jekyll and Hyde emerged suddenly from a dream, but Stevenson had been mulling over its core tenet—the dual (or multiple) nature of individuals—from early in his life. "I had long been trying to write a story on this subject, to find a body, a vehicle, for that strong sense of man's double being which must at times come in upon and overwhelm the mind of every thinking creature."[7] About a decade before *Jekyll and Hyde*, he had argued "that man is twofold at least; that he is not a rounded and autonomous empire; but that in the same body with him there dwell other powers tributary but independent."[8] And then a year before *Jekyll and Hyde*, he wrote "Markheim," a short story about a murderer who meets a kind of doppelganger soon after his crime—an unearthly creature who reads his inmost thoughts. He destroyed another story, "The Travelling Companion," because he felt that *Jekyll and Hyde* had replaced it. Primed in this way, the story ripened quickly. He told a friend that "Jekyll was conceived, written, rewritten, re-rewritten, and printed inside ten weeks."[9] Yet it wasn't his last word on the self being a dwelling place for many. He continued toying with these notions, most notably in his 1889 novel *The Master of Ballantrae*. The plot centers on Lord Durrisdeer's eerie, intensely psychological obsession with his brother James, a devil-like figure who seems not fully mortal. Lord Durrisdeer says of James, "He is bound upon my back to all eternity—to all God's eternity!"[1] In a letter Stevenson wrote in 1892, he brings up duality once again, observing during a severe illness "my other self" emerge, which he also called "the other fellow"—a hallucinating, irrational side that he watched and studied dispassionately from within his "real" self.[2] Not surprisingly, around the time Stevenson dreamt of Jekyll, he had been reading essays about the mind's multiplicity—its unknowable, shadowy parts—written by Freud's immediate predecessors.[3]

Jekyll and Hyde is grounded in the body, not just the mind or spirit. More aware of his body than most because of his chronic illness, Stevenson shoots into his characters an attention to the physical self, especially Hyde's "deformity." This embodiment is lost in the popular usage of the term "Jekyll and Hyde personality" to refer to someone strikingly changeable in character. The confusion has developed because people feel they don't need to read the story—

---

7. Stevenson, "A Chapter on Dreams," *The Travels and Essays of Robert Louis Stevenson* (Scribner's, 1918), p. 263. See the excerpt in the Composition section of this volume.
8. Stevenson, *Lay Morals and Other Papers* (1896; Scribner's, 1923), p. 28.
9. *Letters*, vol. 5, p. 216.
1. Stevenson, *The Master of Ballantrae* (Everyman, 1992), p. 129.
2. *Letters*, vol. 7, pp. 331–32.
3. Stevenson, *Collected Works*, Tusitala Edition (Heinemann, 1923), vol. 5, p. xvi.

it's so famous that they think they know what it's about.[4] They are wrong in this. Key to the power of Stevenson's story, full of rich ambiguity, is that when Jekyll swallows the chemical, he puts on a different body, not merely a different nature. And the confusion about what is "wrong" with this second body (Hyde), and what it does that is so "sinful," lends a universality to the whole, opens it up so that readers can understand it in their own way, project onto it a host of possible insights. The indeterminacy of Hyde's appearance is carefully maintained, despite the many accounts of it. Those who encounter him feel they must describe him, but are always unsuccessful. Enfield, the first character who meets him, says, "there is something wrong with his appearance; something displeasing, something downright detestable" (9). So wrong is it that some men, like a doctor who arrives at the scene of one of Hyde's early crimes, have "the desire to kill him" (7). Enfield goes on, "I never saw a man I so disliked, and yet I scarce know why. He must be deformed somewhere; he gives a strong feeling of deformity, although I couldn't specify the point" (9). Utterson also has a confused unease with Hyde's body, how it "gave an impression of deformity without any nameable malformation." He struggles to pinpoint what brings out his "disgust, loathing, and fear" (15). He speaks to himself, perplexed:

> There must be something else. . . . There *is* something more, if I could find a name for it. God bless me, the man seems hardly human! Something troglodytic . . . or is it the mere radiance of a foul soul that thus transpires through, and transfigures, its clay continent? The last, I think; for O my poor old Harry Jekyll, if ever I read Satan's signature upon a face, it is on that of your new friend. (15)

What is it about this body—its strangeness to the upright Victorian men who narrate the story—that so unsettles everyone? The fact that Stevenson never answers this question, maintaining the mystery, with Hyde as a blank cypher to be filled by others, is his masterstroke.

The temper of the novella owes much to anxious debates about social degeneration in the years following the publication of Cesare Lombroso's *Criminal Man*, in 1876. An Italian physician, Lombroso argued that criminality is innate from birth and is visible in apish signs on a person's anatomy. People born with certain anatomical features like "enormous jaws" and "high cheek bones" would

---

4. *Jekyll and Hyde* has had a rich and long-lasting afterlife with many adaptations, starting with stage versions within a year after it was published, and then multiple films and television shows in the twentieth century. See, for instance, Scott Allen Nollen, *Robert Louis Stevenson: Life, Literature and the Silver Screen* (McFarland, 1994).

become savage brutes.[5] Hyde is fathered by such fears, growing out of Charles Darwin's theories about evolution, but reversing them, imagining a "de-volution," a sinking backward into crime, poverty, drug and alcohol abuse, and "moral perversion." In this light, Hyde was a throwback to something ancient or ancestral, or, as Utterson calls him, troglodytic, a cave-dweller. If such "regression" can be read on the body, then Hyde's became a kind of screen for the shadow play of Victorian fears: of prejudices about how skin color, physiognomy, gestures, and other physical features marked one through and through as bad. In practice, Lombroso's ideas were applied to already-marginalized groups, such as the poor and people of color, as a way to shift the blame for institutionalized cruelty and discrimination onto them, the victims.

Later readers have drawn many meanings out of this indefinite horror for Hyde's physical self. Some have seen him as a working-class or poor man, used by the upper-class Jekyll (with his class written into his title of doctor) as a kind of deep disguise to work through his "demeaning," fierce desires.[6] Does Hyde have a disability, evidence to these Victorian men, written on the body, of moral corruption and evil?[7] Perhaps he is Irish, Jewish, or from another culture believed by some Britons at this time to be innately inferior?[8] The desire to transform one's body into something different also leads us today to think about the "trans" more broadly, not so much *trans*form, but "transgender," another lens through which Hyde's body might be understood.[9] Even though Jekyll does not change his sex or gender with this second physical self, he does manage to find, temporarily, a sense of truth not available in the body he was born into. When he looks in the mirror at Hyde for the first time, he feels "a leap of welcome. This, too, was myself. It seemed natural and human" (48). He could, with his new flesh, "strip off these lendings and spring headlong into the sea of liberty" (49). At first transformation Jekyll discovers "something indescribably new and, from its very novelty, incredibly sweet. I felt younger, lighter, happier in body; within I was conscious of a heady recklessness . . . a solution of the bonds of obligation, an unknown but not an innocent freedom of the soul" (47). While the term "transgender" did not take on its current meaning until about a hundred years after

5. Quoted in Stephen Jay Gould, *The Mismeasure of Man* (Norton, 1981), p. 152.
6. See Martin Danahay, "Dr. Jekyll's Two Bodies," *Nineteenth-Century Contexts* 35.1 (2013): 25. An excerpt appears in the Criticism section of this volume.
7. See, for instance, Sami Schalk, "What Makes Mr. Hyde So Scary?: Disability as a Result of Evil and Cause of Fear," *Disability Studies Quarterly* 28. 4 (2008): 13–19.
8. See Jack Halberstam, *Skin Shows: Gothic Horror and the Technology of Monsters* (Duke UP, 1995), chapter 3.
9. See Jay Prosser, *Second Skins: The Body Narratives of Transsexuality* (Columbia UP, 1998).

Stevenson's novella, some Victorians understood a feeling of being in the wrong body, or of wishing one's body could express a broader spectrum of significance than the restricting gender roles of the time. Yet this lovely feeling in his new body breaks down quickly into self-loathing, his Hyde ("hide") presence seems to him decayed, like a corpse. Another moral to the story, very different from that drawn by Victorian preachers, emerges: Embrace one's transgressive side, run with subversive tendencies, because suppression leads to self-alienation and suicide.

The body (or bodies) is a dwelling place, or a "clay continent" (15). Stevenson starts with this most basic space where one is, and broadens his attention to include the rooms, houses, and apartments that contain these bodies.[1] Here, too, we find the theme of the singular multiplying in a dreamlike way. Jekyll's residence has two entrances that correspond with its two parts, connected by an interior courtyard. So different and seemingly unrelated, they are hard for the reader to reconcile with one property. The "Story of the Door" tells of the most "sinister" of these entrances, "equipped with neither bell nor knocker . . . blistered and distained" and set in a "blind forehead of discolored wall" that "bore in every feature, the marks of prolonged and sordid negligence" (6). Is this the opening to a haunted house, with a history (or future) of violence, madness, and criminality? What "black secrets" (16) does this house conceal? Utterson "began to haunt the door" (13), guessing it will be a clue to the mystery he is trying to solve of the relationship between Jekyll and Hyde.[2] The reader discovers eventually that this is the entrance to the "old dissecting rooms" where bodies were once cut up by a "celebrated surgeon" in order to better understand the workings of the interior (22). Also called a "theater," the space was "once crowded with eager students" but now lay "gaunt and silent" (22), making the equation between the building and the body—a corpse, in this case—apparent. Above the anatomy theater is Jekyll's "cabinet" where he does his chemical experiments that lead to the body-changing medicine, and below a spacious cellar "filled with crazy lumber" (37). A gothic house with old dusty rooms works as a figure for the mind, with its neglected parts as the sub- or unconscious, just as the mind has spaces, as Utterson finds when he gropes "in all the corners of memory" (16). Hyde steps out of these types of "corners" (cabinets, cellars, theaters) of Jekyll's head, fully embodied.

---

1. See Alex Clunas, "Comely External Utterance: Reading Space in *The Strange Case of Dr. Jekyll and Mr. Hyde*," *The Journal of Narrative Technique* 24.3 (1994): 173–89.
2. See Stephen Heath, "Psychopathia Sexualis: Stevenson's Strange Case," *Critical Quarterly* 28. 1–2 (1986), for more about doors.

Windows, thresholds similar to doors, also open onto secrets and madness. Characters look from the outside into intimate interiors, as if windows were eyes that show the soul within. Or they sit inside them, peering out, "like some disconsolate prisoner" (29). In the "Incident at the Window," Enfield and Utterson stroll around the city one evening, eventually spotting Jekyll in a window of his cabinet. They speak to him from the street, until he suddenly has "an expression of such abject terror and despair, as froze the very blood of the two gentlemen below" (29–30). Thinking they see Jekyll descending into some sort of madness, they seem to gain access to some back room of his mind. Earlier, a maidservant sits at her bedroom window at night, in a kind of reverie, and witnesses a violent murder in the street below, illuminated by the moon. Like walls, doors, and windows, skin is another liminal that divides the inner and outer, hinting at concealment and permeability.[3] A different way to think about Jekyll's transformation involves the soul or personality entering into another body through skin or orifices, like a ghostly or demonic possession. *Jekyll and Hyde* is, to some extent, an unconventional ghost story, and Jekyll haunts himself in the form of the supernatural figure of Hyde. In the end, Jekyll must kill himself to cast out this ghost, must destroy the house of life, the continent of clay.

City Haunting

If *Jekyll and Hyde* is a ghost story, then all of London is a haunted house. Depicted as a dreamscape, like other aspects of the tale, fin-de-siècle London is a place of dark secrets and crimes to be tracked down, possibly exposed. This is the metropolis where Sherlock Holmes plied his trade, in stories that began to be published in 1887, a year after *Jekyll and Hyde*. Like Arthur Conan Doyle, Stevenson presents the urban landscape as dangerous, a theme he was already working on in *The Dynamiter*, written in collaboration with Fanny a year before *Jekyll and Hyde*. The danger in this tale, based in part on the early 1880s bombings by campaigners for Home Rule for Ireland, lay in being blown up by a group of political radicals. Stevenson doesn't agree with the bombers' actions, but he does present their motives as worthy of consideration. One plotter explains his reasons thus:

> I was born a hater of injustice; from my most tender years my blood boiled against heaven when I beheld the sick, and against men when I witnessed the sorrows of the poor; the pauper's

---

3. See Halberstam, *Skin Shows*, chapter 1. An excerpt appears in the Criticism section of this volume.

crust stuck in my throat when I sat down to eat my dainties, and the crippled child has set me weeping. . . . What hope was there in kings? What hope in these well-feathered classes that now roll in money? I had observed the course of history; I knew the burgess, our ruler of today, to be base, cowardly, and dull; I saw him, in every age, combine . . . to prey upon those that were below.[4]

And another plotter states more directly, "In this dark period of time, a star—the star of dynamite—has risen for the oppressed" (*Dynamiter*, 183). Such extreme actions don't help the powerless in the story—or anyone—but the sense of a city crazed into fragments, set up for violent revolution, persists. *The Dynamiter* destabilizes any rosy picture of London as a modern city, its inhabitants treated fairly. More closely wedded to the central events of *Jekyll and Hyde*, although they happened two years after the book was published, were the sensationalized Jack the Ripper murders of 1888. In news accounts of the crimes, journalists evoked *Jekyll and Hyde*, describing the Whitechapel murderer as a sexual sadist like Hyde, as if Stevenson had predicted this type of killer with his novella.[5] For many, the Jekyll tale seemed to explain these murders, to simplify them into a tidy plot, and in this way the story influenced ideas about London rather than merely representing it. Yet the Ripper murders do not fit easily with *Jekyll and Hyde* (or the other way around). Hyde murders no women (although he does trample a girl), and it's hard to argue convincingly that he's a sexual sadist. He does murder a man, but rather than a premeditated killing of a downtrodden prostitute, it's a sudden, thoughtless beating of an upper-class, powerful politician. Read in a certain way, Hyde, not a misogynist like the Ripper, aligns more clearly with the anarchist dynamiters, perhaps fighting a kind of class war in a city of slums and palaces.

These urban class divisions exist in Stevenson's work, yet the ruling image of the city in both *Jekyll and Hyde* and *The Dynamiter* is of a threatening emptiness and deadness. A strange contradiction permeates these stories, with characters "in the midst of the chief mass of people," with "the nocturnal crowd dense upon the pavement," and "the high tides of London" roaring about one, but also fully alone (*Dynamiter* 7, 102, 216). This paradox of dreadful absence in the middle of crowds reminds us of the city as a haunted mind,

---

4. Robert Louis Stevenson and Fanny Van de Grift Stevenson, *The Dynamiter* (Books for Libraries Press, 1971), pp. 141–42. Further citations will be in-text.
5. See Judith Walkowitz, *City of Dreadful Delight: Narratives of Sexual Danger in Late-Victorian London* (U of Chicago P, 1992), p. 206. An excerpt appears in the Historical and Cultural Contexts section of this volume.

caught up in existential despair. Such a state strikes the character Mr. Edward Challoner in *The Dynamiter*, who reflects that "here, in broad day, the streets [are] secret as in the blackest night of January, and in the midst of some four million sleepers, solitary as the woods of Yucatan. If I but raise my voice I could summon up the number of an army, and yet the grave is not more silent than this city of sleep" (13–14). Street lamps, rather than illuminating, make light feel menacing, and the quiet can be frightening in a city that should be loud. Enfield's first encounter with Hyde happens at 3:00 a.m., when he walks home.

> My way lay through a part of town where there was literally nothing to be seen but lamps. Street after street, and all the folks asleep—street after street, all lighted up as if for a procession and all as empty as a church—till at last I got into that state of mind when a man listens and listens and begins to long for the sight of a policeman. (6)

This urban desert, ready for a procession that never comes, with a religious flavor in its comparison to a church, erupts with Hyde's appearance, when he tramples the girl at the beginning of the story. The already dreamlike scene becomes more so in the imagination of Utterson after he hears about it. Suffering from insomnia, he finds that Enfield's "tale went by before his mind in a scroll of lighted pictures. He would be aware of the great field of lamps of a nocturnal city; then of the figure of a man walking . . ." (12). Tormented by this image all night, Utterson finally dozes, only to see the figure of Hyde "glide more stealthily through sleeping houses, or move the more swiftly and still the more swiftly, even to dizziness, through wider labyrinths of lamplighted city" (12). He comments later when entering Soho that London is like "some city in a nightmare" (20–21). As with Hyde, Jekyll, Enfield, and others, not only does Utterson himself haunt the city by roaming about the streets at all hours, but the city haunts him, entering his mind and dreams.

London evokes queasiness, with its heavy fogs and confusing spaces. Utterson's first encounter with Hyde happens at night, "the streets as clean as a ballroom floor" (13), a setting that turns the outside into an uncanny interior, as does the fact that "even in the houses the fog began to lie thickly" (23). Utterson describes the backdrop of this first meeting at great length, first with light— "the lamps, unshaken by any wind, drawing a regular pattern of light and shadow"—then with sound, with the sensing of absence then presence:

> By ten o'clock, when the shops were closed, the by-street was very solitary and, in spite of the low growl of London from all

round, very silent. Small sounds carried far; domestic sounds out of the houses were clearly audible on either side of the roadway; and the rumour of the approach of any passenger preceded him by a long time. . . . In the course of his nightly patrols, he had long grown accustomed to the quaint effect with which the footfalls of a single person, while he is still a great way off, suddenly spring out distinct from the vast hum and clatter of the city. (13)

Victorian London has a particular texture to those who inhabit it, and Stevenson wants his readers to experience being in it, with all of the bodily senses attuned, like Jekyll in his Hyde, his skin. The tale, delving into the flesh, is grounded in place and time, lending it a local feel. The pall of fog that repeatedly appears gives the city a further tactile thickness. Even at "nine in the morning . . . a great chocolate-coloured pall lowered over heaven, but the wind was continually charging and routing these embattled vapours so that . . . Mr. Utterson beheld a marvelous number of degrees and hues of twilight; for here would be dark like the back-end of evening; and there would be a glow of a rich, lurid brown, like the light of some strange conflagration . . ." (20). The city tricks the eyes and baffles nature, making its own weather and also putting on and taking off disguises. The characters have the city impressed on them; they are caught up in it. They sink deeper into its interior, like a descent into a mind or into the bowels of a haunted house.

Yet there is also something potentially freeing about this city haunting. Henry James, who came to London in 1876, described it as "dreadfully delightful . . . a strangely mingled monster . . . so clumsy and brutal," gathering "together so many of the darkest sides of life." But in it he found "complete liberty . . . I used to take long walks in the rain. I took possession of London; I felt it to be the right place."[6] Like James, the *flâneurs* in *Jekyll and Hyde*, especially Enfield, Utterson, and Hyde, roam the pavement, observing and sometimes sampling the cosmopolitan delights. In his Hyde body, Jekyll gives full rein to his desires in the metropolis, a center for prostitution, opium dens, gambling halls, and homosexual cruising. Another book that echoes, and was influenced by, *Jekyll and Hyde*, Oscar Wilde's *The Picture of Dorian Gray* (serialized in 1890), presents London as a rich pleasure ground. Wilde's story has even stronger hints of the "crime" of straight and gay pickups and prostitution on the city streets. Such pleasures lead to the downfall of Dorian Gray through another doppelgänger plot, yet this moral rings false. Why not hit the city streets and drink one's fill?

6. Quoted in Walkowitz, *City of Dreadful Delight*, p. 15.

Regent's Park, scene of Jekyll's involuntary transformation

Cavendish Square, site of Dr. Lanyon's house

Soho District, site of Hyde's apartment

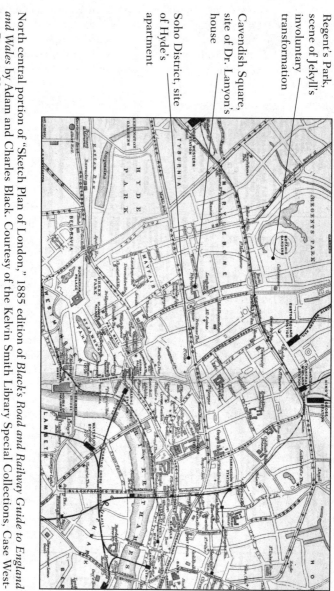

North central portion of "Sketch Plan of London," 1885 edition of *Black's Road and Railway Guide to England and Wales* by Adam and Charles Black. Courtesy of the Kelvin Smith Library Special Collections, Case Western Reserve University.

The different neighborhoods of London in *Jekyll and Hyde* at first appear deeply divided, mirroring the dualities of Jekyll's body and his home. The city's variegated nature, seen best by the wanderer on foot, corresponds to the different bodies Jekyll puts on, as if neighborhoods are also costumes one can dress in and then take off, another means of performing identity through the physical. The body is also a city in this story: Jekyll, after Hyde commits murder and is being hunted around London, sees his Jekyll body as "my city of refuge" (54). But when Utterson passes through neighborhoods, rich and poor, what he finds breaks down these dualities, lending a general instability to the idea of binary oppositions, in bodies as well as cities. The second living space Jekyll sets up for Hyde, in Soho, seems at first to confirm this fragmentation along class lines. Utterson describes his visit to the area: "As the cab drew up before the address indicated, the fog lifted a little and showed him a dingy street, a gin palace, a low French eating house, a shop for the retail of penny numbers and two penny salads, many ragged children huddled in the doorways . . . and the next moment the fog settled down again upon that part, as brown as umber, and cut him off from his blackguardly surroundings" (21). Jekyll's home, which is not far from Hyde's, has a professional and middle-class sheen. But what at first seems like a sharp contrast becomes confused and porous. We've already heard about the backdoor, part of a "sinister block of building" where "tramps slouched" (6), but even the area in the front of Jekyll's place has seen better days. "Round the corner from the by-street, there was a square of ancient, handsome houses, now for the most part decayed from their high estate and let in flats and chambers to all sorts and conditions of men" (15). As with Jekyll himself, the city is multiple and "queer" (just as there is "something queer" about Hyde) rather than dual.

The reader feels bodily placed in 1880s London, and as *Jekyll and Hyde* nears its deathly conclusion, the city itself also seems to be exhaling, expiring. "The fog still slept on the wing above the drowned city, where the lamps glimmered like carbuncles" (25). Under water, or beneath a more sinister substance, characters feel that the city, "full of wind and dust," had never seemed "so deserted" (31). Missing bodies and present ones people the novella, open always to be filled with meaning. *Strange Case of Dr. Jekyll and Mr. Hyde* draws its lasting power from this focus on how we desire and inhabit spaces—cities, bodies—and the ways we want to shape them, but how they often shape and distort us instead.

The Text of
STRANGE CASE OF
DR. JEKYLL AND MR. HYDE

TO

KATHARINE DE MATTOS.[1]

It's ill to loose the bands that God decreed to bind;[2]
Still will we be the children of the heather and the wind.
Far away from home, O it's still for you and me
That the broom is blowing bonnie[3] in the north countrie.

---

1. A favorite cousin of Stevenson's. The poem here appearing beneath her name was adapted by Stevenson from a longer poem he had written her several months earlier celebrating their shared Scottish background. See his letter to her of January 1, 1886, reproduced below, p. 89.
2. Stevenson's original version of this line read, "We cannae break the bonds that God decreed to bind."
3. I.e., that the Scotch broom (a flowering bush) is blooming handsomely.

CONTENTS

Story of the Door

Mr. Utterson the lawyer was a man of a rugged countenance, that was never lighted by a smile; cold, scanty and embarrassed in discourse; backward in sentiment; lean, long, dusty, dreary and yet somehow lovable. At friendly meetings, and when the wine was to his taste, something eminently human beaconed from his eye; something indeed which never found its way into his talk, but which spoke not only in these silent symbols of the after-dinner face, but more often and loudly in the acts of his life. He was austere with himself; drank gin when he was alone, to mortify a taste for vintages; and though he enjoyed the theatre, had not crossed the doors of one for twenty years. But he had an approved[1] tolerance for others; sometimes wondering, almost with envy, at the high pressure of spirits involved in their misdeeds; and in any extremity inclined to help rather than to reprove. "I incline to Cain's heresy," he used to say quaintly: "I let my brother go to the devil in his own way."[2] In this character, it was frequently his fortune to be the last reputable acquaintance and the last good influence in the lives of down-going men. And to such as these, so long as they came about his chambers, he never marked a shade of change in his demeanour.

No doubt the feat was easy to Mr. Utterson; for he was undemonstrative at the best, and even his friendships seemed to be founded in a similar catholicity[3] of good-nature. It is the mark of a modest man to accept his friendly circle ready-made from the hands of opportunity; and that was the lawyer's way. His friends were those of his own blood or those whom he had known the longest; his affections, like ivy, were the growth of time, they implied no aptness in the object. Hence, no doubt, the bond that united him to Mr. Richard Enfield, his distant kinsman, the well-known man about town. It was a nut to crack for many, what these two could see in each other or what subject they could find in common. It was reported by those who encountered them in their Sunday walks, that they said nothing, looked singularly dull, and would hail with obvious relief the appearance of a friend. For all that, the two men put the greatest store by these excursions, counted them the chief jewel of each week, and not only set aside occasions of pleasure, but even resisted the calls of business, that they might enjoy them uninterrupted.

1. Proven.
2. Adam and Eve's firstborn son Cain murdered his brother Abel and afterward asked, "Am I my brother's keeper?" (Genesis 4:5).
3. Breadth.

It chanced on one of these rambles that their way led them down a by-street in a busy quarter of London. The street was small and what is called quiet, but it drove a thriving trade on the week-days. The inhabitants were all doing well, it seemed, and all emulously hoping to do better still, and laying out the surplus of their gains in coquetry; so that the shop fronts stood along that thoroughfare with an air of invitation, like rows of smiling saleswomen. Even on Sunday, when it veiled its more florid charms and lay comparatively empty of passage, the street shone out in contrast to its dingy neighbourhood, like a fire in a forest; and with its freshly painted shutters, well-polished brasses, and general cleanliness and gaiety of note, instantly caught and pleased the eye of the passenger.[4]

Two doors from one corner, on the left hand going east, the line was broken by the entry of a court; and just at that point, a certain sinister block of building thrust forward its gable on the street. It was two storeys high; showed no window, nothing but a door on the lower storey and a blind forehead of discoloured wall on the upper; and bore in every feature, the marks of prolonged and sordid negligence. The door, which was equipped with neither bell nor knocker, was blistered and distained.[5] Tramps slouched into the recess and struck matches on the panels; children kept shop upon the steps; the schoolboy had tried his knife on the mouldings; and for close on a generation, no one had appeared to drive away these random visitors or to repair their ravages.

Mr. Enfield and the lawyer were on the other side of the by-street; but when they came abreast of the entry, the former lifted up his cane and pointed.

"Did you ever remark that door?" he asked; and when his companion had replied in the affirmative, "It is connected in my mind," added he, "with a very odd story."

"Indeed?" said Mr. Utterson, with a slight change of voice, "and what was that?"

"Well, it was this way," returned Mr. Enfield: "I was coming home from some place at the end of the world, about three o'clock of a black winter morning, and my way lay through a part of town where there was literally nothing to be seen but lamps. Street after street, and all the folks asleep—street after street, all lighted up as if for a procession and all as empty as a church—till at last I got into that state of mind when a man listens and listens and begins to long for the sight of a policeman. All at once, I saw two figures: one a little man who was stumping along eastward at a good walk, and the other a girl of maybe eight or ten who was running as hard as she

4. Passer-by.
5. Discolored.

was able down a cross street. Well, sir, the two ran into one another naturally enough at the corner; and then came the horrible part of the thing; for the man trampled calmly over the child's body and left her screaming on the ground. It sounds nothing to hear, but it was hellish to see. It wasn't like a man; it was like some damned Juggernaut.[6] I gave a view halloa,[7] took to my heels, collared my gentleman, and brought him back to where there was already quite a group about the screaming child. He was perfectly cool and made no resistance, but gave me one look, so ugly that it brought out the sweat on me like running. The people who had turned out were the girl's own family; and pretty soon, the doctor, for whom she had been sent, put in his appearance. Well, the child was not much the worse, more frightened, according to the Sawbones;[8] and there you might have supposed would be an end to it. But there was one curious circumstance. I had taken a loathing to my gentleman at first sight. So had the child's family, which was only natural. But the doctor's case was what struck me. He was the usual cut and dry apothecary,[9] of no particular age and colour, with a strong Edinburgh accent, and about as emotional as a bagpipe. Well, sir, he was like the rest of us; every time he looked at my prisoner, I saw that Sawbones turn sick and white with the desire to kill him. I knew what was in his mind, just as he knew what was in mine; and killing being out of the question, we did the next best. We told the man we could and would make such a scandal out of this, as should make his name stink from one end of London to the other. If he had any friends or any credit, we undertook that he should lose them. And all the time, as we were pitching it in red hot, we were keeping the women off him as best we could, for they were as wild as harpies.[1] I never saw a circle of such hateful faces; and there was the man in the middle, with a kind of black, sneering coolness— frightened too, I could see that—but carrying it off, sir, really like Satan. 'If you choose to make capital out of this accident,' said he, 'I am naturally helpless. No gentleman but wishes to avoid a scene,' says he. 'Name your figure.' Well, we screwed him up to a hundred pounds[2] for the child's family; he would have clearly liked to stick out; but there was something about the lot of us that meant

6. An inexorable destructive force; the term derives from accounts given by early European travelers to India of religious worshippers being crushed to death beneath the wheels of the huge processional chariot of the Hindu deity Jagganath.
7. The shout given by a huntsman on seeing a fox break cover.
8. Slang for a doctor, especially a surgeon.
9. A dispenser of drugs; here an archaic and hence semi-facetious term for a doctor.
1. In Greek mythology, hungry birds with the heads of women who carry off people.
2. A large sum at the time; as a rough point of comparison, consider the figure mentioned in George Gissing's novel *The Odd Women* (1893) as the salary of a character working as a mathematical lecturer at a London college in 1888, namely, one hundred and fifty pounds a year.

mischief, and at last he struck.[3] The next thing was to get the money; and where do you think he carried us but to that place with the door?—whipped out a key, went in, and presently came back with the matter of ten pounds in gold and a cheque for the balance on Coutts's,[4] drawn payable to bearer and signed with a name that I can't mention, though it's one of the points of my story, but it was a name at least very well known and often printed. The figure was stiff; but the signature was good for more than that, if it was only genuine. I took the liberty of pointing out to my gentleman that the whole business looked apocryphal,[5] and that a man does not, in real life, walk into a cellar door at four in the morning and come out of it with another man's cheque for close upon a hundred pounds. But he was quite easy and sneering. 'Set your mind at rest,' says he, 'I will stay with you till the banks open and cash the cheque myself.' So we all set off, the doctor, and the child's father, and our friend and myself, and passed the rest of the night in my chambers; and next day, when we had breakfasted, went in a body to the bank. I gave in the cheque myself, and said I had every reason to believe it was a forgery. Not a bit of it. The cheque was genuine."

"Tut-tut," said Mr. Utterson.

"I see you feel as I do," said Mr. Enfield. "Yes, it's a bad story. For my man was a fellow that nobody could have to do with, a really damnable man; and the person that drew the cheque is the very pink of the proprieties;[6] celebrated too, and (what makes it worse) one of your fellows who do what they call good. Black mail, I suppose; an honest man paying through the nose for some of the capers of his youth. Black Mail House is what I call that place with the door, in consequence. Though even that, you know, is far from explaining all," he added, and with the words fell into a vein of musing.

From this he was recalled by Mr. Utterson asking rather suddenly: "And you don't know if the drawer of the cheque lives there?"

"A likely place, isn't it?" returned Mr. Enfield. "But I happen to have noticed his address; he lives in some square or other."

"And you never asked about—the place with the door?" said Mr. Utterson.

"No, sir: I had a delicacy," was the reply. "I feel very strongly about putting questions; it partakes too much of the style of the day of judgment. You start a question, and it's like starting a stone. You

---

3. Surrendered; from the nautical term "strike," meaning to lower the topsails or haul down the flag as a sign of surrender or salute.
4. The most elite bank in Great Britain, catering to a wealthy, respectable clientele that at its upper end included the British royal family.
5. Suspicious, unlikely.
6. The height of proper conduct or respectability.

sit quietly on the top of a hill; and away the stone goes, starting others; and presently some bland old bird (the last you would have thought of) is knocked on the head in his own back garden and the family have to change their name. No, sir, I make it a rule of mine: the more it looks like Queer Street,[7] the less I ask."

"A very good rule, too," said the lawyer.

"But I have studied the place for myself," continued Mr. Enfield. "It seems scarcely a house. There is no other door, and nobody goes in or out of that one but, once in a great while, the gentleman of my adventure. There are three windows looking on the court on the first floor;[8] none below; the windows are always shut but they're clean. And then there is a chimney which is generally smoking; so somebody must live there. And yet it's not so sure; for the buildings are so packed together about that court; that it's hard to say where one ends and another begins."

The pair walked on again for a while in silence; and then "Enfield," said Mr. Utterson, "that's a good rule of yours."

"Yes, I think it is," returned Enfield.

"But for all that," continued the lawyer, "there's one point I want to ask: I want to ask the name of that man who walked over the child."

"Well," said Mr. Enfield, "I can't see what harm it would do. It was a man of the name of Hyde."

"Hm," said Mr. Utterson. "What sort of a man is he to see?"

"He is not easy to describe. There is something wrong with his appearance; something displeasing, something downright detestable. I never saw a man I so disliked, and yet I scarce know why. He must be deformed somewhere; he gives a strong feeling of deformity, although I couldn't specify the point. He's an extraordinary looking man, and yet I really can name nothing out of the way. No, sir; I can make no hand of it; I can't describe him. And it's not want of memory; for I declare I can see him this moment."

Mr. Utterson again walked some way in silence and obviously under a weight of consideration. "You are sure he used a key?" he inquired at last.

"My dear sir . . ." began Enfield, surprised out of himself.

"Yes, I know," said Utterson; "I know it must seem strange. The fact is, if I do not ask you the name of the other party, it is because I know it already. You see, Richard, your tale has gone home. If you have been inexact in any point, you had better correct it."

---

7. In London slang, a figurative allusion to living in troubled circumstances, especially debt.
8. I.e., the first floor above the ground floor, or what North Americans would call the second floor.

"I think you might have warned me," returned the other with a touch of sullenness. "But I have been pedantically exact, as you call it. The fellow had a key; and what's more, he has it still. I saw him use it, not a week ago."

Mr. Utterson sighed deeply but said never a word; and the young man presently resumed. "Here is another lesson to say nothing," said he. "I am ashamed of my long tongue. Let us make a bargain never to refer to this again."

"With all my heart," said the lawyer. "I shake hands on that, Richard."

Search for Mr. Hyde

That evening, Mr. Utterson came home to his bachelor house in sombre spirits and sat down to dinner without relish. It was his custom of a Sunday, when this meal was over, to sit close by the fire, a volume of some dry divinity[9] on his reading desk, until the clock of the neighbouring church rang out the hour of twelve, when he would go soberly and gratefully to bed. On this night, however, as soon as the cloth was taken away, he took up a candle and went into his business room. There he opened his safe, took from the most private part of it a document endorsed on the envelope as Dr. Jekyll's[1] Will, and sat down with a clouded brow to study its contents. The will was holograph,[2] for Mr. Utterson, though he took charge of it now that it was made, had refused to lend the least assistance in the making of it; it provided not only that, in case of the decease of Henry Jekyll, M.D., D.C.L., LL.D., F.R.S.,[3] &c., all his possessions were to pass into the hands of his "friend and bene-factor Edward Hyde," but that in case of Dr. Jekyll's "disappearance or unexplained absence for any period exceeding three calendar months," the said Edward Hyde should step into the said Henry Jekyll's shoes without further delay and free from any burthen or obligation, beyond the payment of a few small sums to the members of the doctor's household. This document had long been the

---

9. Theology.
1. Pronounced as though it were spelled "jee-kill," according to Stevenson in an interview with the *San Francisco Examiner* (June 8, 1888).
2. Wholly written by the person in whose name it appears.
3. Doctor of Medicine, Doctor of Civil Law, Doctor of Laws, and Fellow of the Royal Society. The first two credentials reflect Jekyll's professional training in medicine and law. The second two reflect his subsequent professional achievement: Doctor of Laws was commonly an honorary degree; and fellowship in the venerable Royal Society (members since its founding in the seventeenth century included Sir Isaac Newton, Sir William Herschel, and Michael Faraday) was by invitation only, with just fifteen new fellows being chosen each year on the basis of distinguished contributions to natural science.

lawyer's eyesore. It offended him both as a lawyer and as a lover of the sane and customary sides of life, to whom the fanciful was the immodest. And hitherto it was his ignorance of Mr. Hyde that had swelled his indignation; now, by a sudden turn, it was his knowledge. It was already bad enough when the name was but a name of which he could learn no more. It was worse when it began to be clothed upon with detestable attributes; and out of the shifting, insubstantial mists that had so long baffled his eye, there leaped up the sudden, definite presentment[4] of a fiend.

"I thought it was madness," he said, as he replaced the obnoxious paper in the safe, "and now I begin to fear it is disgrace."

With that he blew out his candle, put on a great coat and set forth in the direction of Cavendish Square, that citadel of medicine,[5] where his friend, the great Dr. Lanyon, had his house and received his crowding patients. "If anyone knows, it will be Lanyon," he had thought.

The solemn butler knew and welcomed him; he was subjected to no stage of delay, but ushered direct from the door to the dining-room where Dr. Lanyon sat alone over his wine. This was a hearty, healthy, dapper, red-faced gentleman, with a shock of hair prematurely white, and a boisterous and decided manner. At sight of Mr. Utterson, he sprang up from his chair and welcomed him with both hands. The geniality, as was the way of the man, was somewhat theatrical to the eye; but it reposed on genuine feeling. For these two were old friends, old mates both at school and college, both thorough respecters of themselves and of each other, and, what does not always follow, men who thoroughly enjoyed each other's company.

After a little rambling talk, the lawyer led up to the subject which so disagreeably preoccupied his mind.

"I suppose, Lanyon," said he, "you and I must be the two oldest friends that Henry Jekyll has?"

"I wish the friends were younger," chuckled Dr. Lanyon. "But I suppose we are. And what of that? I see little of him now."

"Indeed?" said Utterson. "I thought you had a bond of common interest."

"We had," was the reply. "But it is more than ten years since Henry Jekyll became too fanciful for me. He began to go wrong, wrong in mind; and though of course I continue to take an interest in him for old sake's sake as they say, I see and I have seen devilish little of the man. Such unscientific balderdash," added the doctor,

4. Image.
5. Fashionable physicians, surgeons, and dentists had by late Victorian times become the chief tenants of the once-aristocratic homes in this square at the foot of Harley Street in west-central London.

flushing suddenly purple, "would have estranged Damon and Pythias."[6]

This little spirt of temper was somewhat of a relief to Mr. Utterson. "They have only differed on some point of science," he thought; and being a man of no scientific passions (except in the matter of conveyancing)[7] he even added: "It is nothing worse than that!" He gave his friend a few seconds to recover his composure, and then approached the question he had come to put. "Did you ever come across a protégé of his—one Hyde?" he asked.

"Hyde?" repeated Lanyon. "No. Never heard of him. Since my time."

That was the amount of information that the lawyer carried back with him to the great, dark bed on which he tossed to and fro, until the small hours of the morning began to grow large. It was a night of little ease to his toiling mind, toiling in mere[8] darkness and besieged by questions.

Six o'clock struck on the bells of the church that was so conveniently near to Mr. Utterson's dwelling, and still he was digging at the problem. Hitherto it had touched him on the intellectual side alone; but now his imagination also was engaged or rather enslaved; and as he lay and tossed in the gross darkness of the night and the curtained room, Mr. Enfield's tale went by before his mind in a scroll of lighted pictures. He would be aware of the great field of lamps of a nocturnal city; then of the figure of a man walking swiftly; then of a child running from the doctor's; and then these met, and that human Juggernaut trod the child down and passed on regardless of her screams. Or else he would see a room in a rich house, where his friend lay asleep, dreaming and smiling at his dreams; and then the door of that room would be opened, the curtains of the bed plucked apart, the sleeper recalled, and lo! there would stand by his side a figure to whom power was given, and even at that dead hour, he must rise and do its bidding. The figure in these two phases haunted the lawyer all night; and if at any time he dozed over, it was but to see it glide more stealthily through sleeping houses, or move the more swiftly and still the more swiftly, even to dizziness, through wider labyrinths of lamplighted city, and at every street corner crush a child and leave her screaming. And still the figure had no face by which he might know it; even in his dreams, it had no face, or one that baffled him and melted before his eyes; and thus it was that there sprang up and grew apace in the

6. Damon and Phintias, usually called Pythias, were two philosophers of ancient Greece whose friendship was proverbial: when Pythias was condemned to death, Damon temporarily took his friend's place in captivity at the risk of his own life.
7. The drawing of deeds for transfer of property.
8. Absolute, pure (an obsolete usage that occurs again later in the tale).

lawyer's mind a singularly strong, almost an inordinate, curiosity to behold the features of the real Mr. Hyde. If he could but once set eyes on him, he thought the mystery would lighten and perhaps roll altogether away, as was the habit of mysterious things when well examined. He might see a reason for his friend's strange preference or bondage (call it which you please) and even for the startling clauses of the will. And at least it would be a face worth seeing: the face of a man who was without bowels of mercy:[9] a face which had but to show itself to raise up, in the mind of the unimpressionable Enfield, a spirit of enduring hatred.

From that time forward, Mr. Utterson began to haunt the door in the by-street of shops. In the morning before office hours, at noon when business was plenty and time scarce, at night under the face of the fogged city moon, by all lights and at all hours of solitude or concourse, the lawyer was to be found on his chosen post.

"If he be Mr. Hyde," he had thought, "I shall be Mr. Seek."

And at last his patience was rewarded. It was a fine dry night; frost in the air; the streets as clean as a ballroom floor; the lamps, unshaken by any wind, drawing a regular pattern of light and shadow. By ten o'clock, when the shops were closed, the by-street was very solitary and, in spite of the low growl of London from all round, very silent. Small sounds carried far; domestic sounds out of the houses were clearly audible on either side of the roadway; and the rumour of the approach of any passenger preceded him by a long time. Mr. Utterson had been some minutes at his post, when he was aware of an odd, light footstep drawing near. In the course of his nightly patrols, he had long grown accustomed to the quaint effect with which the footfalls of a single person, while he is still a great way off, suddenly spring out distinct from the vast hum and clatter of the city. Yet his attention had never before been so sharply and decisively arrested; and it was with a strong, superstitious prevision of success that he withdrew into the entry of the court.

The steps drew swiftly nearer, and swelled out suddenly louder as they turned the end of the street. The lawyer, looking forth from the entry, could soon see what manner of man he had to deal with. He was small and very plainly dressed, and the look of him, even at that distance, went somehow strongly against the watcher's inclination. But he made straight for the door, crossing the roadway to save time; and as he came, he drew a key from his pocket like one approaching home.

Mr. Utterson stepped out and touched him on the shoulder as he passed. "Mr. Hyde, I think?"

9. Compassion (from an old notion of bowels as the body's center of sympathetic emotions); cf. Colossians 3:12, "bowels of mercy."

Mr. Hyde shrank back with a hissing intake of the breath. But his fear was only momentary; and though he did not look the lawyer in the face, he answered coolly enough: "That is my name. What do you want?"

"I see you are going in," returned the lawyer. "I am an old friend of Dr. Jekyll's—Mr. Utterson of Gaunt Street—you must have heard my name; and meeting you so conveniently, I thought you might admit me."

"You will not find Dr. Jekyll; he is from home," replied Mr. Hyde, blowing in the key.[1] And then suddenly, but still without looking up, "How did you know me?" he asked.

"On your side," said Mr. Utterson, "will you do me a favour?"

"With pleasure," replied the other. "What shall it be?"

"Will you let me see your face?" asked the lawyer.

Mr. Hyde appeared to hesitate, and then, as if upon some sudden reflection, fronted about with an air of defiance; and the pair stared at each other pretty fixedly for a few seconds. "Now I shall know you again," said Mr. Utterson. "It may be useful."

"Yes," returned Mr. Hyde, "it is as well we have met; and à propos, you should have my address." And he gave a number of a street in Soho.[2]

"Good God!" thought Mr. Utterson, "can he too have been thinking of the will?" But he kept his feelings to himself and only grunted in acknowledgement of the address.

"And now," said the other, "how did you know me?"

"By description," was the reply.

"Whose description?"

"We have common friends," said Mr. Utterson.

"Common friends?" echoed Mr. Hyde, a little hoarsely. "Who are they?"

"Jekyll, for instance," said the lawyer.

"He never told you," cried Mr. Hyde, with a flush of anger. "I did not think you would have lied."

"Come," said Mr. Utterson, "that is not fitting language."

The other snarled aloud into a savage laugh; and the next moment, with extraordinary quickness, he had unlocked the door and disappeared into the house.

The lawyer stood awhile when Mr. Hyde had left him, the picture of disquietude. Then he began slowly to mount the street, pausing every step or two and putting his hand to his brow like a man in

---

1. Probably blowing into a type of key, constructed on a hollow shank that fit over a pin in the lock mechanism, that needed the dirt or lint cleaned out before using.
2. A district in central London known in Victorian times for its crowded immigrant populations and squalid entertainments, including taverns, music halls, and brothels. It is roughly a mile east of fashionable Cavendish Square where Dr. Lanyon lives.

mental perplexity. The problem he was thus debating as he walked, was one of a class that is rarely solved. Mr. Hyde was pale and dwarfish, he gave an impression of deformity without any nameable malformation, he had a displeasing smile, he had borne himself to the lawyer with a sort of murderous mixture of timidity and boldness, and he spoke with a husky, whispering and somewhat broken voice; all these were points against him, but not all of these together could explain the hitherto unknown disgust, loathing and fear with which Mr. Utterson regarded him. "There must be something else," said the perplexed gentleman. "There *is* something more, if I could find a name for it. God bless me, the man seems hardly human! Something troglodytic,[3] shall we say? or can it be the old story of Dr. Fell?[4] or is it the mere radiance of a foul soul that thus transpires through, and transfigures, its clay continent? The last, I think; for O my poor old Harry Jekyll, if ever I read Satan's signature upon a face, it is on that of your new friend."

Round the corner from the by-street, there was a square of ancient, handsome houses, now for the most part decayed from their high estate and let in flats and chambers to all sorts and conditions of men: map-engravers, architects, shady lawyers and the agents of obscure enterprises. One house, however, second from the corner, was still occupied entire; and at the door of this, which wore a great air of wealth and comfort, though it was now plunged in darkness except for the fan-light,[5] Mr. Utterson stopped and knocked. A well-dressed, elderly servant opened the door.

"Is Dr. Jekyll at home, Poole?" asked the lawyer.

"I will see, Mr. Utterson," said Poole, admitting the visitor, as he spoke, into a large, low-roofed, comfortable hall, paved with flags,[6] warmed (after the fashion of a country house) by a bright, open fire, and furnished with costly cabinets of oak. "Will you wait here by the fire, sir? or shall I give you a light in the dining-room?"

"Here, thank you," said the lawyer, and he drew near and leaned on the tall fender.[7] This hall, in which he was now left alone, was a pet fancy of his friend the doctor's; and Utterson himself was wont to speak of it as the pleasantest room in London. But to-night there was a shudder in his blood; the face of Hyde sat heavy on his memory; he felt (what was rare with him) a nausea and distaste of life; and in

3. Characteristic of a troglodyte, or cave-dweller.
4. A man who inspires an unspeakable or unfathomable repugnance. The allusion derives from a verse written by a seventeenth-century Oxford student, Thomas Brown, who retaliated against a disciplinarian dean, Dr. John Fell, by loosely translating a Latin epigram by Martial to read: "I do not love thee, Dr. Fell, / The reason why I cannot tell; / But this I know, and know full well, / I do not love thee, Dr. Fell."
5. Semicircular window over a door with radiating sections that look like an open fan.
6. I.e., flagstones.
7. A metal frame put in front of a fireplace to keep embers from rolling out onto the floor.

the gloom of his spirits, he seemed to read a menace in the flickering of the firelight on the polished cabinets and the uneasy starting of the shadow on the roof. He was ashamed of his relief, when Poole presently returned to announce that Dr. Jekyll was gone out.

"I saw Mr. Hyde go in by the old dissecting room door, Poole," he said. "Is that right, when Dr. Jekyll is from home?"

"Quite right, Mr. Utterson, sir," replied the servant. "Mr. Hyde has a key."

"Your master seems to repose a great deal of trust in that young man, Poole," resumed the other musingly.

"Yes, sir, he do indeed," said Poole. "We have all orders to obey him."

"I do not think I ever met Mr. Hyde?" asked Utterson.

"O, dear no, sir. He never *dines* here," replied the butler. "Indeed we see very little of him on this side of the house; he mostly comes and goes by the laboratory."

"Well, good night, Poole."

"Good night, Mr. Utterson."

And the lawyer set out homeward with a very heavy heart. "Poor Harry Jekyll," he thought, "my mind misgives me he is in deep waters! He was wild when he was young; a long while ago to be sure; but in the law of God, there is no statute of limitations. Ay, it must be that; the ghost of some old sin, the cancer of some concealed disgrace: punishment coming, *pede claudo*,[8] years after memory has forgotten and self-love condoned the fault." And the lawyer, scared by the thought, brooded awhile on his own past, groping in all the corners of memory, lest by chance some Jack-in-the-Box of an old iniquity should leap to light there. His past was fairly blameless; few men could read the rolls of their life with less apprehension; yet he was humbled to the dust by the many ill things he had done, and raised up again into a sober and fearful gratitude by the many that he had come so near to doing, yet avoided. And then by a return on his former subject, he conceived a spark of hope. "This Master Hyde, if he were studied," thought he, "must have secrets of his own: black secrets, by the look of him; secrets compared to which poor Jekyll's worst would be like sunshine. Things cannot continue as they are. It turns me cold to think of this creature stealing like a thief to Harry's bedside; poor Harry, what a wakening! And the danger of it; for if this Hyde suspects the existence of the will, he may grow impatient to inherit. Ay, I must put my shoulder to the wheel—if Jekyll will but let me,"

---

8. Latin, "on limping foot." Utterson is recalling the closing line of an ode on male virtue by the Roman poet Horace (65–8 BCE), "*raro antecedentem scelestum / deseruit pede Poena claudo*": "seldom has Vengeance abandoned a wicked man through lameness of foot though he has got a start on her" (Horace, *Odes*, 3.2.32).

he added, "if Jekyll will only let me." For once more he saw before his mind's eye, as clear as a transparency, the strange clauses of the will.

Dr. Jekyll Was Quite at Ease

A fortnight later, by excellent good fortune, the doctor gave one of his pleasant dinners to some five or six old cronies, all intelligent, reputable men and all judges of good wine; and Mr. Utterson so contrived that he remained behind after the others had departed. This was no new arrangement, but a thing that had befallen many scores of times. Where Utterson was liked, he was liked well. Hosts loved to detain the dry lawyer, when the light-hearted and the loose-tongued had already their foot on the threshold; they liked to sit awhile in his unobtrusive company, practicing for solitude; sobering their minds in the man's rich silence after the expense and strain of gaiety. To this rule, Dr. Jekyll was no exception; and as he now sat on the opposite side of the fire—a large, well-made, smooth-faced man of fifty, with something of a slyish cast perhaps, but every mark of capacity and kindness—you could see by his looks that he cherished for Mr. Utterson a sincere and warm affection.

"I have been wanting to speak to you, Jekyll," began the latter. "You know that will of yours?"

A close observer might have gathered that the topic was distasteful; but the doctor carried it off gaily. "My poor Utterson," said he, "you are unfortunate in such a client. I never saw a man so distressed as you were by my will; unless it were that hide-bound pedant, Lanyon, at what he called my scientific heresies. O, I know he's a good fellow—you needn't frown—an excellent fellow, and I always mean to see more of him; but a hide-bound pedant for all that; an ignorant, blatant pedant. I was never more disappointed in any man than Lanyon."

"You know I never approved of it," pursued Utterson, ruthlessly disregarding the fresh topic.

"My will? Yes, certainly, I know that," said the doctor, a trifle sharply. "You have told me so."

"Well, I tell you so again," continued the lawyer. "I have been learning something of young Hyde."

The large handsome face of Dr. Jekyll grew pale to the very lips, and there came a blackness about his eyes. "I do not care to hear more," said he. "This is a matter I thought we had agreed to drop."

"What I heard was abominable," said Utterson.

"It can make no change. You do not understand my position," returned the doctor, with a certain incoherency of manner. "I am painfully situated, Utterson; my position is a very strange—a very strange one. It is one of those affairs that cannot be mended by talking."

"Jekyll," said Utterson, "you know me: I am a man to be trusted. Make a clean breast of this in confidence; and I make no doubt I can get you out of it."

"My good Utterson," said the doctor, "this is very good of you, this is downright good of you, and I cannot find words to thank you in. I believe you fully; I would trust you before any man alive, ay, before myself, if I could make the choice; but indeed it isn't what you fancy; it is not so bad as that; and just to put your good heart at rest, I will tell you one thing: the moment I choose, I can be rid of Mr. Hyde. I give you my hand upon that; and I thank you again and again; and I will just add one little word, Utterson, that I'm sure you'll take in good part: this is a private matter, and I beg of you to let it sleep."

Utterson reflected a little looking in the fire.

"I have no doubt you are perfectly right," he said at last, getting to his feet.

"Well, but since we have touched upon this business, and for the last time I hope," continued the doctor, "there is one point I should like you to understand. I have really a very great interest in poor Hyde. I know you have seen him; he told me so; and I fear he was rude. But I do sincerely take a great, a very great interest in that young man; and if I am taken away, Utterson, I wish you to promise me that you will bear with him and get his rights for him. I think you would, if you knew all; and it would be a weight off my mind if you would promise."

"I can't pretend that I shall ever like him," said the lawyer.

"I don't ask that," pleaded Jekyll, laying his hand upon the other's arm; "I only ask for justice; I only ask you to help him for my sake, when I am no longer here."

Utterson heaved an irrepressible sigh. "Well," said he. "I promise."

The Carew Murder Case

Nearly a year later, in the month of October 18—,[9] London was startled by a crime of singular ferocity and rendered all the more notable by the high position of the victim. The details were few

9. Stevenson followed a then-familiar literary convention in using a dash for the final two digits of a date so as to leave the exact year unspecified. Draft fragments of the tale show that at an earlier stage of composition he included several fully specified dates that set the action of the story in the years 1883–85.

and startling. A maid servant living alone in a house not far from the river, had gone upstairs to bed about eleven. Although a fog rolled over the city in the small hours, the early part of the night was cloudless, and the lane, which the maid's window overlooked, was brilliantly lit by the full moon. It seems she was romantically given, for she sat down upon her box, which stood immediately under the window, and fell into a dream of musing. Never (she used to say, with streaming tears, when she narrated that experience) never had she felt more at peace with all men or thought more kindly of the world. And as she so sat she became aware of an aged and beautiful gentleman with white hair, drawing near along the lane; and advancing to meet him, another and very small gentleman, to whom at first she paid less attention. When they had come within speech (which was just under the maid's eyes) the older man bowed and accosted the other with a very pretty manner of politeness. It did not seem as if the subject of his address were of great importance; indeed, from his pointing, it sometimes appeared as if he were only inquiring his way; but the moon shone on his face as he spoke, and the girl was pleased to watch it, it seemed to breathe such an innocent and old-world kindness of disposition, yet with something high too, as of a well-founded self-content. Presently her eye wandered to the other, and she was surprised to recognise in him a certain Mr. Hyde, who had once visited her master and for whom she had conceived a dislike. He had in his hand a heavy cane, with which he was trifling; but he answered never a word, and seemed to listen with an ill-contained impatience. And then all of a sudden he broke out in a great flame of anger, stamping with his foot, brandishing the cane, and carrying on (as the maid described it) like a madman. The old gentleman took a step back, with the air of one very much surprised and a trifle hurt; and at that Mr. Hyde broke out of all bounds and clubbed him to the earth. And next moment, with ape-like fury, he was trampling his victim under foot, and hailing down a storm of blows, under which the bones were audibly shattered and the body jumped upon the roadway. At the horror of these sights and sounds, the maid fainted.

It was two o'clock when she came to herself and called for the police. The murderer was gone long ago; but there lay his victim in the middle of the lane, incredibly mangled. The stick with which the deed had been done, although it was of some rare and very tough and heavy wood, had broken in the middle under the stress of this insensate cruelty; and one splintered half had rolled in the neighbouring gutter—the other, without doubt, had been carried away by the murderer. A purse and a gold watch were found upon the victim; but no cards or papers, except a sealed and stamped envelope, which he had been probably carrying to the post, and which bore the name and address of Mr. Utterson.

This was brought to the lawyer the next morning, before he was out of bed; and he had no sooner seen it, and been told the circumstances, than he shot out a solemn lip. "I shall say nothing till I have seen the body," said he; "this may be very serious. Have the kindness to wait while I dress." And with the same grave countenance he hurried through his breakfast and drove to the police station, whither the body had been carried. As soon as he came into the cell, he nodded.

"Yes," said he, "I recognise him. I am sorry to say that this is Sir Danvers Carew."

"Good God, sir," exclaimed the officer, "is it possible?" And the next moment his eye lighted up with professional ambition. "This will make a deal of noise," he said. "And perhaps you can help us to the man." And he briefly narrated what the maid had seen, and showed the broken stick.

Mr. Utterson had already quailed at the name of Hyde; but when the stick was laid before him, he could doubt no longer: broken and battered as it was, he recognised it for one that he had himself presented many years before to Henry Jekyll.

"Is this Mr. Hyde a person of small stature?" he inquired.

"Particularly small and particularly wicked-looking, is what the maid calls him," said the officer.

Mr. Utterson reflected; and then, raising his head, "If you will come with me in my cab," he said, "I think I can take you to his house."

It was by this time about nine in the morning, and the first fog of the season.[1] A great chocolate-coloured pall lowered over heaven, but the wind was continually charging and routing these embattled vapours; so that as the cab crawled from street to street, Mr. Utterson beheld a marvellous number of degrees and hues of twilight; for here it would be dark like the back-end of evening; and there would be a glow of a rich, lurid brown, like the light of some strange conflagration; and here, for a moment, the fog would be quite broken up, and a haggard shaft of daylight would glance in between the swirling wreaths. The dismal quarter of Soho seen under these changing glimpses, with its muddy ways, and slatternly passengers, and its lamps, which had never been extinguished or had been kindled afresh to combat this mournful reinvasion of darkness, seemed, in the lawyer's eyes, like a district of some city

---

1. In modern terms, smog; by the late nineteenth century, smoke pollution in industrialized London had become so thick that when mixed with fog, especially during the winter months, it produced famously sky-darkening, choking hazes that could last for days or weeks on end.

in a nightmare. The thoughts of his mind, besides, were of the gloomiest dye; and when he glanced at the companion of his drive, he was conscious of some touch of that terror of the law and the law's officers, which may at times assail the most honest.

As the cab drew up before the address indicated, the fog lifted a little and showed him a dingy street, a gin palace,[2] a low French eating house, a shop for the retail of penny numbers[3] and twopenny salads, many ragged children huddled in the doorways, and many women of many different nationalities passing out, key in hand, to have a morning glass; and the next moment the fog settled down again upon that part, as brown as umber, and cut him off from his blackguardly surroundings. This was the home of Henry Jekyll's favourite; of a man who was heir to quarter of a million sterling.[4]

An ivory-faced and silvery-haired old woman opened the door. She had an evil face, smoothed by hypocrisy; but her manners were excellent. Yes, she said, this was Mr. Hyde's, but he was not at home; he had been in that night very late, but had gone away again in less than an hour; there was nothing strange in that; his habits were very irregular, and he was often absent; for instance, it was nearly two months since she had seen him till yesterday.

"Very well then, we wish to see his rooms," said the lawyer; and when the woman began to declare it was impossible, "I had better tell you who this person is," he added. "This is Inspector Newcomen of Scotland Yard."

A flash of odious joy appeared upon the woman's face. "Ah!" said she, "he is in trouble! What has he done?"

Mr. Utterson and the inspector exchanged glances. "He don't seem a very popular character," observed the latter. "And now, my good woman, just let me and this gentleman have a look about us."

In the whole extent of the house, which but for the old woman remained otherwise empty, Mr. Hyde had only used a couple of rooms; but these were furnished with luxury and good taste. A closet was filled with wine; the plate was of silver, the napery[5] elegant; a good picture hung upon the walls, a gift (as Utterson supposed) from Henry Jekyll, who was much of a connoisseur; and the carpets were of many plies and agreeable in colour. At this moment, however, the rooms bore every mark of having been recently and hurriedly ransacked; clothes lay about the floor, with their pockets

---

2. The phrase was used contemptuously of the cheapest type of drinking establishment.
3. Cheap serial installments of popular sensation fiction, also known as "penny dreadfuls."
4. I.e., pounds sterling.
5. Domestic linens, especially table linens.

inside out; lockfast[6] drawers stood open; and on the hearth there lay a pile of gray ashes, as though many papers had been burned. From these embers the inspector disinterred the butt end of a green cheque book, which had resisted the action of the fire; the other half of the stick was found behind the door; and as this clinched his suspicions, the officer declared himself delighted. A visit to the bank, where several thousand pounds were found to be lying to the murderer's credit, completed his gratification.

"You may depend upon it, sir," he told Mr. Utterson: "I have him in my hand. He must have lost his head, or he never would have left the stick or, above all, burned the cheque book. Why, money's life to the man. We have nothing to do but wait for him at the bank, and get out the handbills."[7]

This last, however, was not so easy of accomplishment; for Mr. Hyde had numbered few familiars—even the master of the servant maid had only seen him twice; his family could nowhere be traced; he had never been photographed; and the few who could describe him differed widely, as common observers will. Only on one point, were they agreed; and that was the haunting sense of unexpressed deformity with which the fugitive impressed his beholders.

Incident of the Letter

It was late in the afternoon, when Mr. Utterson found his way to Dr. Jekyll's door, where he was at once admitted by Poole, and carried down by the kitchen offices[8] and across a yard which had once been a garden, to the building which was indifferently known as the laboratory or the dissecting rooms. The doctor had bought the house from the heirs of a celebrated surgeon; and his own tastes being rather chemical than anatomical, had changed the destination of the block[9] at the bottom of the garden. It was the first time that the lawyer had been received in that part of his friend's quarters; and he eyed the dingy windowless structure with curiosity, and gazed round with a distasteful sense of strangeness as he crossed the theatre,[1] once crowded with eager students and now lying gaunt and silent, the tables laden with chemical apparatus, the floor strewn with crates and littered with packing

6. Fastened or secured by a lock (Scottish usage).
7. Printed sheets circulated locally by hand describing known or suspected criminals and seeking information from the public to aid in their identification and arrest.
8. Rooms devoted to kitchen functions.
9. I.e., had changed the purpose of the building.
1. A surgical or anatomical theater, with seats for students arranged around a central lecturing or demonstration platform.

straw, and the light falling dimly through the foggy cupola. At the further end, a flight of stairs mounted to a door covered with red baize; and through this, Mr. Utterson was at last received into the doctor's cabinet. It was a large room, fitted round with glass presses,[2] furnished, among other things, with a cheval-glass[3] and a business table, and looking out upon the court by three dusty windows barred with iron. The fire burned in the grate; a lamp was set lighted on the chimney shelf, for even in the houses the fog began to lie thickly; and there, close up to the warmth, sat Dr. Jekyll, looking deadly sick. He did not rise to meet his visitor, but held out a cold hand and bade him welcome in a changed voice.

"And now," said Mr. Utterson, as soon as Poole had left them, "you have heard the news?"

The doctor shuddered. "They were crying it in the square," he said. "I heard them in my dining room."

"One word," said the lawyer. "Carew was my client, but so are you, and I want to know what I am doing. You have not been mad enough to hide this fellow?"

"Utterson, I swear to God," cried the doctor, "I swear to God I will never set eyes on him again. I bind my honour to you that I am done with him in this world. It is all at an end. And indeed he does not want my help; you do not know him as I do; he is safe, he is quite safe; mark my words, he will never more be heard of."

The lawyer listened gloomily; he did not like his friend's feverish manner. "You seem pretty sure of him," said he; "and for your sake, I hope you may be right. If it came to a trial, your name might appear."

"I am quite sure of him," replied Jekyll; "I have grounds for certainty that I cannot share with anyone. But there is one thing on which you may advise me. I have—I have received a letter; and I am at a loss whether I should show it to the police. I should like to leave it in your hands, Utterson; you would judge wisely I am sure; I have so great a trust in you."

"You fear, I suppose, that it might lead to his detection?" asked the lawyer.

"No," said the other. "I cannot say that I care what becomes of Hyde; I am quite done with him. I was thinking of my own character, which this hateful business has rather exposed."

Utterson ruminated awhile; he was surprised at his friend's selfishness, and yet relieved by it. "Well," said he, at last, "let me see the letter."

2. Shelved cupboards with glass doors.
3. A full-length mirror pivotally attached to a stationary frame in which it may be tilted.

The letter was written in an odd, upright hand and signed "Edward Hyde": and it signified, briefly enough, that the writer's benefactor, Dr. Jekyll, whom he had long so unworthily repaid for a thousand generosities, need labour under no alarm for his safety as he had means of escape on which he placed a sure dependence. The lawyer liked this letter well enough; it put a better colour on the intimacy than he had looked for; and he blamed himself for some of his past suspicions.

"Have you the envelope?" he asked.

"I burned it," replied Jekyll, "before I thought what I was about. But it bore no postmark. The note was handed in."

"Shall I keep this and sleep upon it?" asked Utterson.

"I wish you to judge for me entirely," was the reply. "I have lost confidence in myself."

"Well, I shall consider," returned the lawyer. "And now one word more: it was Hyde who dictated the terms in your will about that disappearance?"

The doctor seemed seized with a qualm of faintness; he shut his mouth tight and nodded.

"I knew it," said Utterson. "He meant to murder you. You have had a fine escape."

"I have had what is far more to the purpose," returned the doctor solemnly: "I have had a lesson—O God, Utterson, what a lesson I have had!" And he covered his face for a moment with his hands.

On his way out, the lawyer stopped and had a word or two with Poole. "By the by," said he "there was a letter handed in to-day: what was the messenger like?" But Poole was positive nothing had come except by post; "and only circulars by that," he added.

This news sent off the visitor with his fears renewed. Plainly the letter had come by the laboratory door; possibly, indeed, it had been written in the cabinet; and if that were so, it must be differently judged, and handled with the more caution. The newsboys, as he went, were crying themselves hoarse along the footways: "Special edition. Shocking murder of an M.P."[4] That was the funeral oration of one friend and client; and he could not help a certain apprehension lest the good name of another should be sucked down in the eddy of the scandal. It was, at least, a ticklish decision that he had to make; and self-reliant as he was by habit, he began to cherish a longing for advice. It was not to be had directly; but perhaps, he thought, it might be fished for.

Presently after, he sat on one side of his own hearth, with Mr. Guest, his head clerk, upon the other, and midway between, at a nicely calculated distance from the fire, a bottle of a particular

4. Member of Parliament.

old wine that had long dwelt unsunned in the foundations of his house. The fog still slept on the wing above the drowned city, where the lamps glimmered like carbuncles; and through the muffle and smother of these fallen clouds, the procession of the town's life was still rolling in through the great arteries with a sound as of a mighty wind. But the room was gay with firelight. In the bottle the acids were long ago resolved; the imperial dye had softened with time, as the colour grows richer in stained windows; and the glow of hot autumn afternoons on hillside vineyards, was ready to be set free and to disperse the fogs of London. Insensibly the lawyer melted. There was no man from whom he kept fewer secrets than Mr. Guest; and he was not always sure that he kept as many as he meant. Guest had often been on business to the doctor's; he knew Poole; he could scarce have failed to hear of Mr. Hyde's familiarity about the house; he might draw conclusions: was it not as well, then, that he should see a letter which put that mystery to rights? and above all since Guest, being a great student and critic of handwriting, would consider the step natural and obliging? The clerk, besides, was a man of counsel; he would scarce read so strange a document without dropping a remark; and by that remark Mr. Utterson might shape his future course.

"This is a sad business about Sir Danvers," he said.

"Yes, sir, indeed. It has elicited a great deal of public feeling," returned Guest. "The man, of course, was mad."

"I should like to hear your views on that," replied Utterson. "I have a document here in his handwriting; it is between ourselves, for I scarce know what to do about it; it is an ugly business at the best. But there it is; quite in your way: a murderer's autograph."

Guest's eyes brightened, and he sat down at once and studied it with passion. "No, sir," he said; "not mad; but it is an odd hand."

"And by all accounts a very odd writer," added the lawyer.

Just then the servant entered with a note.

"Is that from Dr. Jekyll, sir?" inquired the clerk. "I thought I knew the writing. Anything private, Mr. Utterson?"

"Only an invitation to dinner. Why? do you want to see it?"

"One moment. I thank you, sir;" and the clerk laid the two sheets of paper alongside and sedulously compared their contents. "Thank you, sir," he said at last, returning both; "it's a very interesting autograph."

There was a pause, during which Mr. Utterson struggled with himself. "Why did you compare them, Guest?" he inquired suddenly.

"Well, sir," returned the clerk, "there's a rather singular resemblance; the two hands are in many points identical: only differently sloped."

"Rather quaint," said Utterson.

"It is, as you say, rather quaint," returned Guest.

"I wouldn't speak of this note, you know," said the master.

"No, sir," said the clerk. "I understand."

But no sooner was Mr. Utterson alone that night, than he locked the note into his safe where it reposed from that time forward. "What!" he thought. "Henry Jekyll forge for a murderer!" And his blood ran cold in his veins.

Remarkable Incident of Dr. Lanyon

Time ran on; thousands of pounds were offered in reward, for the death of Sir Danvers was resented as a public injury; but Mr. Hyde had disappeared out of the ken[5] of the police as though he had never existed. Much of his past was unearthed, indeed, and all disreputable: tales came out of the man's cruelty, at once so callous and violent, of his vile life, of his strange associates, of the hatred that seemed to have surrounded his career; but of his present whereabouts, not a whisper. From the time he had left the house in Soho on the morning of the murder, he was simply blotted out; and gradually, as time drew on, Mr. Utterson began to recover from the hotness of his alarm, and to grow more at quiet with himself. The death of Sir Danvers was, to his way of thinking, more than paid for by the disappearance of Mr. Hyde. Now that that evil influence had been withdrawn, a new life began for Dr. Jekyll. He came out of his seclusion, renewed relations with his friends, became once more their familiar guest and entertainer; and whilst he had always been known for charities, he was now no less distinguished for religion. He was busy, he was much in the open air, he did good; his face seemed to open and brighten, as if with an inward consciousness of service; and for more than two months, the doctor was at peace.

On the 8th of January Utterson had dined at the doctor's with a small party; Lanyon had been there; and the face of the host had looked from one to the other as in the old days when the trio were inseparable friends. On the 12th, and again on the 14th, the door was shut against the lawyer. "The doctor was confined to the house," Poole said, "and saw no one." On the 15th, he tried again, and was again refused; and having now been used for the last two months to see his friend almost daily, he found this return of solitude to weigh upon his spirits. The fifth night, he had in Guest to dine with him; and the sixth he betook himself to Dr. Lanyon's.

There at least he was not denied admittance; but when he came in, he was shocked at the change which had taken place in the

5. Sight; knowledge.

doctor's appearance. He had his death-warrant written legibly upon his face. The rosy man had grown pale; his flesh had fallen away; he was visibly balder and older; and yet it was not so much these tokens of a swift physical decay that arrested the lawyer's notice, as a look in the eye and quality of manner that seemed to testify to some deep-seated terror of the mind. It was unlikely that the doctor should fear death; and yet that was what Utterson was tempted to suspect. "Yes," he thought, "he is a doctor, he must know his own state and that his days are counted; and the knowledge is more than he can bear." And yet when Utterson remarked on his ill-looks, it was with an air of great firmness that Lanyon declared himself a doomed man.

"I have had a shock," he said, "and I shall never recover. It is a question of weeks. Well, life has been pleasant; I liked it; yes, sir, I used to like it. I sometimes think if we knew all, we should be more glad to get away."

"Jekyll is ill, too," observed Utterson. "Have you seen him?"

But Lanyon's face changed, and he held up a trembling hand. "I wish to see or hear no more of Dr. Jekyll," he said in a loud, unsteady voice. "I am quite done with that person; and I beg that you will spare me any allusion to one whom I regard as dead."

"Tut-tut," said Mr. Utterson; and then after a considerable pause, "Can't I do anything?" he inquired. "We are three very old friends, Lanyon; we shall not live to make others."

"Nothing can be done," returned Lanyon; "ask himself."

"He will not see me," said the lawyer.

"I am not surprised at that," was the reply.

"Some day, Utterson, after I am dead, you may perhaps come to learn the right and wrong of this. I cannot tell you. And in the meantime, if you can sit and talk with me of other things, for God's sake, stay and do so; but if you cannot keep clear of this accursed topic, then, in God's name, go, for I cannot bear it."

As soon as he got home, Utterson sat down and wrote to Jekyll, complaining of his exclusion from the house, and asking the cause of this unhappy break with Lanyon; and the next day brought him a long answer, often very pathetically worded, and sometimes darkly mysterious in drift. The quarrel with Lanyon was incurable. "I do not blame our old friend," Jekyll wrote, "but I share his view that we must never meet. I mean from henceforth to lead a life of extreme seclusion; you must not be surprised, nor must you doubt my friendship, if my door is often shut even to you. You must suffer me to go my own dark way. I have brought on myself a punishment and a danger that I cannot name. If I am the chief of sinners, I am the chief of sufferers also. I could not think that this earth con-tained a place for sufferings and terrors so unmanning; and you can do but one thing, Utterson, to lighten this destiny, and that is to respect my silence." Utterson was amazed; the dark influence of Hyde had been withdrawn, the doctor had returned to his old tasks and amities; a week ago, the prospect had smiled with every promise of a cheerful and an honoured age; and now in a moment, friendship, and peace of mind and the whole tenor of his life were wrecked. So great and unprepared a change pointed to madness; but in view of Lanyon's manner and words, there must lie for it some deeper ground.

A week afterwards Dr. Lanyon took to his bed, and in something less than a fortnight he was dead. The night after the funeral, at which he had been sadly affected, Utterson locked the door of his business room, and sitting there by the light of a melancholy candle, drew out and set before him an envelope addressed by the hand and sealed with the seal of his dead friend. "PRIVATE: for the hands of J. G. Utterson ALONE and in case of his predecease *to be destroyed unread*," so it was emphatically superscribed; and the lawyer dreaded to behold the contents. "I have buried one friend to-day," he thought: "what if this should cost me another?" And then he condemned the fear as a disloyalty, and broke the seal. Within there was another enclosure, likewise sealed, and marked upon the cover as "not to be opened till the death or disappearance of Dr. Henry Jekyll." Utterson could not trust his eyes. Yes, it was disappearance; here again, as in the mad will which he had long ago restored to its author, here again were the idea of a disappearance and the name of Henry Jekyll bracketed. But in the will, that idea had sprung from the sinister suggestion of the man Hyde; it was set there with a purpose all too plain and horrible. Written by the hand of Lanyon, what should it mean? A great curiosity came on the trustee, to disregard the prohibition and dive at once to the bottom of these mysteries; but professional honour and faith to his dead friend were stringent obligations; and the packet slept in the inmost corner of his private safe.

It is one thing to mortify curiosity, another to conquer it; and it may be doubted if, from that day forth, Utterson desired the society of his surviving friend with the same eagerness. He thought of him kindly; but his thoughts were disquieted and fearful. He went to call indeed; but he was perhaps relieved to be denied admittance; perhaps, in his heart, he preferred to speak with Poole upon the doorstep and surrounded by the air and sounds of the open city, rather than to be admitted into that house of voluntary bondage, and to sit and speak with its inscrutable recluse. Poole had, indeed, no very pleasant news to communicate. The doctor, it appeared, now more than ever confined himself to the cabinet over the laboratory, where he would sometimes even sleep; he was out of spirits, he had grown very silent, he did not read; it seemed as if he had something on his mind. Utterson became so used to the unvarying character of these reports, that he fell off little by little in the frequency of his visits.

Incident at the Window

It chanced on Sunday, when Mr. Utterson was on his usual walk with Mr. Enfield, that their way lay once again through the by-street; and that when they came in front of the door, both stopped to gaze on it.

"Well," said Enfield, "that story's at an end at least. We shall never see more of Mr. Hyde."

"I hope not," said Utterson. "Did I ever tell you that I once saw him, and shared your feeling of repulsion?"

"It was impossible to do the one without the other," returned Enfield. "And by the way what an ass you must have thought me, not to know that this was a back way to Dr. Jekyll's! It was partly your own fault that I found it out, even when I did."

"So you found it out, did you?" said Utterson.

"But if that be so, we may step into the court and take a look at the windows. To tell you the truth, I am uneasy about poor Jekyll; and even outside, I feel as if the presence of a friend might do him good."

The court was very cool and a little damp, and full of premature twilight, although the sky, high up overhead, was still bright with sunset. The middle one of the three windows was half way open; and sitting close beside it, taking the air with an infinite sadness of mien, like some disconsolate prisoner, Utterson saw Dr. Jekyll.

"What! Jekyll!" he cried. "I trust you are better."

"I am very low, Utterson," replied the doctor drearily, "very low. It will not last long, thank God."

"You stay too much indoors," said the lawyer. "You should be out, whipping up the circulation like Mr. Enfield and me. (This is my cousin—Mr. Enfield—Dr. Jekyll.) Come now; get your hat and take a quick turn with us."

"You are very good," sighed the other. "I should like to very much; but no, no, no, it is quite impossible; I dare not. But indeed, Utterson, I am very glad to see you; this is really a great pleasure; I would ask you and Mr. Enfield up, but the place is really not fit."

"Why then," said the lawyer, good-naturedly, "the best thing we can do is to stay down here and speak with you from where we are."

"That is just what I was about to venture to propose," returned the doctor with a smile. But the words were hardly uttered, before the smile was struck out of his face and succeeded by an expression of such abject terror and despair, as froze the very blood of the two gentlemen below. They saw it but for a glimpse, for the window was instantly thrust down; but that glimpse had been sufficient, and they turned and left the court without a word. In silence, too, they traversed the by-street; and it was not until they had come into a neighbouring thoroughfare, where even upon a Sunday there were still some stirrings of life, that Mr. Utterson at last turned and looked at his companion. They were both pale; and there was an answering horror in their eyes.

"God forgive us, God forgive us," said Mr. Utterson.

But Mr. Enfield only nodded his head very seriously, and walked on once more in silence.

The Last Night

Mr. Utterson was sitting by his fireside one evening after dinner, when he was surprised to receive a visit from Poole.

"Bless me, Poole, what brings you here?" he cried; and then taking a second look at him, "What ails you?" he added, "is the doctor ill?"

"Mr. Utterson," said the man, "there is something wrong."

"Take a seat, and here is a glass of wine for you," said the lawyer. "Now, take your time, and tell me plainly what you want."

"You know the doctor's ways, sir," replied Poole, "and how he shuts himself up. Well, he's shut up again in the cabinet; and I don't like it, sir—I wish I may die if I like it. Mr. Utterson, sir, I'm afraid."

"Now, my good man," said the lawyer, "be explicit. What are you afraid of?"

"I've been afraid for about a week," returned Poole, doggedly disregarding the question, "and I can bear it no more."

The man's appearance amply bore out his words; his manner was altered for the worse; and except for the moment when he had first announced his terror, he had not once looked the lawyer in the face. Even now, he sat with the glass of wine untasted on his knee, and his eyes directed to a corner of the floor. "I can bear it no more," he repeated.

"Come," said the lawyer, "I see you have some good reason, Poole; I see there is something seriously amiss. Try to tell me what it is."

"I think there's been foul play," said Poole, hoarsely.

"Foul play!" cried the lawyer, a good deal frightened and rather inclined to be irritated in consequence. "What foul play? What does the man mean?"

"I daren't say, sir," was the answer; "but will you come along with me and see for yourself?"

Mr. Utterson's only answer was to rise and get his hat and great coat; but he observed with wonder the greatness of the relief that appeared upon the butler's face, and perhaps with no less, that the wine was still untasted when he set it down to follow.

It was a wild, cold, seasonable night of March, with a pale moon, lying on her back as though the wind had tilted her, and a flying wrack of the most diaphanous and lawny texture. The wind made talking difficult, and flecked the blood into the face. It seemed to have swept the streets unusually bare of passengers, besides; for Mr. Utterson thought he had never seen that part of London so deserted. He could have wished it otherwise; never in his life had he been conscious of so sharp a wish to see and touch his fellow-creatures; for struggle as he might, there was borne in upon his mind a crushing anticipation of calamity. The square, when they got there, was all full of wind and dust, and the thin trees in the garden were lashing themselves along the railing. Poole, who had kept all the way a pace or two ahead, now pulled up in the middle of the pavement, and in spite of the biting weather, took off his hat and mopped his brow with a red pocket-handkerchief. But for all the hurry of his coming, these were not the dews of exertion that he wiped away, but the moisture of some strangling anguish; for his face was white and his voice, when he spoke, harsh and broken.

"Well, sir," he said, "here we are, and God grant there be nothing wrong."

"Amen, Poole," said the lawyer.

Thereupon the servant knocked in a very guarded manner; the door was opened on the chain; and a voice asked from within, "Is that you, Poole?"

"It's all right," said Poole. "Open the door."

The hall, when they entered it, was brightly lighted up; the fire was built high; and about the hearth the whole of the servants, men and women, stood huddled together like a flock of sheep. At the sight of Mr. Utterson, the housemaid broke into hysterical whimpering; and the cook, crying out "Bless God! it's Mr. Utterson," ran forward as if to take him in her arms.

"What, what? Are you all here?" said the lawyer peevishly. "Very irregular, very unseemly; your master would be far from pleased."

"They're all afraid," said Poole.

Blank silence followed, no one protesting; only the maid lifted up her voice and now wept loudly.

"Hold your tongue!" Poole said to her, with a ferocity of accent that testified to his own jangled nerves; and indeed, when the girl had so suddenly raised the note of her lamentation, they had all started and turned towards the inner door with faces of dreadful expectation. "And now," continued the butler, addressing the knife-boy, "reach me a candle, and we'll get this through hands at once."

And then he begged Mr. Utterson to follow him, and led the way to the back garden.

"Now, sir," said he, "you come as gently as you can. I want you to hear, and I don't want you to be heard. And see here, sir, if by any chance he was to ask you in, don't go."

Mr. Utterson's nerves, at this unlooked-for termination, gave a jerk that nearly threw him from his balance; but he recollected his courage and followed the butler into the laboratory building and through the surgical theatre, with its lumber of crates and bottles, to the foot of the stair. Here Poole motioned him to stand on one side and listen; while he himself, setting down the candle and making a great and obvious call on his resolution, mounted the steps and knocked with a somewhat uncertain hand on the red baize of the cabinet door.

"Mr. Utterson, sir, asking to see you," he called; and even as he did so, once more violently signed to the lawyer to give ear.

A voice answered from within: "Tell him I cannot see anyone," it said complainingly.

"Thank you, sir," said Poole, with a note of something like triumph in his voice; and taking up his candle, he led Mr. Utterson back across the yard and into the great kitchen, where the fire was out and the beetles were leaping on the floor.

"Sir," he said, looking Mr. Utterson in the eyes, "was that my master's voice?"

"It seems much changed," replied the lawyer, very pale, but giving look for look.

"Changed? Well, yes, I think so," said the butler. "Have I been twenty years in this man's house, to be deceived about his voice? No, sir; master's made away with; he was made away with, eight days ago, when we heard him cry out upon the name of God; and who's in there instead of him, and why it stays there, is a thing that cries to Heaven, Mr. Utterson!"

"This is a very strange tale, Poole; this is rather a wild tale, my man," said Mr. Utterson, biting his finger. "Suppose it were as you suppose, supposing Dr. Jekyll to have been—well, murdered, what could induce the murderer to stay? That won't hold water; it doesn't commend itself to reason."

"Well, Mr. Utterson, you are a hard man to satisfy, but I'll do it yet," said Poole. "All this last week (you must know) him, or it, or whatever it is that lives in that cabinet, has been crying night and day for some sort of medicine and cannot get it to his mind.[6] It was sometimes his way—the master's, that is—to write his orders on a sheet of paper and throw it on the stair. We've had nothing else this week back; nothing but papers, and a closed door, and the very meals left there to be smuggled in when nobody was looking. Well,

6. To his liking.

sir, every day, ay, and twice and thrice in the same day, there have been orders and complaints, and I have been sent flying to all the wholesale chemists in town. Every time I brought the stuff back, there would be another paper telling me to return it, because it was not pure, and another order to a different firm. This drug is wanted bitter bad, sir, whatever for."

"Have you any of these papers?" asked Mr. Utterson.

Poole felt in his pocket and handed out a crumpled note, which the lawyer, bending nearer to the candle, carefully examined. Its contents ran thus: "Dr. Jekyll presents his compliments to Messrs. Maw. He assures them that their last sample is impure and quite useless for his present purpose. In the year 18—, Dr. J. purchased a somewhat large quantity from Messrs. M. He now begs them to search with the most sedulous care, and should any of the same quality be left, to forward it to him at once. Expense is no consider-ation. The importance of this to Dr. J. can hardly be exaggerated." So far the letter had run composedly enough, but here with a sud-den splutter of the pen, the writer's emotion had broken loose. "For God's sake," he had added, "find me some of the old."

"This is a strange note," said Mr. Utterson; and then sharply, "How do you come to have it open?"

"The man at Maw's was main[7] angry, sir, and he threw it back to me like so much dirt," returned Poole.

"This is unquestionably the doctor's hand, do you know?" resumed the lawyer.

"I thought it looked like it," said the servant rather sulkily; and then, with another voice, "But what matters hand of write," he said. "I've seen him!"

"Seen him?" repeated Mr. Utterson. "Well?"

"That's it!" said Poole. "It was this way. I came suddenly into the theatre from the garden. It seems he had slipped out to look for this drug or whatever it is; for the cabinet door was open, and there he was at the far end of the room digging among the crates. He looked up when I came in, gave a kind of cry, and whipped upstairs into the cabinet. It was but for one minute that I saw him, but the hair stood upon my head like quills. Sir, if that was my master, why had he a mask upon his face? If it was my master, why did he cry out like a rat, and run from me? I have served him long enough. And then . . ." the man paused and passed his hand over his face.

"These are all very strange circumstances," said Mr. Utterson, "but I think I begin to see daylight. Your master, Poole, is plainly seized with one of those maladies that both torture and deform the sufferer; hence, for aught I know, the alteration of his voice; hence the mask and his avoidance of his friends; hence his eagerness to find this drug, by means of which the poor soul retains some hope

7. Exceedingly (working-class dialect).

of ultimate recovery—God grant that he be not deceived! There is my explanation; it is sad enough, Poole, ay, and appalling to consider; but it is plain and natural, hangs well together and delivers us from all exorbitant alarms."

"Sir," said the butler, turning to a sort of mottled pallor, "that thing was not my master, and there's the truth. My master"—here he looked round him and began to whisper—"is a tall fine build of a man, and this was more of a dwarf." Utterson attempted to protest. "O, sir," cried Poole, "do you think I do not know my master after twenty years? do you think I do not know where his head comes to in the cabinet door, where I saw him every morning of my life? No, sir, that thing in the mask was never Dr. Jekyll—God knows what it was, but it was never Dr. Jekyll; and it is the belief of my heart that there was murder done."

"Poole," replied the lawyer, "if you say that, it will become my duty to make certain. Much as I desire to spare your master's feelings, much as I am puzzled by this note which seems to prove him to be still alive, I shall consider it my duty to break in that door."

"Ah, Mr. Utterson, that's talking!" cried the butler.

"And now comes the second question," resumed Utterson: "Who is going to do it?"

"Why, you and me, sir," was the undaunted reply.

"That is very well said," returned the lawyer; "and whatever comes of it, I shall make it my business to see you are no loser."

"There is an axe in the theatre," continued Poole, "and you might take the kitchen poker for yourself."

The lawyer took that rude but weighty instrument into his hand, and balanced it. "Do you know, Poole," he said, looking up, "that you and I are about to place ourselves in a position of some peril?"

"You may say so, sir, indeed," returned the butler.

"It is well, then, that we should be frank," said the other. "We both think more than we have said; let us make a clean breast. This masked figure that you saw, did you recognise it?"

"Well, sir, it went so quick, and the creature was so doubled up, that I could hardly swear to that," was the answer. "But if you mean, was it Mr. Hyde?—why, yes, I think it was! You see, it was much of the same bigness; and it had the same quick light way with it; and then who else could have got in by the laboratory door? You have not forgot, sir, that at the time of the murder he had still the key with him? But that's not all. I don't know, Mr. Utterson, if ever you met this Mr. Hyde?"

"Yes," said the lawyer, "I once spoke with him."

"Then you must know as well as the rest of us that there was something queer about that gentleman—something that gave a man a turn—I don't know rightly how to say it, sir, beyond this: that you felt it in your marrow kind of cold and thin."

"I own I felt something of what you describe," said Mr. Utterson.

"Quite so, sir," returned Poole. "Well, when that masked thing like a monkey jumped from among the chemicals and whipped into the cabinet, it went down my spine like ice. O, I know it's not evidence, Mr. Utterson; I'm book-learned enough for that; but a man has his feelings, and I give you my bible-word it was Mr. Hyde!"

"Ay, ay," said the lawyer. "My fears incline to the same point. Evil, I fear, founded—evil was sure to come—of that connection. Ay, truly, I believe you; I believe poor Harry is killed; and I believe his murderer (for what purpose, God alone can tell) is still lurking in his victim's room. Well, let our name be vengeance. Call Bradshaw."

The footman came at the summons, very white and nervous.

"Pull yourself together, Bradshaw," said the lawyer. "This suspense, I know, is telling upon all of you; but it is now our intention to make an end of it. Poole, here, and I are going to force our way into the cabinet. If all is well, my shoulders are broad enough to bear the blame. Meanwhile, lest anything should really be amiss, or any malefactor seek to escape by the back, you and the boy must go round the corner with a pair of good sticks, and take your post at the laboratory door. We give you ten minutes, to get to your stations."

As Bradshaw left, the lawyer looked at his watch. "And now, Poole, let us get to ours," he said; and taking the poker under his arm, he led the way into the yard. The scud[8] had banked over the moon, and it was now quite dark. The wind, which only broke in puffs and draughts into that deep well of building, tossed the light of the candle to and fro about their steps, until they came into the shelter of the theatre, where they sat down silently to wait. London hummed solemnly all around; but nearer at hand, the stillness was only broken by the sound of a footfall moving to and fro along the cabinet floor.

"So it will walk all day, sir," whispered Poole; "ay, and the better part of the night. Only when a new sample comes from the chemist, there's a bit of a break. Ah, it's an ill-conscience that's such an enemy to rest! Ah, sir, there's blood foully shed in every step of it! But hark again, a little closer—put your heart in your ears, Mr. Utterson, and tell me, is that the doctor's foot?"

The steps fell lightly and oddly, with a certain swing, for all they went so slowly; it was different indeed from the heavy creaking tread of Henry Jekyll. Utterson sighed. "Is there never anything else?" he asked.

Poole nodded. "Once," he said. "Once I heard it weeping!"

8. Wind-driven clouds.

"Weeping? how that?" said the lawyer, conscious of a sudden chill of horror.

"Weeping like a woman or a lost soul," said the butler. "I came away with that upon my heart, that I could have wept too."

But now the ten minutes drew to an end. Poole disinterred the axe from under a stack of packing straw; the candle was set upon the nearest table to light them to the attack; and they drew near with bated breath to where that patient foot was still going up and down, up and down, in the quiet of the night.

"Jekyll," cried Utterson, with a loud voice, "I demand to see you." He paused a moment, but there came no reply. "I give you fair warning, our suspicions are aroused, and I must and shall see you," he resumed; "if not by fair means, then by foul—if not of your consent, then by brute force!"

"Utterson," said the voice, "for God's sake, have mercy!"

"Ah, that's not Jekyll's voice—it's Hyde's!" cried Utterson. "Down with the door, Poole."

Poole swung the axe over his shoulder; the blow shook the building, and the red baize door leaped against the lock and hinges. A dismal screech, as of mere animal terror, rang from the cabinet. Up went the axe again, and again the panels crashed and the frame bounded; four times the blow fell; but the wood was tough and the fittings were of excellent workmanship; and it was not until the fifth, that the lock burst in sunder and the wreck of the door fell inwards on the carpet.

The besiegers, appalled by their own riot and the stillness that had succeeded, stood back a little and peered in. There lay the cabinet before their eyes in the quiet lamplight, a good fire glowing and chattering on the hearth, the kettle singing its thin strain, a drawer or two open, papers neatly set forth on the business table, and nearer the fire, the things laid out for tea: the quietest room, you would have said, and, but for the glazed presses full of chemicals, the most commonplace that night in London.

Right in the midst there lay the body of a man sorely contorted and still twitching. They drew near on tiptoe, turned it on its back and beheld the face of Edward Hyde. He was dressed in clothes far too large for him, clothes of the doctor's bigness; the cords of his face still moved with a semblance of life, but life was quite gone; and by the crushed phial in the hand and the strong smell of kernels that hung upon the air, Utterson knew that he was looking on the body of a self-destroyer.[9]

"We have come too late," he said sternly, "whether to save or punish. Hyde is gone to his account; and it only remains for us to find the body of your master."

---

9. Cyanide, an extremely fast-acting poison, has a characteristic smell of bitter almond kernels.

The far greater proportion of the building was occupied by the theatre, which filled almost the whole ground story and was lighted from above, and by the cabinet, which formed an upper story at one end and looked upon the court. A corridor joined the theatre to the door on the by-street; and with this, the cabinet communicated separately by a second flight of stairs. There were besides a few dark closets and a spacious cellar. All these they now thoroughly examined. Each closet needed but a glance, for all were empty and all, by the dust that fell from their doors, had stood long unopened. The cellar, indeed, was filled with crazy lumber, mostly dating from the times of the surgeon who was Jekyll's predecessor; but even as they opened the door, they were advertised of the uselessness of further search, by the fall of a perfect mat of cobweb which had for years sealed up the entrance. Nowhere was there any trace of Henry Jekyll, dead or alive.

Poole stamped on the flags of the corridor. "He must be buried here," he said, hearkening to the sound.

"Or he may have fled," said Utterson, and he turned to examine the door in the by-street. It was locked; and lying near by on the flags, they found the key, already stained with rust.

"This does not look like use," observed the lawyer.

"Use!" echoed Poole. "Do you not see, sir, it is broken? much as if a man had stamped on it."

"Ay," continued Utterson, "and the fractures, too, are rusty." The two men looked at each other with a scare. "This is beyond me, Poole," said the lawyer. "Let us go back to the cabinet."

They mounted the stair in silence, and still with an occasional awestruck glance at the dead body, proceeded more thoroughly to examine the contents of the cabinet. At one table, there were traces of chemical work, various measured heaps of some white salt being laid on glass saucers, as though for an experiment in which the unhappy man had been prevented.

"That is the same drug that I was always bringing him," said Poole; and even as he spoke, the kettle with a startling noise boiled over.

This brought them to the fireside, where the easy chair was drawn cosily up, and the tea things stood ready to the sitter's elbow, the very sugar in the cup. There were several books on a shelf; one lay beside the tea things open, and Utterson was amazed to find it a copy of a pious work, for which Jekyll had several times expressed a great esteem, annotated, in his own hand, with startling blasphemies.

Next, in the course of their review of the chamber, the searchers came to the cheval glass, into whose depths they looked with an involuntary horror. But it was so turned as to show them nothing but the rosy glow playing on the roof, the fire sparkling in a hundred repetitions along the glazed front of the presses, and their own pale and fearful countenances stooping to look in.

"This glass have seen some strange things, sir," whispered Poole.

"And surely none stranger than itself," echoed the lawyer in the same tones. "For what did Jekyll"—he caught himself up at the word with a start, and then conquering the weakness: "what could Jekyll want with it?" he said.

"You may say that!" said Poole.

Next they turned to the business table. On the desk among the neat array of papers, a large envelope was uppermost, and bore, in the doctor's hand, the name of Mr. Utterson. The lawyer unsealed it, and several enclosures fell to the floor. The first was a will, drawn in the same eccentric terms as the one which he had returned six months before, to serve as a testament in case of death and as a deed of gift in case of disappearance; but in place of the name of Edward Hyde, the lawyer, with indescribable amazement, read the name of Gabriel John Utterson. He looked at Poole, and then back at the paper, and last of all at the dead malefactor stretched upon the carpet.

"My head goes round," he said. "He has been all these days in possession; he had no cause to like me; he must have raged to see himself displaced; and he has not destroyed this document."

He caught up the next paper; it was a brief note in the doctor's hand and dated at the top. "O Poole!" the lawyer cried, "he was alive and here this day. He cannot have been disposed of in so short a space, he must be still alive, he must have fled! And then, why fled? and how? and in that case, can we venture to declare this suicide? O, we must be careful. I foresee that we may yet involve your master in some dire catastrophe."

"Why don't you read it, sir?" asked Poole.

"Because I fear," replied the lawyer solemnly. "God grant I have no cause for it!" And with that he brought the paper to his eyes and read as follows.

"My dear Utterson,—When this shall fall into your hands, I shall have disappeared, under what circumstances I have not the penetration to foresee, but my instinct and all the circumstances of my nameless situation tell me that the end is sure and must be early. Go then, and first read the narrative which Lanyon warned me he was to place in your hands; and if you care to hear more, turn to the confession of

"Your unworthy and unhappy friend,

"HENRY JEKYLL."

"There was a third enclosure?" asked Utterson.

"Here, sir," said Poole, and gave into his hands a considerable packet sealed in several places.

The lawyer put it in his pocket. "I would say nothing of this paper. If your master has fled or is dead, we may at least save his credit.[1] It is now ten; I must go home and read these documents in quiet; but I shall be back before midnight, when we shall send for the police."

They went out, locking the door of the theatre behind them; and Utterson, once more leaving the servants gathered about the fire in the hall, trudged back to his office to read the two narratives in which this mystery was now to be explained.

Dr. Lanyon's Narrative

On the ninth of January, now four days ago, I received by the evening delivery a registered envelope, addressed in the hand of my colleague and old school-companion, Henry Jekyll. I was a good deal surprised by this; for we were by no means in the habit of correspondence; I had seen the man, dined with him, indeed, the night before; and I could imagine nothing in our intercourse that should justify the formality of registration. The contents increased my wonder; for this is how the letter ran:

10th December, 18—[2]

"Dear Lanyon,—You are one of my oldest friends; and although we may have differed at times on scientific questions, I cannot remember, at least on my side, any break in our affection. There was never a day when, if you had said to me, 'Jekyll, my life, my honour, my reason, depend upon you,' I would not have sacrificed my fortune or my left hand to help you. Lanyon, my life, my honour, my reason, are all at your mercy; if you fail me to-night, I am lost. You might suppose, after this preface, that I am going to ask you for something dishonourable to grant. Judge for yourself.

"I want you to postpone all other engagements for to-night—ay, even if you were summoned to the bedside of an emperor; to take a cab, unless your carriage should be actually at the door; and with this letter in your hand for consultation, to drive straight to my house. Poole, my butler, has his orders; you will find him waiting your arrival with a locksmith. The door of my cabinet is then to be forced; you are to go in alone; to open the glazed press (letter E) on the left hand, breaking the lock if it be shut; and to draw out, *with*

---

1. I.e., reputation, good name.
2. This letter should be dated 9th January, 18—, judging not only by Lanyon's opening mention of having received the letter late on January 9 after seeing Jekyll the night before, but also by chronology established elsewhere in the story. Stevenson apparently simply slipped up in putting the December 10 date here, very likely as a result of what he later called the "white-hot haste" in which the story was initially drafted.

all its contents as they stand, the fourth drawer from the top or (which is the same thing) the third from the bottom. In my extreme distress of mind, I have a morbid fear of misdirecting you; but even if I am in error, you may know the right drawer by its contents: some powders, a phial and a paper book. This drawer I beg of you to carry back with you to Cavendish Square exactly as it stands.

"That is the first part of the service: now for the second. You should be back, if you set out at once on the receipt of this, long before midnight; but I will leave you that amount of margin, not only in the fear of one of those obstacles that can neither be prevented nor foreseen, but because an hour when your servants are in bed is to be preferred for what will then remain to do. At midnight, then, I have to ask you to be alone in your consulting room, to admit with your own hand into the house a man who will present himself in my name, and to place in his hands the drawer that you will have brought with you from my cabinet. Then you will have played your part and earned my gratitude completely. Five minutes afterwards, if you insist upon an explanation, you will have understood that these arrangements are of capital importance; and that by the neglect of one of them, fantastic as they must appear, you might have charged your conscience with my death or the shipwreck of my reason.

"Confident as I am that you will not trifle with this appeal, my heart sinks and my hand trembles at the bare thought of such a possibility. Think of me at this hour, in a strange place, labouring under a blackness of distress that no fancy can exaggerate, and yet well aware that, if you will but punctually serve me, my troubles will roll away like a story that is told. Serve me, my dear Lanyon, and save

"Your friend,
"H. J.

"P.S. I had already sealed this up when a fresh terror struck upon my soul. It is possible that the post office may fail me, and this letter not come into your hands until to-morrow morning. In that case, dear Lanyon, do my errand when it shall be most convenient for you in the course of the day; and once more expect my messenger at midnight. It may then already be too late; and if that night passes without event, you will know that you have seen the last of Henry Jekyll."

Upon the reading of this letter, I made sure[3] my colleague was insane; but till that was proved beyond the possibility of doubt, I felt bound to do as he requested. The less I understood of this

---

3. I.e., I felt sure.

farrago,[4] the less I was in a position to judge of its importance; and an appeal so worded could not be set aside without a grave responsibility. I rose accordingly from table, got into a hansom,[5] and drove straight to Jekyll's house. The butler was awaiting my arrival; he had received by the same post as mine a registered letter of instruction, and had sent at once for a locksmith and a carpenter. The tradesmen came while we were yet speaking; and we moved in a body to old Dr. Denman's surgical theatre, from which (as you are doubtless aware) Jekyll's private cabinet is most conveniently entered. The door was very strong, the lock excellent; the carpenter avowed he would have great trouble and have to do much damage, if force were to be used; and the locksmith was near despair. But this last was a handy fellow, and after two hours' work, the door stood open. The press marked E was unlocked; and I took out the drawer, had it filled up with straw and tied in a sheet, and returned with it to Cavendish Square.

Here I proceeded to examine its contents. The powders were neatly enough made up, but not with the nicety of the dispensing chemist; so that it was plain they were of Jekyll's private manufacture; and when I opened one of the wrappers, I found what seemed to me a simple, crystalline salt of a white colour. The phial, to which I next turned my attention, might have been about half-full of a blood-red liquor, which was highly pungent to the sense of smell and seemed to me to contain phosphorus and some volatile ether. At the other ingredients, I could make no guess. The book was an ordinary version book[6] and contained little but a series of dates. These covered a period of many years, but I observed that the entries ceased nearly a year ago and quite abruptly. Here and there a brief remark was appended to a date, usually no more than a single word: "double" occurring perhaps six times in a total of several hundred entries; and once very early in the list and followed by several marks of exclamation, "total failure!!!" All this, though it whetted my curiosity, told me little that was definite. Here were a phial of some tincture, a paper of some salt, and the record of a series of experiments that had led (like too many of Jekyll's investigations) to no end[7] of practical usefulness. How could the presence of these articles in my house affect either the honour, the sanity, or the life of my flighty colleague? If his messenger could go to one place, why could he not go to another? And even granting some impediment, why was this gentleman to be received by me in secret?

---

4. A confusing jumble or mixture.
5. A two-wheeled horsedrawn cab.
6. A blank notebook designed for the school exercise of doing "versions," i.e., language translations (Scottish usage).
7. No outcome.

The more I reflected, the more convinced I grew that I was dealing with a case of cerebral disease; and though I dismissed my servants to bed, I loaded an old revolver that I might be found in some posture of self-defence.

Twelve o'clock had scarce rung out over London, ere the knocker sounded very gently on the door. I went myself at the summons, and found a small man crouching against the pillars of the portico.

"Are you come from Dr. Jekyll?" I asked.

He told me "yes" by a constrained gesture; and when I had bidden him enter, he did not obey me without a searching backward glance into the darkness of the square. There was a policeman not far off, advancing with his bull's eye open;[8] and at the sight, I thought my visitor started and made greater haste.

These particulars struck me, I confess, disagreeably; and as I followed him into the bright light of the consulting room, I kept my hand ready on my weapon. Here, at last, I had a chance of clearly seeing him. I had never set eyes on him before, so much was certain. He was small, as I have said; I was struck besides with the shocking expression of his face, with his remarkable combination of great muscular activity and great apparent debility of constitution, and—last but not least—with the odd, subjective disturbance caused by his neighbourhood. This bore some resemblance to incipient rigor, and was accompanied by a marked sinking of the pulse. At the time, I set it down to some idiosyncratic, personal distaste, and merely wondered at the acuteness of the symptoms; but I have since had reason to believe the cause to lie much deeper in the nature of man, and to turn on some nobler hinge than the principle of hatred.

This person (who had thus, from the first moment of his entrance, struck in me what I can only describe as a disgustful curiosity) was dressed in a fashion that would have made an ordinary person laughable: his clothes, that is to say, although they were of rich and sober fabric, were enormously too large for him in every measurement—the trousers hanging on his legs and rolled up to keep them from the ground, the waist of the coat below his haunches, and the collar sprawling wide upon his shoulders. Strange to relate, this ludicrous accoutrement was far from moving me to laughter. Rather, as there was something abnormal and misbegotten in the very essence of the creature that now faced me— something seizing, surprising and revolting—this fresh disparity seemed but to fit in with and to reinforce it; so that to my interest in

8. I.e., the sliding door of his lantern open (to emit light).

the man's nature and character, there was added a curiosity as to his origin, his life, his fortune and status in the world.

These observations, though they have taken so great a space to be set down in, were yet the work of a few seconds. My visitor was, indeed, on fire with sombre excitement.

"Have you got it?" he cried. "Have you got it?" And so lively was his impatience that he even laid his hand upon my arm and sought to shake me.

I put him back, conscious at his touch of a certain icy pang along my blood. "Come, sir," said I. "You forget that I have not yet the pleasure of your acquaintance. Be seated, if you please." And I showed him an example, and sat down myself in my customary seat and with as fair an imitation of my ordinary manner to a patient, as the lateness of the hour, the nature of my preoccupations, and the horror I had of my visitor, would suffer me to muster.

"I beg your pardon, Dr. Lanyon," he replied civilly enough. "What you say is very well founded; and my impatience has shown its heels to my politeness. I come here at the instance of your colleague, Dr. Henry Jekyll, on a piece of business of some moment; and I understood . . ." he paused and put his hand to his throat, and I could see, in spite of his collected manner, that he was wrestling against the approaches of the hysteria—"I understood, a drawer . . ."

But here I took pity on my visitor's suspense, and some perhaps on my own growing curiosity.

"There it is, sir," said I, pointing to the drawer, where it lay on the floor behind a table and still covered with the sheet.

He sprang to it, and then paused, and laid his hand upon his heart; I could hear his teeth grate with the convulsive action of his jaws; and his face was so ghastly to see that I grew alarmed both for his life and reason.

"Compose yourself," said I.

He turned a dreadful smile to me, and as if with the decision of despair, plucked away the sheet. At sight of the contents, he uttered one loud sob of such immense relief that I sat petrified. And the next moment, in a voice that was already fairly well under control, "Have you a graduated glass?" he asked.

I rose from my place with something of an effort and gave him what he asked.

He thanked me with a smiling nod, measured out a few minims of the red tincture and added one of the powders. The mixture, which was at first of a reddish hue, began, in proportion as the crystals melted, to brighten in colour, to effervesce audibly, and to throw off small fumes of vapour. Suddenly and at the same moment, the ebullition ceased and the compound changed to a dark purple, which faded again more slowly to a watery green. My visitor, who had watched these metamorphoses with a keen eye, smiled, set down the glass upon the table, and then turned and looked upon me with an air of scrutiny.

"And now," said he, "to settle what remains. Will you be wise? will you be guided? will you suffer me to take this glass in my hand and to go forth from your house without further parley? or has the greed of curiosity too much command of you? Think before you answer, for it shall be done as you decide. As you decide, you shall be left as you were before, and neither richer nor wiser, unless the sense of service rendered to a man in mortal distress may be counted as a kind of riches of the soul. Or, if you shall so prefer to choose, a new province of knowledge and new avenues to fame and power shall be laid open to you, here, in this room, upon the instant; and your sight shall be blasted by a prodigy to stagger the unbelief of Satan."

"Sir," said I, affecting a coolness that I was far from truly possessing, "you speak enigmas, and you will perhaps not wonder that I hear you with no very strong impression of belief. But I have gone too far in the way of inexplicable services to pause before I see the end."

"It is well," replied my visitor. "Lanyon, you remember your vows: what follows is under the seal of our profession. And now, you who have so long been bound to the most narrow and material views, you who have denied the virtue of transcendental medicine, you who have derided your superiors—behold!"

He put the glass to his lips and drank at one gulp. A cry followed; he reeled, staggered, clutched at the table and held on, staring with injected[9] eyes, gasping with open mouth; and as I looked there came, I thought, a change—he seemed to swell—his face became suddenly black and the features seemed to melt and alter—and the next moment, I had sprung to my feet and leaped back against the wall, my arm raised to shield me from that prodigy, my mind submerged in terror.

"O God!" I screamed, and "O God!" again and again; for there before my eyes—pale and shaken, and half fainting, and groping before him with his hands, like a man restored from death—there stood Henry Jekyll!

What he told me in the next hour, I cannot bring my mind to set on paper. I saw what I saw, I heard what I heard, and my soul sickened at it; and yet now when that sight has faded from my eyes, I ask myself if I believe it, and I cannot answer. My life is shaken to its roots; sleep has left me; the deadliest terror sits by me at all hours of the day and night; I feel that my days are numbered, and

9. Swollen.

that I must die; and yet I shall die incredulous. As for the moral turpitude that man unveiled to me, even with tears of penitence, I cannot, even in memory, dwell on it without a start of horror. I will say but one thing, Utterson, and that (if you can bring your mind to credit it) will be more than enough. The creature who crept into my house that night was, on Jekyll's own confession, known by the name of Hyde and hunted for in every corner of the land as the murderer of Carew.

HASTIE LANYON.

Henry Jekyll's Full Statement of the Case

I was born in the year 18— to a large fortune, endowed besides with excellent parts,[1] inclined by nature to industry, fond of the respect of the wise and good among my fellow-men, and thus, as might have been supposed, with every guarantee of an honourable and distinguished future. And indeed the worst of my faults was a certain impatient gaiety of disposition, such as has made the happiness of many, but such as I found it hard to reconcile with my imperious desire to carry my head high, and wear a more than commonly grave countenance before the public. Hence it came about that I concealed my pleasures; and that when I reached years of reflection, and began to look round me and take stock of my progress and position in the world, I stood already committed to a profound duplicity of life. Many a man would have even blazoned such irregularities as I was guilty of; but from the high views that I had set before me, I regarded and hid them with an almost morbid sense of shame. It was thus rather the exacting nature of my aspirations than any particular degradation in my faults, that made me what I was and, with even a deeper trench than in the majority of men, severed in me those provinces of good and ill which divide and compound man's dual nature. In this case, I was driven to reflect deeply and inveterately on that hard law of life, which lies at the root of religion and is one of the most plentiful springs of distress. Though so profound a double-dealer, I was in no sense a hypocrite; both sides of me were in dead earnest; I was no more myself when I laid aside restraint and plunged in shame, than when I laboured, in the eye of day, at the furtherance of knowledge or the relief of sorrow and suffering. And it chanced that the direction of my scientific studies, which led wholly towards the mystic and the transcendental, reacted and shed a strong light on this

---

1. Abilities.

consciousness of the perennial war among my members.[2] With every day, and from both sides of my intelligence, the moral and the intellectual, I thus drew steadily nearer to that truth, by whose partial discovery I have been doomed to such a dreadful shipwreck: that man is not truly one, but truly two. I say two, because the state of my own knowledge does not pass beyond that point. Others will follow, others will outstrip me on the same lines; and I hazard the guess that man will be ultimately known for a mere polity of multifarious, incongruous and independent denizens. I for my part, from the nature of my life, advanced infallibly in one direction and in one direction only. It was on the moral side, and in my own person, that I learned to recognise the thorough and primitive duality of man; I saw that, of the two natures that contended in the field of my consciousness, even if I could rightly be said to be either, it was only because I was radically both; and from an early date, even before the course of my scientific discoveries had begun to suggest the most naked possibility of such a miracle, I had learned to dwell with pleasure, as a beloved daydream, on the thought of the separation of these elements. If each, I told myself, could but be housed in separate identities, life would be relieved of all that was unbearable; the unjust might go his way, delivered from the aspirations and remorse of his more upright twin; and the just could walk steadfastly and securely on his upward path, doing the good things in which he found his pleasure, and no longer exposed to disgrace and penitence by the hands of this extraneous evil. It was the curse of mankind that these incongruous faggots[3] were thus bound together—that in the agonised womb of consciousness, these polar twins should be continuously struggling. How, then, were they dissociated?

I was so far in my reflections when, as I have said, a side light began to shine upon the subject from the laboratory table. I began to perceive more deeply than it has ever yet been stated, the trembling immateriality, the mist-like transience, of this seemingly so solid body in which we walk attired. Certain agents I found to have the power to shake and to pluck back that fleshly vestment, even as a wind might toss the curtains of a pavilion.[4] For two good reasons, I will not enter deeply into this scientific branch of my confession. First, because I have been made to learn that the doom and burthen of our life is bound forever on man's shoulders, and when the

---

2. Conflict among parts of the self, especially between body and spirit. The phrase echoes James 4:1, "From whence come wars and fightings among you? come they not hence, even of your lusts that war in your members?"
3. A faggot is a collection of twigs or sticks bundled together for use as fuel; or, figuratively, a collection of things not forming any genuine unity.
4. A large, often stately tent.

attempt is made to cast it off, it but returns upon us with more unfamiliar and more awful pressure. Second, because as my narrative will make alas! too evident, my discoveries were incomplete. Enough, then, that I not only recognised my natural body for the mere aura and effulgence of certain of the powers that made up my spirit, but managed to compound a drug by which these powers should be dethroned from their supremacy, and a second form and countenance substituted, none the less natural to me because they were the expression, and bore the stamp, of lower elements in my soul.

I hesitated long before I put this theory to the test of practice. I knew well that I risked death; for any drug that so potently controlled and shook the very fortress of identity, might by the least scruple of an overdose or at the least inopportunity in the moment of exhibition, utterly blot out that immaterial tabernacle[5] which I looked to it to change. But the temptation of a discovery so singular and profound, at last overcame the suggestions of alarm. I had long since prepared my tincture; I purchased at once, from a firm of wholesale chemists, a large quantity of a particular salt which I knew, from my experiments, to be the last ingredient required; and late one accursed night, I compounded the elements, watched them boil and smoke together in the glass, and when the ebullition had subsided, with a strong glow of courage, drank off the potion.

The most racking pangs succeeded: a grinding in the bones, deadly nausea, and a horror of the spirit that cannot be exceeded at the hour of birth or death. Then these agonies began swiftly to subside, and I came to myself as if out of a great sickness. There was something strange in my sensations, something indescribably new and, from its very novelty, incredibly sweet. I felt younger, lighter, happier in body; within I was conscious of a heady recklessness, a current of disordered sensual images running like a mill race in my fancy, a solution[6] of the bonds of obligation, an unknown but not an innocent freedom of the soul. I knew myself, at the first breath of this new life, to be more wicked, tenfold more wicked, sold a slave to my original evil; and the thought, in that moment, braced and delighted me like wine. I stretched out my hands, exulting in the freshness of these sensations; and in the act, I was suddenly aware that I had lost in stature.

There was no mirror, at that date, in my room; that which stands beside me as I write, was brought there later on and for the very

---

5. I.e., the body (a usage found in 2 Corinthians 5:1–4 and 2 Peter 1:13–14, where the body, as a perishable abode for the soul, is likened to the "tabernacle," or tent sanctuary, used for religious worship during the Israelite wandering in the wilderness). *Scruple*: a very small unit of weight or measurement (20 grams or 1/24th ounce).
6. Dissolving. *Mill race*: the current of water that drives a mill-wheel.

purpose of these transformations. The night, however, was far gone into the morning—the morning, black as it was, was nearly ripe for the conception of the day—the inmates of my house were locked in the most rigorous hours of slumber; and I determined, flushed as I was with hope and triumph, to venture in my new shape as far as to my bedroom. I crossed the yard, wherein the constellations looked down upon me, I could have thought, with wonder, the first creature of that sort that their unsleeping vigilance had yet disclosed to them; I stole through the corridors, a stranger in my own house; and coming to my room, I saw for the first time the appearance of Edward Hyde.

I must here speak by theory alone, saying not that which I know, but that which I suppose to be most probable. The evil side of my nature, to which I had now transferred the stamping efficacy,[7] was less robust and less developed than the good which I had just deposed. Again, in the course of my life, which had been, after all, nine tenths a life of effort, virtue and control, it had been much less exercised and much less exhausted. And hence, as I think, it came about that Edward Hyde was so much smaller, slighter and younger than Henry Jekyll. Even as good shone upon the countenance of the one, evil was written broadly and plainly on the face of the other. Evil besides (which I must still believe to be the lethal side of man) had left on that body an imprint of deformity and decay. And yet when I looked upon that ugly idol in the glass, I was conscious of no repugnance, rather of a leap of welcome. This, too, was myself. It seemed natural and human. In my eyes it bore a livelier image of the spirit, it seemed more express and single, than the imperfect and divided countenance, I had been hitherto accustomed to call mine. And in so far I was doubtless right. I have observed that when I wore the semblance of Edward Hyde, none could come near to me at first without a visible misgiving of the flesh. This, as I take it, was because all human beings, as we meet them, are commingled out of good and evil: and Edward Hyde, alone in the ranks of mankind, was pure evil.

I lingered but a moment at the mirror: the second and conclusive experiment had yet to be attempted; it yet remained to be seen if I had lost my identity beyond redemption and must flee before daylight from a house that was no longer mine; and hurrying back to my cabinet, I once more prepared and drank the cup, once more suffered the pangs of dissolution, and came to myself once more with the character, the stature and the face of Henry Jekyll.

That night I had come to the fatal cross roads. Had I approached my discovery in a more noble spirit, had I risked the experiment while under the empire of generous or pious aspirations, all must

7. I.e., the shape-giving power.

have been otherwise, and from these agonies of death and birth, I had come forth an angel instead of a fiend. The drug had no discriminating action; it was neither diabolical nor divine; it but shook the doors of the prisonhouse of my disposition; and like the captives of Philippi, that which stood within ran forth.[8] At that time my virtue slumbered; my evil, kept awake by ambition, was alert and swift to seize the occasion; and the thing that was projected was Edward Hyde. Hence, although I had now two characters as well as two appearances, one was wholly evil, and the other was still the old Henry Jekyll, that incongruous compound of whose reformation and improvement I had already learned to despair. The movement was thus wholly toward the worse.

Even at that time, I had not yet conquered my aversion to the dryness of a life of study. I would still be merrily disposed at times; and as my pleasures were (to say the least) undignified, and I was not only well known and highly considered, but growing towards the elderly man, this incoherency of my life was daily growing more unwelcome. It was on this side that my new power tempted me until I fell in slavery. I had but to drink the cup, to doff at once the body of the noted professor, and to assume, like a thick cloak, that of Edward Hyde. I smiled at the notion; it seemed to me at the time to be humorous; and I made my preparations with the most studious care. I took and furnished that house in Soho, to which Hyde was tracked by the police; and engaged as housekeeper a creature whom I well knew to be silent and unscrupulous. On the other side, I announced to my servants that a Mr. Hyde (whom I described) was to have full liberty and power about my house in the square; and to parry mishaps, I even called and made myself a familiar object, in my second character. I next drew up that will to which you so much objected; so that if anything befell me in the person of Dr. Jekyll, I could enter on that of Edward Hyde without pecuniary loss. And thus fortified, as I supposed, on every side, I began to profit by the strange immunities of my position.

Men have before hired bravos[9] to transact their crimes, while their own person and reputation sat under shelter. I was the first that ever did so for his pleasures. I was the first that could thus plod in the public eye with a load of genial respectability, and in a moment, like a schoolboy, strip off these lendings[1] and spring headlong into

---

8. As recounted in Acts 16:26, when God visited an earthquake upon the prison in Philippi where the apostle Paul and his companion Silas were being held captive, "immediately all the doors were opened, and every one's bands were loosed." Paul and Silas, however, rather than fleeing, honorably turned themselves over to their captors.
9. Paid desperadoes or assassins.
1. Something lent, here referring to clothes in an echo of King Lear's line, "Off, off, you lendings!" as he tears off his garments on the heath in a sudden access of fellow-feeling for the naked madman he encounters there (*King Lear*, 3.4.114).

the sea of liberty. But for me, in my impenetrable mantle, the safety was complete. Think of it—I did not even exist! Let me but escape into my laboratory door, give me but a second or two to mix and swallow the draught that I had always standing ready; and whatever he had done, Edward Hyde would pass away like the stain of breath upon a mirror; and there in his stead, quietly at home, trimming the midnight lamp in his study, a man who could afford to laugh at suspicion, would be Henry Jekyll.

The pleasures which I made haste to seek in my disguise were, as I have said, undignified; I would scarce use a harder term. But in the hands of Edward Hyde, they soon began to turn towards the monstrous. When I would come back from these excursions, I was often plunged into a kind of wonder at my vicarious depravity. This familiar that I called out of my own soul, and sent forth alone to do his good pleasure,[2] was a being inherently malign and villainous; his every act and thought centered on self; drinking pleasure with bestial avidity from any degree of torture to another; relentless like a man of stone. Henry Jekyll stood at times aghast before the acts of Edward Hyde; but the situation was apart from ordinary laws, and insidiously relaxed the grasp of conscience. It was Hyde, after all, and Hyde alone, that was guilty. Jekyll was no worse; he woke again to his good qualities seemingly unimpaired; he would even make haste, where it was possible, to undo the evil done by Hyde. And thus his conscience slumbered.

Into the details of the infamy at which I thus connived (for even now I can scarce grant that I committed it) I have no design of entering; I mean but to point out the warnings and the successive steps with which my chastisement approached. I met with one accident which, as it brought on no consequence, I shall no more than mention. An act of cruelty to a child aroused against me the anger of a passer by, whom I recognised the other day in the person of your kinsman; the doctor and the child's family joined him; there were moments when I feared for my life; and at last, in order to pacify their too just resentment, Edward Hyde had to bring them to the door, and pay them in a cheque drawn in the name, of Henry Jekyll. But this danger was easily eliminated from the future, by opening an account at another bank in the name of Edward Hyde himself; and when, by sloping my own hand backward, I had supplied my double with a signature, I thought I sat beyond the reach of fate.

2. I.e., pleasure that is satisfying or suitable to him (the phrase occurs frequently in the Bible in reference to God's "good pleasure," e.g., Psalms 51:18, Luke 12:32, Philippians 2:13). *Familiar:* a spirit or demon supposed to be in association with or under the power of a particular person.

Some two months before the murder of Sir Danvers, I had been out for one of my adventures, had returned at a late hour, and woke the next day in bed with somewhat odd sensations. It was in vain I looked about me; in vain I saw the decent furniture and tall proportions of my room in the square; in vain that I recognised the pattern of the bed curtains and the design of the mahogany frame; something still kept insisting that I was not where I was, that I had not wakened where I seemed to be, but in the little room in Soho where I was accustomed to sleep in the body of Edward Hyde. I smiled to myself, and, in my psychological way, began lazily to inquire into the elements of this illusion, occasionally, even as I did so, dropping back into a comfortable morning doze. I was still so engaged when, in one of my more wakeful moments, my eye fell upon my hand. Now the hand of Henry Jekyll (as you have often remarked) was professional in shape and size: it was large, firm, white and comely. But the hand which I now saw, clearly enough, in the yellow light of a mid-London morning, lying half shut on the bed clothes, was lean, corded, knuckly, of a dusky pallor and thickly shaded with a swart[3] growth of hair. It was the hand of Edward Hyde.

I must have stared upon it for near half a minute, sunk as I was in the mere stupidity of wonder, before terror woke up in my breast as sudden and startling as the crash of cymbals; and bounding from my bed, I rushed to the mirror. At the sight that met my eyes, my blood was changed into something exquisitely thin and icy. Yes, I had gone to bed Henry Jekyll, I had awakened Edward Hyde. How was this to be explained? I asked myself; and then, with another bound of terror—how was it to be remedied? It was well on in the morning; the servants were up; all my drugs were in the cabinet—a long journey, down two pair of stairs, through the back passage, across the open court and through the anatomical theatre, from where I was then standing horror-struck. It might indeed be possible to cover my face; but of what use was that, when I was unable to conceal the alteration in my stature? And then with an overpowering sweetness of relief, it came back upon my mind that the servants were already used to the coming and going of my second self. I had soon dressed, as well as I was able, in clothes of my own size: had soon passed through the house, where Bradshaw stared and drew back at seeing Mr. Hyde at such an hour and in such a strange array; and ten minutes later, Dr. Jekyll had returned to his own shape and was sitting down, with a darkened brow, to make a feint of breakfasting.

---

3. Swarthy, dark.

Small indeed was my appetite. This inexplicable incident, this reversal of my previous experience, seemed, like the Babylonian finger on the wall, to be spelling out the letters of my judgment;[4] and I began to reflect more seriously than ever before on the issues and possibilities of my double existence. That part of me which I had the power of projecting, had lately been much exercised and nourished; it had seemed to me of late as though the body of Edward Hyde had grown in stature, as though (when I wore that form) I were conscious of a more generous tide of blood; and I began to spy a danger that, if this were much prolonged, the balance of my nature might be permanently overthrown, the power of voluntary change be forfeited, and the character of Edward Hyde become irrevocably mine. The power of the drug had not been always equally displayed. Once, very early in my career, it had totally failed me; since then I had been obliged on more than one occasion to double, and once, with infinite risk of death, to treble the amount; and these rare uncertainties had cast hitherto the sole shadow on my contentment. Now, however, and in the light of that morning's accident, I was led to remark that whereas, in the beginning, the difficulty had been to throw off the body of Jekyll, it had of late, gradually but decidedly transferred itself to the other side. All things therefore seemed to point to this: that I was slowly losing hold of my original and better self, and becoming slowly incorporated with my second and worse.

Between these two, I now felt I had to choose. My two natures had memory in common, but all other faculties were most unequally shared between them. Jekyll (who was composite) now with the most sensitive apprehensions, now with a greedy gusto, projected and shared in the pleasures and adventures of Hyde; but Hyde was indifferent to Jekyll, or but remembered him as the mountain bandit remembers the cavern in which he conceals himself from pursuit. Jekyll had more than a father's interest; Hyde had more than a son's indifference. To cast in my lot with Jekyll, was to die to those appetites which I had long secretly indulged and had of late begun to pamper. To cast it in with Hyde, was to die to a thousand interests and aspirations, and to become, at a blow and forever, despised and friendless. The bargain might appear unequal; but there was still another consideration in the scales; for while Jekyll would suffer smartingly in the fires of abstinence, Hyde would be not even conscious of all that he had lost. Strange as my circumstances were, the terms of this debate are as old and commonplace as man;

4. Refers to the biblical episode in which King Belshazzar of Babylon sees "fingers of a man's hand" writing onto the wall of his palace a mysterious message, which the prophet Daniel reveals to be a sign of God's imminent punishment of Belshazzar for having "lifted" himself "up against the Lord of heaven" (Daniel 5:5 and 5:23).

much the same inducements and alarms cast the die for any tempted and trembling sinner; and it fell out with me, as it falls with so vast a majority of my fellows, that I chose the better part and was found wanting in the strength to keep to it.

Yes, I preferred the elderly and discontented doctor, surrounded by friends and cherishing honest hopes; and bade a resolute farewell to the liberty, the comparative youth, the light step, leaping pulses and secret pleasures, that I had enjoyed in the disguise of Hyde. I made this choice perhaps with some unconscious reservation, for I neither gave up the house in Soho, nor destroyed the clothes of Edward Hyde, which still lay ready in my cabinet. For two months, however, I was true to my determination; for two months, I led a life of such severity as I had never before attained to, and enjoyed the compensations of an approving conscience. But time began at last to obliterate the freshness of my alarm; the praises of conscience began to grow into a thing of course; I began to be tortured with throes and longings, as of Hyde struggling after freedom; and at last, in an hour of moral weakness, I once again compounded and swallowed the transforming draught.

I do not suppose that, when a drunkard reasons with himself upon his vice, he is once out of five hundred times affected by the dangers that he runs through his brutish, physical insensibility; neither had I, long as I had considered my position, made enough allowance for the complete moral insensibility and insensate readiness to evil, which were the leading characters of Edward Hyde. Yet it was by these that I was punished. My devil had been long caged, he came out roaring. I was conscious, even when I took the draught, of a more unbridled, a more furious propensity to ill. It must have been this, I suppose, that stirred in my soul that tempest of impatience with which I listened to the civilities of my unhappy victim; I declare at least, before God, no man morally sane could have been guilty of that crime upon so pitiful a provocation; and that I struck in no more reasonable spirit than that in which a sick child may break a plaything. But I had voluntarily stripped myself of all those balancing instincts, by which even the worst of us continues to walk with some degree of steadiness among temptations; and in my case, to be tempted, however slightly, was to fall.

Instantly the spirit of hell awoke in me and raged. With a transport of glee, I mauled the unresisting body, tasting delight from every blow; and it was not till weariness had begun to succeed,[5] that I was suddenly, in the top fit of my delirium, struck through the heart by a cold thrill of terror. A mist dispersed; I saw my life to be forfeit; and fled from the scene of these excesses, at once glorying

5. Follow.

and trembling, my lust of evil gratified and stimulated, my love of life screwed to the topmost peg.[6] I ran to the house in Soho, and (to make assurance doubly sure) destroyed my papers; thence I set out through the lamplit streets, in the same divided ecstasy of mind, gloating on my crime, light-headedly devising others in the future, and yet still hastening and still hearkening in my wake for the steps of the avenger. Hyde had a song upon his lips as he compounded the draught, and as he drank it, pledged the dead man. The pangs of transformation had not done tearing him, before Henry Jekyll, with streaming tears of gratitude and remorse, had fallen upon his knees and lifted his clasped hands to God. The veil of self-indulgence was rent from head to foot, I saw my life as a whole: I followed it up from the days of childhood, when I had walked with my father's hand, and through the self-denying toils of my professional life, to arrive again and again, with the same sense of unreality, at the damned horrors of the evening. I could have screamed aloud; I sought with tears and prayers to smother down the crowd of hideous images and sounds with which my memory swarmed against me; and still, between the petitions, the ugly face of my iniquity stared into my soul. As the acuteness of this remorse began to die away, it was succeeded by a sense of joy. The problem of my conduct was solved. Hyde was thenceforth impossible; whether I would or not, I was now confined to the better part of my existence; and O, how I rejoiced to think it! with what willing humility, I embraced anew the restrictions of natural life! with what sincere renunciation, I locked the door by which I had so often gone and come, and ground the key under my heel!

The next day, came the news that the murder had been overlooked,[7] that the guilt of Hyde was patent to the world, and that the victim was a man high in public estimation. It was not only a crime, it had been a tragic folly. I think I was glad to know it; I think I was glad to have my better impulses thus buttressed and guarded by the terrors of the scaffold. Jekyll was now my city of refuge; let but Hyde peep out an instant, and the hands of all men would be raised to take and slay him.

I resolved in my future conduct to redeem the past; and I can say with honesty that my resolve was fruitful of some good. You know yourself how earnestly in the last months of last year, I laboured to relieve suffering; you know that much was done for others, and that the days passed quietly, almost happily for myself. Nor can I truly say that I wearied of this beneficent and innocent life; I think instead that I daily enjoyed it more completely; but I was still cursed

6. Raised to its highest pitch (as in tuning a string instrument).
7. Seen from above (by the maidservant at the upstairs window).

with my duality of purpose; and as the first edge of my penitence wore off, the lower side of me, so long indulged, so recently chained down, began to growl for license. Not that I dreamed of resuscitating Hyde; the bare idea of that would startle me to frenzy: no, it was in my own person, that I was once more tempted to trifle with my conscience; and it was as an ordinary secret sinner, that I at last fell before the assaults of temptation.

There comes an end to all things; the most capacious measure is filled at last; and this brief condescension to my evil finally destroyed the balance of my soul. And yet I was not alarmed; the fall seemed natural, like a return to the old days before I had made my discovery. It was a fine, clear, January day, wet under foot where the frost had melted, but cloudless overhead; and the Regent's Park[8] was full of winter chirrupings and sweet with Spring odours. I sat in the sun on a bench; the animal within me licking the chops of memory; the spiritual side a little drowsed, promising subsequent penitence, but not yet moved to begin. After all, I reflected, I was like my neighbours; and then I smiled, comparing myself with other men, comparing my active goodwill with the lazy cruelty of their neglect. And at the very moment of that vainglorious thought, a qualm came over me, a horrid nausea and the most deadly shuddering. These passed away, and left me faint; and then as in its turn the faintness subsided, I began to be aware of a change in the temper of my thoughts, a greater boldness, a contempt of danger, a solution of the bonds of obligation. I looked down; my clothes hung formlessly on my shrunken limbs; the hand that lay on my knee was corded and hairy. I was once more Edward Hyde. A moment before I had been safe of all men's respect, wealthy, beloved—the cloth laying for me in the dining room at home; and now I was the common quarry of mankind, hunted, houseless, a known murderer, thrall to the gallows.

My reason wavered, but it did not fail me utterly. I have more than once observed that, in my second character, my faculties seemed sharpened to a point and my spirits more tensely elastic; thus it came about that, where Jekyll perhaps might have succumbed, Hyde rose to the importance of the moment. My drugs were in one of the presses of my cabinet; how was I to reach them? That was the problem that (crushing my temples in my hands) I set myself to solve. The laboratory door I had closed. If I sought to enter by the house, my own servants would consign me to the gallows. I saw I must employ another hand, and thought of Lanyon. How was he to be reached? how persuaded? Supposing that I

8. A large public park just north of the west-central London neighborhood where Dr. Lanyon lives.

escaped capture in the streets, how was I to make my way into his presence? and how should I, an unknown and displeasing visitor, prevail on the famous physician to rifle the study of his colleague, Dr. Jekyll? Then I remembered that of my original character, one part remained to me: I could write my own hand; and once I had conceived that kindling spark, the way that I must follow became lighted up from end to end.

Thereupon, I arranged my clothes as best I could, and summoning a passing hansom, drove to an hotel in Portland Street, the name of which I chanced to remember. At my appearance (which was indeed comical enough, however tragic a fate these garments covered) the driver could not conceal his mirth. I gnashed my teeth upon him with a gust of devilish fury; and the smile withered from his face—happily for him—yet more happily for myself, for in another instant I had certainly dragged him from his perch. At the inn, as I entered, I looked about me with so black a countenance as made the attendants tremble; not a look did they exchange in my presence; but obsequiously took my orders, led me to a private room, and brought me wherewithal to write. Hyde in danger of his life was a creature new to me: shaken with inordinate anger, strung to the pitch of murder, lusting to inflict pain. Yet the creature was astute; mastered his fury with a great effort of the will; composed his two important letters, one to Lanyon and one to Poole; and that he might receive actual evidence of their being posted, sent them out with directions that they should be registered.

Thenceforward, he sat all day over the fire in the private room, gnawing his nails; there he dined, sitting alone with his fears, the waiter visibly quailing before his eye; and thence, when the night was fully come, he set forth in the corner of a closed cab, and was driven to and fro about the streets of the city. He, I say—I cannot say, I. That child of Hell had nothing human; nothing lived in him but fear and hatred. And when at last, thinking the driver had begun to grow suspicious, he discharged the cab and ventured on foot, attired in his misfitting clothes, an object marked out for observation, into the midst of the nocturnal passengers, these two base passions raged within him like a tempest. He walked fast, hunted by his fears, chattering to himself, skulking through the less frequented thoroughfares, counting the minutes that still divided him from midnight. Once a woman spoke to him, offering, I think, a box of lights.[9] He smote her in the face, and she fled.

When I came to myself at Lanyon's, the horror of my old friend perhaps affected me somewhat: I do not know; it was at least but a

9. Matches.

drop in the sea to the abhorrence with which I looked back upon these hours. A change had come over me. It was no longer the fear of the gallows, it was the horror of being Hyde that racked me. I received Lanyon's condemnation partly in a dream; it was partly in a dream that I came home to my own house and got into bed. I slept after the prostration of the day, with a stringent and profound slumber which not even the nightmares that wrung me could avail to break. I awoke in the morning shaken, weakened, but refreshed. I still hated and feared the thought of the brute that slept within me, and I had not of course forgotten the appalling dangers of the day before; but I was once more at home, in my own house and close to my drugs; and gratitude for my escape shone so strong in my soul that it almost rivalled the brightness of hope.

I was stepping leisurely across the court after breakfast, drinking the chill of the air with pleasure, when I was seized again with those indescribable sensations that heralded the change; and I had but the time to gain the shelter of my cabinet, before I was once again raging and freezing with the passions of Hyde. It took on this occasion a double dose to recall me to myself; and alas, six hours after, as I sat looking sadly in the fire, the pangs returned, and the drug had to be re-administered. In short, from that day forth it seemed only by a great effort as of gymnastics, and only under the immediate stimulation of the drug, that I was able to wear the countenance of Jekyll. At all hours of the day and night, I would be taken with the premonitory shudder; above all, if I slept, or even dozed for a moment in my chair, it was always as Hyde that I awakened. Under the strain of this continually impending doom and by the sleeplessness to which I now condemned myself, ay, even beyond what I had thought possible to man, I became, in my own person, a creature eaten up and emptied by fever, languidly weak both in body and mind, and solely occupied by one thought: the horror of my other self. But when I slept, or when the virtue of the medicine wore off, I would leap almost without transition (for the pangs of transformation grew daily less marked) into the possession of a fancy brimming with images of terror, a soul boiling with causeless hatreds, and a body that seemed not strong enough to contain the raging energies of life. The powers of Hyde seemed to have grown with the sickliness of Jekyll. And certainly the hate that now divided them was equal on each side. With Jekyll, it was a thing of vital instinct. He had now seen the full deformity of that creature that shared with him some of the phenomena of consciousness, and was co-heir with him to death: and beyond these links of community, which in themselves made the most poignant part of his distress, he thought of Hyde, for all his energy of life, as of something not only hellish but inorganic. This was the shocking thing; that the slime of the pit seemed to utter cries and voices; that the amorphous dust gesticulated and sinned; that what was dead, and had no shape, should usurp the offices of life. And this again, that that insurgent horror was knit to him closer than a wife, closer than an eye; lay caged in his flesh, where he heard it mutter and felt it struggle to be born; and at every hour of weakness, and in the confidence of slumber, prevailed against him, and deposed him out of life. The hatred of Hyde for Jekyll, was of a different order. His terror of the gallows drove him continually to commit temporary suicide, and return to his subordinate station of a part instead of a person; but he loathed the necessity, he loathed the despondency into which Jekyll was now fallen, and he resented the dislike with which he was himself regarded. Hence the apelike tricks that he would play me, scrawling in my own hand blasphemies on the pages of my books, burning the letters and destroying the portrait of my father; and indeed, had it not been for his fear of death, he would long ago have ruined himself in order to involve me in the ruin. But his love of life is wonderful; I go further: I, who sicken and freeze at the mere thought of him, when I recall the abjection and passion of this attachment, and when I know how he fears my power to cut him off by suicide, I find it in my heart to pity him.

It is useless, and the time awfully fails me, to prolong this description; no one has ever suffered such torments, let that suffice; and yet even to these, habit brought—no, not alleviation—but a certain callousness of soul, a certain acquiescence of despair; and my punishment might have gone on for years, but for the last calamity which has now fallen, and which has finally severed me from my own face and nature. My provision of the salt, which had never been renewed since the date of the first experiment, began to run low. I sent out for a fresh supply, and mixed the draught; the ebullition followed, and the first change of colour, not the second; I drank it and it was without efficiency. You will learn from Poole how I have had London ransacked; it was in vain; and I am now persuaded that my first supply was impure, and that it was that unknown impurity which lent efficacy to the draught.

About a week has passed, and I am now finishing this statement under the influence of the last of the old powders. This, then, is the last time, short of a miracle, that Henry Jekyll can think his own thoughts or see his own face (now how sadly altered!) in the glass. Nor must I delay too long to bring my writing to an end; for if my narrative has hitherto escaped destruction, it has been by a combination of great prudence and great good luck. Should the throes of change take me in the act of writing it, Hyde will tear it in pieces; but if some time shall have elapsed after I have laid it by, his wonderful selfishness and circumscription to the moment[1] will probably save it once again from the action of his apelike spite. And indeed the doom that is closing on us both, has already changed and crushed him. Half an hour from now, when I shall again and forever reindue[2] that hated personality, I know how I shall sit shuddering and weeping in my chair, or continue, with the most strained and fearstruck ecstasy[3] of listening, to pace up and down this room (my last earthly refuge) and give ear to every sound of menace. Will Hyde die upon the scaffold? or will he find the courage to release himself at the last moment? God knows; I am careless;[4] this is my true hour of death, and what is to follow concerns another than myself. Here then, as I lay down the pen and proceed to seal up my confession, I bring the life of that unhappy Henry Jekyll to an end.

1. I.e., his astonishing selfishness and limitation of attention to each present moment.
2. Put on again.
3. Transport; frenzy.
4. Indifferent.

Notes on the Manuscript

Numerous mysteries surround the manuscript of *Strange Case of Dr. Jekyll and Mr. Hyde*. Substantial portions of the final draft—the one Stevenson sent to the printers, called here the "printer's copy"—are missing, or no longer exist. Parts of an earlier draft (called here the "notebook draft") are also extant, but with, again, large fractions lost. What remains of these two drafts has been separated and now resides in four different archives. This fragmentation and dispersal of the whole seems fitting for a story about, in part, varied versions of the same tale—told from the point of view of Utterson, Lanyon, Jekyll, and others—with deliberate gaps, partially filled in by letters, memoranda, wills, and other documents. Studying what is left of Stevenson's drafts, one feels like Utterson piecing together scattered bits of handwriting to solve a mystery. The only complete version Stevenson directly approved is the first edition published in Britain (on which this Norton Critical Edition is based). He read and corrected the proofs for it, making more revisions on the page. These proofs have, not surprisingly, gone missing.

The longest segment of manuscript that survives is thirty-four pages of the printer's copy Stevenson sent to his publisher, Longmans, Green, and Co., copied out in his hand. These sheets were used by the printers to produce the first edition, as can be seen by notations made by the compositors in margins and next to chapter headings. Despite being a "final" draft, the changes Stevenson made on some of these leaves—inserting and deleting words, phrases, and even sections—are not minor. All of these thirty-four pages are at the Morgan Library, in New York City, except for one, which is at the Silverado Museum in California. Confusingly, these pages are not one continuous block of the story, but two sections making up the first quarter and final third. Stevenson's handwriting on this partial draft is easy to read, but the paper holds the marks of use and time. The sheets, pre-lined like modern notebook paper, are worn, stained, and have been folded down the middle, with the crease running so deep that some sheets have come apart and been repaired to hold them together. One especially grubby leaf, hand-paginated by Stevenson as 43, has been folded four times. On the back, he penciled part of an earlier draft, then crossed it out. The last section of the printer's copy, "Henry Jekyll's Full Statement of the Case," is the most heavily marked up, as if Stevenson, even on what was supposed to be the clean copy, still couldn't get it right. Yet the mystery remains: where are the missing pages from the middle of the tale? Might they still turn up, having been squirreled away somewhere and forgotten?

The extant fragments of the notebook draft add up to twenty-seven pages in total and are split between three libraries. Based on Stevenson remarking in a letter that he wrote three drafts and his wife and stepson's account that he burned the first draft, the notebook draft is probably the second draft.[1] Clearly a rougher sketch because of the messier handwriting and the more substantial changes, these pre-lined pages are smaller—6½ by 8 inches—than the printer's draft (measuring 8 by 13 inches). Not one continuous segment, the leaves contain incomplete passages from different parts of the plot. The largest one is held by the Beinecke Rare Book and Manuscript Library at Yale University, and one sheet that fits neatly into this portion is at the Silverado Museum. From the last part of the book, although not including the very end, the pages were "found in an old trunk which had not been opened for a long time" by Stevenson's stepdaughter Belle Strong.[2]

Two additional pages of what seems to be this draft, at Princeton University, tell of events from earlier in the plot, and only survive because Stevenson used the blank sides to write to his cousin and close friend Bob Stevenson in October 1885. "Excuse the use of ancient scraps of MS; I have no other paper here," Stevenson writes in the letter, surely exaggerating since he started working on the story in late September or early October, so the scraps were, at most, a few weeks old.[3] Stevenson crossed out the text with a large, page-sized "x" on one and on the other one long stroke. While these bits of draft are on paper of the same type and size as the notebook draft at the Beinecke and Silverado, their handwritten page numbers, 33 and 48, are in a different place, and the events they describe don't square well with the plot as written in the notebook draft (or,

1. See Stevenson's letter to F. W. H. Myers, March 1, 1886, *The Letters of Robert Louis Stevenson*, ed. Bradford A. Booth and Ernest Mehew (Yale UP, 1995), vol. 5, p. 216; and Graham Balfour's account in the Composition section of this Norton Critical Edition. See also Roger Swearingen, *The Prose Writings of Robert Louis Stevenson: A Guide* (Archon Books, 1980), pp. 98–101; and William Veeder, "The Texts in Question," in *Dr. Jekyll and Mr. Hyde After One Hundred Years*, ed. William Veeder and Gordon Hirsch (U of Chicago P, 1988), pp. 3–11.
2. Quoted in Veeder, "The Texts in Question," p. 5.
3. *Letters*, vol. 5, p. 133. See p. 128, n. 2, for more about when he started writing *Jekyll and Hyde*.

for that matter, in the printer's copy). Katherine Linehan has speculated that these might be pages of the first draft—the one said to be burned—perhaps put aside for some reason, or an abandoned experimentation not part of any of the three drafts.[4] She observes that the plot as laid out on the other pages of the notebook draft fits fairly neatly into that of the printer's copy. These two spare leaves don't fit. For instance, on page 48 of the Princeton draft, Utterson is described as having been

> dragged all day through scenes and among characters that made his gorge rise. . . . He lay on the outside of his bed in the fall of the foggy night; and he heard the pattering of countless thousands of feet, all, as he now told himself, making haste to do evil, and the rush of the wheels of countless cabs and carriages conveying men . . . to sin and punishment; and the horror of that monstrous seething mud-pot of a city, and of that kindred monster-man's soul, rose up within.

These "scenes" and "characters" Utterson is "dragged" through are no longer part of the plot in later drafts, and his feeling that many men rush about the city "to do evil" has been subdued.

In these two Princeton pages and also the longer sections of the notebook draft, a character called Mr. Lemsome, who disappears by the printer's copy, plays a central role. Page 33 of the Princeton manuscript establishes that Lemsome "was the first independent sign that such a man as Mr. Hyde existed," a role played by Enfield in the final draft. Lemsome, described here as "an uncurable cad," with "a fine forehead and good features; anemically pale; shielding a pair of suffering eyes under blue spectacles; and dressed with that sort of outward decency that implies both a lack of means and a defect of taste," is the man murdered by Hyde instead of the respectable M.P., Sir Danvers Carew. Stevenson's contemporaries would probably recognize Lemsome as a particular type of voluptuary or aesthete, whose effeminacy would in certain circles associate him with male homosexuality. Deleting this figure tames the sexual deviance of the tale. William Veeder has traced other signs of Stevenson soft-pedaling the sexual nature of Jekyll's desires from the notebook draft to the printer's draft, then through to the published edition with Stevenson's corrections to the proofs. To give just a few examples of many, the notebook draft has Jekyll explaining, "From an early age, I became in secret the slave of

4. Robert Louis Stevenson, *Strange Case of Dr. Jekyll and Mr. Hyde*, ed. Katherine Linehan (Norton, 2003), p. 64. See also the edition by Richard Drury (Edinburgh UP, 2004), p. 169.

Page of the notebook draft that has a letter to Stevenson's cousin Bob written on the back. From the Morris L. Parrish Collection of Victorian Novelists, Manuscript Division, Department of Rare Books and Special Collections, Princeton University Library. Courtesy of the Princeton University Library.

disgraceful pleasures."[5] In the printer's copy, these last two words become "certain appetites," but when the book is published, the sentence is revised to read: "and indeed the worst of my faults was a certain impatient gaiety of disposition, such as has made the happiness of many." Later in the same passage, in the notebook draft, Jekyll is "plunged into the mire of my vices . . . they were at once criminal in the sight of the law and abhorrent in themselves." The printer's copy changes the "criminal" and "abhorrent" to "no worse than those of many who have lived and died with credit." By the first edition, this whole passage is deleted and replaced with: "Many a man would have even blazoned such irregularities as I was guilty of."[6] Disgraceful and criminal vices become irregularities worth bragging about.

Below are reproduced the two Princeton draft pages in their entirety. Following that are the more substantive variations between the notebook draft and the printer's copy. These variants follow the format established by Katherine Linehan, which begins by citing the text, referenced by page and line number in the present Norton Critical Edition of the tale. After a left-facing arrow, the manuscript variant is transcribed, including Stevenson's on-the-page insertions and deletions. In cases where an overlap in textual coverage across manuscript fragments allows us to trace a change back through two stages of drafting, the entry works backward in compositional time, with the printer's copy version being presented before the earlier notebook draft version. The complete set of visual symbols used is as follows:

. . . ← . . .	words left of arrow replaced those on right
PC, followed by roman script	variation found in printer's copy manuscript
ND, followed by *italic script*	variation found in the Beinecke-Silverado notebook draft
\ . . . /	words between slashes inserted in manuscript
< . . . >	words within angled brackets deleted
{ . . .}	words within braces inserted, then deleted
[. . .]	editor's comments, not Stevenson's revisions

Symbols are doubled when there are deletions within deletions (thus: < . . .<< . . .>> . . .>).

5. This quote and the following ones in this paragraph are from Veeder, "The Texts in Question," p. 11.
6. For a full transcription of the drafts of the manuscripts, see Drury, ed., *Strange Case*, pp. 111–62.

Cancelled Princeton page 33[†]

ten years old. For ten years he had kept that preposterous document in his safe; and here was the first <external proof> \indepen-
dent sign/ that such a man as Mr Hyde existed <.>—here, <on>
\from/ the lips of a creature who had come to him bleating for help
under the most ignoble and deserved misfortunes, he <found>
\heard/ the name of the man to whom Henry Jekyll had left everything and whom, <in that> he named his "friend and benefactor."
He studied Mr Lemsome covertly. He was <still> a <youngish>
man of about twenty eight, with a fine forehead and good features;
anæmically pale; shielding a pair of <faint> suffering eyes under
blue spectacles; and dressed with that sort of <external> \outward/
decency that implies \both/ a lack of means and a defect of taste. By
his own confession, Mr Utterson knew him to be a bad fellow; <in
this short scrutiny, he <<read him through and through>> \made
{out very plainly that}/ him out to be a bad fellow of the> he now
saw for himself that he was an incurable cad.

"Sit down," said he. "I will take your business."

No one was more astonished than the client; but as he had been
speaking uninterruptedly for some three minutes, he set down the
success to the score of his own eloquence. <And> there never was a
client who did less credit to his lawyer; but still Mr Utterson stuck
to him on the chance that something might

Cancelled Princeton page 48

Thereupon, Mr Utterson, conceiving he had done <the> all and
more than could be asked of him, went home to his rooms and lay
down upon his bed, <mentally> \like one/ sick. <The last words of
the public officer had been the last straw on his overtaxed endur-
ance; there was something in the beaming air {, as of a man who
said a pleasant and witty thing,} with which that deadly truth had
been communicated that finally unmanned the lawyer.> He had
been dragged all day through scenes and among characters that
made his gorge rise; hunting a low murderer, and himself hag-
ridden by the thought that this murderer was the chosen heir \and/
the secret ally <and the so-called benefactor of the <<good,>>
learned and well beloved Henry Jekyll> \of his friend/; and now, at
the end of that experience, an honest man and active public servant

† The following transcription of cancelled manuscript leaves 33 and 48, from the Morris L. Parrish Collection of Victorian Novelists, Manuscripts Division, Department of
Rare Books and Special Collections, Princeton University Library, is published with
permission of the Princeton University Library.

<tells him with a smile> \spoke out in words what had been for Mr
Utterson the haunting moral and unspoken refrain of the day's
journeyings:/ that all men, high and low, are of the same \pattern/.
He lay on the outside <side> \of/ his bed in the fall of the foggy
night; and <he> heard the pattering of countless thousands of feet,
all, as he now told himself, making haste to do evil, and the rush of
the wheels of countless cabs and carriages conveying men <to
deadly yet> {still} \yet/ more expeditiously to sin and punishment;
and the horror of that monstrous seething mud-pot of a city, and of
that kindred <monster> monster—man's soul, rose up within \him/
to the

Variations from rough-draft notebook pages and printer's copy manuscript[†]

7:29   faces; and ← **PC** faces; <I declare we looked like fiends> and

12:16   besieged by questions. [paragraph break] Six o'clock ← **PC**
besieged by questions. <How could such a man as Henry Jekyll be
bound up with such a man as Edward Hyde? How should he have
chosen as his heir one who was unknown to his oldest intimates?
If it were a case of terrorism, why the will? Or again, if Hyde were
Jekyll's son, why the proviso of the disappearance?> Six o'clock

12:18–13:16   digging at the problem . . . "If he be Mr. Hyde," [The
following eight sentences coming after "digging at the problem"
were deleted in the printer's copy manuscript to allow the insertion,
as page 8A, of Utterson's troubled night visions of Hyde.[1]] ← **PC**
digging at the problem. <And for all that, he had no sooner swallowed his breakfast, than he must put on his hat and greatcoat and
set forth eastward <<of a>> \in/ the teeth of a fine, driving rain,
coming iced out of Siberia, with no more sensible purpose than to

---

† All passages in the following transcriptions headed ND (notebook draft) are, with one
exception, found on manuscript pages in the holding of the Beinecke Rare Book and
Manuscript Library, Yale University, and are published with permission of that library.
All passages headed PC (printer's copy) are, again with one exception, found on manuscript pages in the holding of the Pierpont Morgan Library, New York (accession
number PML 133614) and are published with permission of that library. The two
excepted passages, one belonging to the notebook draft and the other to the printer's
copy, are located on manuscript pages in the holding of the Robert Louis Stevenson
Silverado Museum, St. Helena, California. They are identified by footnotes where they
occur in this list of manuscript variations, and are published with permission of that
museum.
1. The first of the eight sentences occurs on the bottom of Morgan Library's p. 8 of the
printer's copy manuscript. The remaining seven sentences, beginning with an ellipsis
which is Stevenson's own, occur on Silverado Museum's p. 9 of the printer's copy
manuscript.

stand awhile on the opposite pavement and look awhile at the door
with the knocker. . . . This excursion, once taken, seemed to have
laid a spell on the methodical gentleman. In the morning before
office hours, at noon when business was plenty and time scarce, at
night under the glimpses of the fogged city moon or by the cheap
glare of the lamps, a spirit in his feet kept still drawing and guiding
the lawyer to that door in the by street of shops. <<He saw it thus
under all sorts of illumination, and occupied by all kinds of passing
tenants.>> He made long stages on the pavement opposite, studying
the bills of fare stuck on the sweating windows of the cookshop,
reading the labels on the various lotions or watching the bust of the
proud lady swing stonily round upon him on her \velvet/ pedestal at
the perfumers; but <<all the time>> \still/ with one eye over his
shoulder, spying at the door. And all the time the door remained
inexorably closed; none entered in, none came forth; <<it>> the
high tides of the town swarmed close by, but did not touch it. Yet
the lawyer was not to be beaten. He had made a solemn agreement
with himself <<and>> \to/ penetrate this mystery of Mr Hyde.> "If
he be Mr Hyde,"

16:20–21   deep waters! He was wild ← **PC** deep waters! <That
could never be the face of his son, never in this world. No, there is
a secret at the root of it; <<Jekyll>>> \He/ was wild

16:36–37   like sunshine. Things cannot ← **PC** like sunshine. <I
think we might turn the tables; I am sure, if Harry will but let me,
that I ought to try. For> Things cannot

37:31–38:9   glass saucers, as though . . . the business table ← **PC
discarded draft** [The immediately following variation comes from
the cancelled, discontinuous half-page found on the reverse of a
printer's copy manuscript page, as described in the headnote to this
section.] glass saucers, as if for <some> \an/ experiment in which
the unhappy man had been prevented. <At another, as has been
said, tea was set out> The kettle had by this time boiled over; and
they were obliged to take it off the fire; but the tea things were still
set forth with a comfortable orderliness that was in strange contrast to the tumbled corpse upon the floor. <Indeed the> Several
books were on a shelf <beside> \near/ the fire; one lay <beside>
beside the tea things open, and Utterson was <amazed> {somewhat
surprised} \amazed/ to find it <[? illegible word]> \pious/. Next, in
the course of their review of the chamber, the searchers came to
the cheval glass.
     "This glass have seen some queer doings, \sir,/ no doubt," whis-
pered Poole.

"And none stranger than itself," echoed the lawyer \in the same tones/. "What did—what did Jekyll do with a glass?"

"<I can't tell you> \That's what I have/ often asked myself," returned the butler.

Then they found a prayer in the doctor's writing, very eloquently put in words but breathing a spirit of despair and horror worthy of the cells of Bedlam, and the sight of this so ← **ND** *glass saucers <; and>, <these Poole recognised> as if for some purpose in which the unhappy man had been interrupted. On the desk of the business table*

41:25–28 no guess. The book was an ordinary version book and contained little but a series of dates. These covered a period of many years, but I observed that the entries ceased nearly a year ago and quite abruptly. Here and there ← **ND** *no guess. The dates in the version \book/ covered <a consider-> many years, fifteen I think or twenty, but I observed that they had ceased some months before \that day, on about April 1884/.*[2] *Here and there*

42:19 small, as I have said; I was struck ← **ND** *small, I have said; he had besides a slight shortening of some of the cords of the neck which tilted his head upon one side; I was struck*

44:3 with an air of scrutiny. ← **ND** *with a great air of scrutiny and hesitation.*

44:38–45:9 to set on paper . . . Hastie Lanyon ← **ND** *to place on paper. In spite of what I saw, my mind revolts <from> against belief; the shock of that moment has, I feel sure, struck at the very roots of my life, but it has not bowed the pride of my scepticism; I shall die, but I shall die incredulous. As for the moral turpitude that man unveiled to me, it is matter that I disdain to handle. He found me an elderly, a useful and a happy man; that he has blighted and shortened what remains to me of life, is but a small addendum to the monstrous tale of his misdeeds. Hastie Lanyon.*

45:11 I was born in the year 18— to ← **ND** *I was born in the year 1830 to*

45:15–20 distinguished future. And indeed . . . my pleasures; and that when I reached ← **PC** distinguished future. <From an early age, however, I became in secret the slave of certain

---

2. The concluding nine words of this sentence, beginning with "some months," occur on Silverado Museum's p. 68 of the notebook draft manuscript.

appetites;> \And indeed the worst of my faults was a certain impatient gaiety of disposition, such as has made the happiness of many, but such as I found it hard to reconcile with my imperious desire to carry my head high, and wear a more than commonly grave countenance before the public. Hence it came about that I concealed my pleasures;/ and \that when/ I reached ← **ND** *distinguished future. From a very early age, however, I became* <add> *in secret/ the slave of disgraceful pleasures;* <*my life was double;* <<*outwardly*>> *absorbed in scientific toil,* <<*and [?two illegible words]*>> *never indifferent to any noble* <<*opinion*>> *cause or*> *and when I reached*

45:23–28   duplicity of life. Many a man . . . and with an even deeper trench ← **PC** duplicity of life. <On the one side, I was what you have known me, a man of some note, immersed in toils, open to \all/ generous sympathies, never slow to befriend struggling virtue, never backward in <<an honour>> \the course/ of honour; on the other, as soon as night released me from my engagements and <<covered>> \hid/ me from the <<espial>> \notice/ of my friends, <<the iron hand>> indurated habit plunged me again into the mire of my vices. I will trouble you with these no further than to say that they were, at that period, no worse than those of many who have lived and died with credit. It was rather the somewhat high aspiration of my life by daylight> \Many a man would have even blazoned such irregularities as I was guilty of; but from the high views <of conduct> \that I had/ set before me I regarded and hid them with an almost morbid sense of shame, and it was thus rather the exacting nature of my aspirations/ than any particular degradation in my faults, that made me what I was; and with even a deeper trench ← **ND** *duplicity of life. On the one side, I was what you have known me, a man of distinction, immersed in toils, open to generous sympathies, never slow to befriend struggling virtue, never backward in an honourable cause; on the other, as soon as night had fallen and I could shake off my friends, the iron hand of indurated habit plunged me once again into the mire of my vices. I will trouble you with these no further than to say that they were at once criminal in the sight of the law and abhorrent in themselves. They cut me off from the sympathy of those whom I otherwise respected; and with even a deeper trench*

49:11–26   already learned to despair. The movement . . . On the other side I announced to my servants ← **ND** *already learned to despair. You can see now what was the result; for days, I would,* <[? two words illegible]> *as of yore,/ preserve and obey my better* <nature> *instincts/; and then when evil triumphed, I would again*

drink the cup and, impenetrably disguised as <Henry> *Edward*/
Hyde, pass *privately*/ *out of the laboratory door and roll myself in
infamy.*

*The temptation of my present power can hardly be overestimated.
As* <Henry> *Edward*/ *Hyde* (, *for I had so dubbed* <myself> *my second self—God help me—*/ *in pleasantry*), *I was secure of an immu-
nity that never* <man> *before was attained by any criminal. Think of
it—I did not exist! Let me but escape into my laboratory door, give
me but a second to* *mix and*/ *swallow* <that> *the draft that I had
always standing ready, and whatever* <I> *he had done, Edward Hyde
had vanished like a wreath of smoke, and there, in his stead, quietly
at home and trimming the midnight lamp in his laborious study, was
the well-known, the spotless, the benevolent and the beloved Dr
Jekyll!*

*I made my preparations with the most studious care. I announced
to my servants*

49:32–50:27   And thus fortified . . . I mean but to point out ←
ND *And thus fortified as I fondly supposed on every side, I began to
plunge into a career of cruel, soulless and degrading vice.*

Into the details of <this> *my shame, I scorn to enter; I mean but to
point out*

50:28   chastisement approached. I met ←   **PC** chastisement
approached <, and the halter of social responsibility, which I had so
long eluded, \was/ once more tightened about my neck>. I met

50:29–34   shall no more than mention . . . in order to pacify their
too just resentment ←   **ND** *mention only in passing: detected in an
act of infamy, I had to bribe a party of young fools to set me free, and
in order to* <*find* [?] *the money*> *satisfy their demands*/

51:1   Some two months before the murder of Sir Danvers, I ← **ND**
About <*five*> *a*/ *month* <s> *before the Lemsome murder, I*

51:8–9   but in the little room in Soho where ← **ND** *but in the iron
bed and the somewhat dreary and exiguous rooms off Gray's Inn
Road, where*

51:14–16   Now the hand of Henry Jekyll (as you have often
remarked) was professional in shape and size: it was large, firm,
white and comely. But ← **ND** *Now the hand of Henry Jekyll, as we
have often jocularly said, was eminently professional in shape and
size: it was large, firm, white and comely, the hand of a lady's doctor,
in a word.* <Now> *But*

54:35   slay him ← **PC** slay him. <The long drawn hum of anger and horror that sounded through society upon the fall of their favourite [crew? For Carew?] was>

56:31–57:5   driven to and fro about the streets of the city . . . came home to my own house ← **ND** *driven to a remote part of London <, where> \. Here/ I stopped \the driver/ at a door, asked for the first name that came into my head, was of course refused admittance, and was then driven back to the neighbourhood of Cavendish Square not very long before the hour of my appointment.*

   You know already what occurred. Lanyon threw me off from him with horror; it scarcely moved me; I was still so full of my immediate joy. I was already so conscious of the perpetual doom that hung above my head; and when I returned home

57:42–43   to death: and beyond these links of community, which ← **PC** to death: <more bonds he could not now recognise; the thought of him, like the <<sight of something odious>> \killing smell of ammonia/> \and beyond these links of community,/ <he did not stoop to recognise him> which

CONTEXTS

Composition

Stevenson affirmed the importance of dreams and trancelike states to his creativity in a number of his works. The three excerpts in this section explore their strong influence on the production of *Strange Case of Dr. Jekyll and Mr. Hyde*. In the first, Graham Balfour, Stevenson's cousin, describes the drafting of the novella on the heels of a dream, based on accounts by Stevenson's wife, his stepson Lloyd Osbourne, and his publisher Charles Longman. The second excerpt comes from Stevenson's essay on dreams. The third, a letter from Stevenson to the founder of the Society for Psychical Research, F. W. H. Myers, written after the publication of the novella, discusses his lifelong interest in theories of dual selves and altered states of consciousness.

GRAHAM BALFOUR

[Writing the Tale][†]

* * *

A subject much in his thoughts at this time was the duality of man's nature and the alternation of good and evil; and he was for a long while casting about for a story to embody this central idea. Out of this frame of mind had come the sombre imagination of "Markheim,"[1] but that was not what he required. The true story still delayed, till suddenly one night he had a dream. He awoke, and found himself in possession of two, or rather three, of the scenes in *The Strange Case of Dr. Jekyll and Mr. Hyde*.

Its waking existence, however, was by no means without incident. He dreamed these scenes in considerable detail, including the circumstance of the transforming powders, and so vivid was the impression that he wrote the story off at a red heat, just as it had presented itself to him in his sleep.

"In the small hours of one morning," says Mrs. Stevenson, "I was awakened by cries of horror from Louis. Thinking he had a nightmare,

---

† From *The Life of Robert Louis Stevenson*, vol. 2 (New York: Scribner's, 1901), pp. 15–18. Notes are by the editor of this Norton Critical Edition.
1. A short story by Stevenson dealing with similar themes.

I awakened him. He said angrily: 'Why did you wake me? I was dreaming a fine bogey tale.' I had awakened him at the first trans-formation scene."

Mr. Osbourne writes: "I don't believe that there was ever such a literary feat before as the writing of *Dr. Jekyll*. I remember the first reading as though it were yesterday. Louis came downstairs in a fever; read nearly half the book aloud; and then, while we were still gasping, he was away again, and busy writing. I doubt if the first draft took so long as three days."

He had lately had a hemorrhage, and was strictly forbidden all discussion or excitement. No doubt the reading aloud was contrary to the doctor's orders; at any rate Mrs. Stevenson, according to the custom then in force, wrote her detailed criticism of the story as it then stood, pointing out her chief objection—that it was really an allegory, whereas he had treated it purely as if it were a story. In the first draft Jekyll's nature was bad all through, and the Hyde change was worked only for the sake of a disguise. She gave the paper to her husband and left the room. After a while his bell rang; on her return she found him sitting up in bed (the clinical thermometer in his mouth), pointing with a long denunciatory finger to a pile of ashes. He had burned the entire draft. Having realised that he had taken the wrong point of view, that the tale was an allegory and not another "Markheim," he at once destroyed his manu-script, acting not out of pique, but from a fear that he might be tempted to make too much use of it, and not rewrite the whole from a new standpoint.

It was written again in three days ("I drive on with Jekyll: bank-ruptcy at my heels");[2] but the fear of losing the story altogether pre-vented much further criticism. The powder was condemned as too material an agency, but this he could not eliminate, because in the dream it had made so strong an impression upon him.

"The mere physical feat," Mr. Osbourne continues, "was tremen-dous; and instead of harming him, it roused and cheered him inex-pressibly." Of course it must not be supposed that these three days represent all the time that Stevenson spent upon the story, for after this he was working hard for a month or six weeks in bringing it into its present form.

The manuscript was then offered to Messrs. Longmans for their magazine; and on their judgment the decision was taken not to break it up into monthly sections, but to issue it as a shilling book in paper covers. The chief drawbacks of this plan to the author were the loss of immediate payment and the risk of total failure, but these were generously met by an advance payment from the

2. Stevenson wrote this in a letter to his wife, Fanny, dated October 20, 1885.

publishers on account of royalties. "The little book was printed," says Mr. Charles Longman, "but when it was ready the bookstalls were already full of Christmas numbers, etc., and the trade would not look at it. We therefore withdrew it till after Christmas. In January it was launched—not without difficulty. The trade did not feel inclined to take it up, till a review appeared in the *Times* calling attention to the story. This gave it a start, and in the next six months close on forty thousand copies were sold in this country alone." Besides the authorised edition in America, the book was widely pirated, and probably not less than a quarter of a million copies in all have been sold in the United States.

Its success was probably due rather to the moral instincts of the public than to any conscious perception of the merits of its art. It was read by those who never read fiction, it was quoted in pulpits, and made the subject of leading articles in religious newspapers. * * *

But as literature also it was justly received with enthusiasm. * * *

* * *

ROBERT LOUIS STEVENSON

[The Use of Dreams]†

* * *

* * * There are some among us who claimed to have lived longer and more richly than their neighbours; when they lay asleep they claim they were still active; and among the treasures of memory that all men review for their amusement, these count in no second place the harvests of their dreams. There is one of this kind whom I have in my eye, and whose case is perhaps unusual enough to be described.[1] He was from a child an ardent and uncomfortable dreamer. When he had a touch of fever at night, and the room swelled and shrank, and his clothes, hanging on a nail, now loomed up instant to the bigness of a church, and now drew away into a horror of infinite distance and infinite littleness, the poor soul was very well aware of what must follow, and struggled hard against the approaches of that slumber which was the beginning of sorrows. But his struggles were in vain; sooner or later the night-hag would have him by the throat, and pluck him, strangling and screaming,

---

† From "A Chapter on Dreams," *The Travels and Essays of Robert Louis Stevenson* (New York: Scribner's, 1918), pp. 251–58, 262–65. Notes are by the editor of this Norton Critical Edition.
1. Stevenson refers to himself.

from his sleep. His dreams were at times commonplace enough, at times very strange: at times they were almost formless, he would be haunted, for instance, by nothing more definite than a certain hue of brown, which he did not mind in the least while he was awake, but feared and loathed while he was dreaming; at times, again, they took on every detail of circumstance, as when once he supposed he must swallow the populous world, and awoke screaming with the horror of the thought. The two chief troubles of his very narrow existence—the practical and everyday trouble of school tasks and the ultimate and airy one of hell and judgment—were often confounded together into one appalling nightmare. He seemed to himself to stand before the Great White Throne; he was called on, poor little devil, to recite some form of words, on which his destiny depended; his tongue stuck, his memory was blank, hell gaped for him; and he would awake, clinging to the curtain-rod with his knees to his chin.

These were extremely poor experiences, on the whole; and at that time of life my dreamer would have very willingly parted with his power of dreams. But presently, in the course of his growth, the cries and physical contortions passed away, seemingly forever; his visions were still for the most part miserable, but they were more constantly supported; and he would awake with no more extreme symptom than a flying heart, a freezing scalp, cold sweats, and the speechless midnight fear. His dreams, too, as befitted a mind better stocked with particulars, became more circumstantial, and had more the air and continuity of life. The look of the world beginning to take hold on his attention, scenery came to play a part in his sleeping as well as in his waking thoughts, so that he would take long, uneventful journeys and see strange towns and beautiful places as he lay in bed. And, what is more significant, an odd taste that he had for the Georgian costume and for stories laid in that period of English history, began to rule the features of his dreams; so that he masqueraded there in a three-cornered hat, and was much engaged with Jacobite conspiracy between the hour for bed and that for breakfast. About the same time, he began to read in his dreams—tales, for the most part, and for the most part after the manner of G. P. R. James,[2] but so incredibly more vivid and moving than any printed book, that he has ever since been malcontent with literature.

And then, while he was yet a student, there came to him a dream-adventure which he has no anxiety to repeat; he began, that is to say, to dream in sequence and thus to lead a double life—one of the day, one of the night—one that he had every reason to believe was

2. British novelist known for his formulaic historical fiction.

the true one, another that he had no means of proving to be false. I should have said he studied, or was by way of studying, at Edinburgh College, which (it may be supposed) was how I came to know him. Well, in his dream life, he passed a long day in the surgical theatre, his heart in his mouth, his teeth on edge, seeing monstrous malformations and the abhorred dexterity of surgeons. In a heavy, rainy, foggy evening he came forth into the South Bridge, turned up the High Street, and entered the door of a tall *land,* at the top of which he supposed himself to lodge. All night long, in his wet clothes, he climbed the stairs, stair after stair in endless series, and at every second flight a flaring lamp with a reflector. All night long, he brushed by single persons passing downward—beggarly women of the street, great, weary, muddy labourers, poor scarecrows of men, pale parodies of women—but all drowsy and weary like himself, and all single, and all brushing against him as they passed. In the end, out of a northern window, he would see day beginning to whiten over the Firth,[3] give up the ascent, turn to descend, and in a breath be back again upon the streets, in his wet clothes, in the wet, haggard dawn, trudging to another day of monstrosities and operations. Time went quicker in the life of dreams, some seven hours (as near as he can guess) to one; and it went, besides, more intensely, so that the gloom of these fancied experiences clouded the day, and he had not shaken off their shadow ere it was time to lie down and to renew them. I cannot tell how long it was that he endured this discipline; but it was long enough to leave a great black blot upon his memory, long enough to send him, trembling for his reason, to the doors of a certain doctor; whereupon with a simple draught he was restored to the common lot of man.

The poor gentleman has since been troubled by nothing of the sort; indeed, his nights were for some while like other men's, now blank, now chequered with dreams, and these sometimes charming, sometimes appalling, but except for an occasional vividness, of no extraordinary kind. I will just note one of these occasions, ere I pass on to what makes my dreamer truly interesting. It seemed to him that he was in the first floor of a rough hill-farm. The room showed some poor efforts at gentility, a carpet on the floor, a piano, I think, against the wall; but, for all these refinements, there was no mistaking he was in a moorland place, among hillside people, and set in miles of heather. He looked down from the window upon a bare farmyard, that seemed to have been long disused. A great, uneasy stillness lay upon the world. There was no sign of the farm-folk or of any live stock, save for an old, brown, curly dog of the retriever breed, who sat close in against the wall of the house and

3. Firth of Forth: estuary that flows through the city of Edinburgh.

seemed to be dozing. Something about this dog disquieted the dreamer; it was quite a nameless feeling, for the beast looked right enough—indeed, he was so old and dull and dusty and broken-down, that he should rather have awakened pity; and yet the conviction came and grew upon the dreamer that this was no proper dog at all, but something hellish. A great many dozing summer flies hummed about the yard; and presently the dog thrust forth his paw, caught a fly in his open palm, carried it to his mouth like an ape, and looking suddenly up at the dreamer in the window, winked to him with one eye. The dream went on, it matters not how it went; it was a good dream as dreams go; but there was nothing in the sequel worthy of that devilish brown dog. And the point of interest for me lies partly in that very fact: that having found so singular an incident, my imperfect dreamer should prove unable to carry the tale to a fit end and fall back on indescribable noises and indiscriminate horrors. It would be different now; he knows his business better!

For, to approach at last the point: This honest fellow had long been in the custom of setting himself to sleep with tales, and so had his father before him; but these were irresponsible inventions, told for the teller's pleasure, with no eye to the crass public or the thwart reviewer: tales where a thread might be dropped, or one adventure quitted for another, on fancy's least suggestion. So that the little people who manage man's internal theatre had not as yet received a very rigorous training; and played upon their stage like children who should have slipped into the house and found it empty, rather than like drilled actors performing a set piece to a huge hall of faces. But presently my dreamer began to turn his former amusement of story-telling to (what is called) account; by which I mean that he began to write and sell his tales. Here was he, and here were the little people who did that part of his business, in quite new conditions. The stories must now be trimmed and pared and set upon all fours, they must run from a beginning to an end and fit (after a manner) with the laws of life; the pleasure, in one word, had become a business; and that not only for the dreamer, but for the little people of his theatre. These understood the change as well as he. When he lay down to prepare himself for sleep, he no longer sought amusement, but printable and profitable tales; and after he had dozed off in his box-seat, his little people continued their evolutions with the same mercantile designs. All other forms of dream deserted him but two: he still occasionally reads the most delightful books, he still visits at times the most delightful places; and it is perhaps worthy of note that to these same places, and to one in particular, he returns at intervals of months and years, finding new field-paths, visiting new neighbours, beholding that happy valley under new effects of noon and dawn and sunset. But all the rest of the family of visions is quite lost to him: the common, mangled version of yesterday's affairs, the raw-head-and-bloody-bones nightmare, rumoured to be the child of toasted cheese—these and their like are gone; and, for the most part, whether awake or asleep, he is simply occupied—he or his little people—in consciously making stories for the market. This dreamer (like many other persons) has encountered some trifling vicissitudes of fortune. When the bank begins to send letters and the butcher to linger at the back gate, he sets to belabouring his brains after a story, for that is his readiest money-winner; and, behold! at once the little people begin to bestir themselves in the same quest, and labour all night long, and all night long set before him truncheons of tales upon their lighted theatre. No fear of his being frightened now; the flying heart and the frozen scalp are things bygone; applause, growing applause, growing interest, growing exultation in his own cleverness (for he takes all the credit), and at last a jubilant leap to wakefulness, with the cry, "I have it, that'll do!" upon his lips: with such and similar emotions he sits at these nocturnal dramas, with such outbreaks, like Claudius in the play,[4] he scatters the performance in the midst. Often enough the waking is a disappointment: he has been too deep asleep, as I explain the thing; drowsiness has gained his little people, they have gone stumbling and maundering through their parts; and the play, to the awakened mind, is seen to be a tissue of absurdities. And yet how often have these sleepless Brownies done him honest service, and given him, as he sat idly taking his pleasure in the boxes, better tales than he could fashion for himself.

*   *   *

* * * Who are the Little People? They are near connections of the dreamer's, beyond doubt; they share in his financial worries and have an eye to the bank-book; they share plainly in his training; they have plainly learned like him to build the scheme of a considerate story and to arrange emotion in progressive order; only I think they have more talent; and one thing is beyond doubt, they can tell him a story piece by piece, like a serial, and keep him all the while in ignorance of where they aim. Who are they, then? and who is the dreamer?

Well, as regards the dreamer, I can answer that, for he is no less a person than myself;—as I might have told you from the beginning, only that the critics murmur over my consistent egotism;—and as

---

4. In *Hamlet*, by William Shakespeare (1564–1616), King Claudius stops a play put on by his nephew Hamlet when he recognizes in the story an exposure of his crime—his poisoning of his brother, the king, in order to marry the queen and ascend to the throne.

I am positively forced to tell you now, or I could advance but little farther with my story. And for the Little People, what shall I say they are but just my Brownies, God bless them! who do one-half my work for me while I am fast asleep, and in all human likelihood, do the rest for me as well, when I am wide awake and fondly suppose I do it for myself. That part which is done while I am sleeping is the Brownies' part beyond contention; but that which is done when I am up and about is by no means necessarily mine, since all goes to show the Brownies have a hand in it even then. Here is a doubt that much concerns my conscience. For myself—what I call I, my conscious ego, the denizen of the pineal gland unless he has changed his residence since Descartes,[5] the man with the conscience and the variable bank-account, the man with the hat and the boots, and the privilege of voting and not carrying his candidate at the general elections—I am sometimes tempted to suppose he is no story-teller at all, but a creature as matter of fact as any cheesemonger or any cheese, and a realist bemired up to the ears in actuality; so that, by that account, the whole of my published fiction should be the single-handed product of some Brownie, some Familiar,[6] some unseen collaborator, whom I keep locked in a back garret, while I get all the praise and he but a share (which I cannot prevent him getting) of the pudding. I am an excellent adviser, something like Molière's[7] servant; I pull back and I cut down; and I dress the whole in the best words and sentences that I can find and make; I hold the pen, too; and I do the sitting at the table, which is about the worst of it; and when all is done, I make up the manuscript and pay for the registration; so that, on the whole, I have some claim to share, though not so largely as I do, in the profits of our common enterprise.

I can but give an instance or so of what part is done sleeping and what part awake, and leave the reader to share what laurels there are, at his own nod, between myself and my collaborators; and to do this I will first take a book that a number of persons have been polite enough to read, the *Strange Case of Dr. Jekyll and Mr. Hyde*. I had long been trying to write a story on this subject, to find a body, a vehicle, for that strong sense of man's double being which must at times come in upon and overwhelm the mind of every thinking creature. I had even written one, *The Travelling Companion*, which was returned by an editor on the plea that it was a work of genius

---

5. René Descartes (1596–1650), French philosopher who argued that the pineal gland was the main seat of the soul.
6. Supernatural assistant, spirit, or companion to a witch or other practitioner of magic, often taking the form of an animal.
7. Stage and pen name of the French playwright and actor Jean-Baptiste Poquelin (1622–1673), whose works sometimes feature rational and plainspoken servants who advise their employers.

and indecent, and which I burned the other day on the ground that it was not a work of genius, and that *Jekyll* had supplanted it. Then came one of those financial fluctuations to which (with an elegant modesty) I have hitherto referred in the third person. For two days I went about racking my brains for a plot of any sort; and on the second night I dreamed the scene at the window, and a scene afterwards split in two, in which Hyde, pursued for some crime, took the powder and underwent the change in the presence of his pursuers. All the rest was made awake, and consciously, although I think I can trace in much of it the manner of my Brownies. The meaning of the tale is therefore mine, and had long pre-existed in my garden of Adonis, and tried one body after another in vain; indeed, I do most of the morality, worse luck! and my Brownies have not a rudiment of what we call a conscience. Mine, too, is the setting, mine the characters. All that was given me was the matter of three scenes, and the central idea of a voluntary change becoming involuntary. Will it be thought ungenerous, after I have been so liberally ladling out praise to my unseen collaborators, if I here toss them over, bound hand and foot, into the arena of the critics? For the business of the powders, which so many have censured, is, I am relieved to say, not mine at all but the Brownies'. Of another tale, in case the reader should have glanced at it, I may say a word: the not very defensible story of *Olalla*.[8] Here the court, the mother, the mother's niche, Olalla, Olalla's chamber, the meetings on the stair, the broken window, the ugly scene of the bite, were all given me in bulk and detail as I have tried to write them; to this I added only the external scenery (for in my dream I never was beyond the court), the portrait, the characters of Felipe and the priest, the moral, such as it is, and the last pages, such as, alas! they are. And I may even say that in this case the moral itself was given me; for it arose immediately on a comparison of the mother and the daughter, and from the hideous trick of atavism in the first. Sometimes a parabolic sense is still more undeniably present in a dream; sometimes I cannot but suppose my Brownies have been aping Bunyan,[9] and yet in no case with what would possibly be called a moral in a tract; never with the ethical narrowness; conveying hints instead of life's larger limitations and that sort of sense which we seem to perceive in the arabesque of time and space.

For the most part, it will be seen, my Brownies are somewhat fantastic, like their stories hot and hot, full of passion and the

8. Stevenson's short story about a formerly wealthy family's insanity, quasi-vampirism, and degeneration, written in 1886 just after *Strange Case of Dr. Jekyll and Mr. Hyde*.
9. John Bunyan (1628–1688), British writer known for the didactic allegory *The Pilgrim's Progress* (1678).

picturesque, alive with animating incident; and they have no preju-
dice against the supernatural. * * *

[My Other Self][†]

To F. W. H. Myers

14 July 1892   Vailima Plantation[1]

Dear Mr Myers, I am tempted to communicate to you some experiences of mine which seem to me (ignorant as I am) of a high psychological interest.

I had infamous bad health when I was a child and suffered much
from night fears; but from the age of about thirteen until I was past
thirty I did not know what it was to have a high fever or to wander
in my mind. So that these experiences, when they were renewed,
came upon me with entire freshness; and either I am a peculiar
subject, or I was thus enabled to observe them with unusual
closeness.

Experience A. During an illness at Nice I lay awake a whole night
in extreme pain. From the beginning of the evening *one part of my
mind* became possessed of a notion so grotesque and shapeless that
it may best be described as a form of words. I thought the pain was,
or was connected with, a wisp or coil of some sort; I knew not of
what it consisted nor yet where it was, and cared not; only I thought,
if the two ends were brought together the pain would cease. Now
all the time, with *another part of my mind*, which I ventured to
think was *myself*, I was fully alive to the absurdity of this idea, knew
it to be a mark of impaired sanity, and was engaged with *my other
self* in a perpetual conflict. *Myself* had nothing more at heart than
to keep from my wife, who was nursing me, any hint of this ridicu-
lous hallucination; the *other* was bound that she should be told of it
and ordered to effect the cure. I believe it must have been well on
in the morning before the fever (or *the other fellow*) triumphed, and
I called my wife to my bedside, seized her savagely by the wrist, and
looking on her with a face of fury, cried: 'Why do you not put the
two ends together and put me out of pain?'

Experience B. The other day in Sydney I was seized on a Satur-
day with a high fever. Early in the afternoon I began to repeat
mechanically the sound usually written 'mhn' caught myself in the
act, instantly stopped it, and explained to my mother, who was in

---

† From *The Letters of Robert Louis Stevenson*, ed. Bradford A. Booth and Ernest Mehew
(New Haven: Yale UP, 1995), vol. 7, pp. 331–33. Copyright © 1995 Yale University.
Reprinted by permission of the publisher. Notes are by the editor of this Norton Critical Edition.
1. He writes from the estate in Samoa that the Stevensons bought in 1890.

the room, my reasons for so doing. 'That is the beginning of the mind to wander,' I said, 'and has to be resisted at the outset.' I fell asleep and woke, and for the rest of the night repeated to myself mentally a nonsense word which I could not recall next morning. I had been reading the day before the life of Swift,[2] and all night long one part of my mind (*the other fellow*) kept informing me that I was not repeating the word myself, but was only reading in a book that Swift had so repeated it in his last sickness. The temptation to communicate this nonsense was again strongly felt by *myself*, but was on this occasion triumphantly resisted, and my watcher heard from me all night nothing of Dean Swift or the word, nothing but what was rational and to the point. So much for the two consciousnesses when I can disentangle them; but there is a part of my thoughts that I have more difficulty in attributing. One part of my mind continually bid me remark the transrational felicity of the word, examined all the syllables, showed me that not one was in itself significant, and yet the whole expressed to a nicety the voluminous distress of one in a high fever and his annoyance at and recoil from the attentions of his nurses. It was probably the same part (and for a guess *the other fellow*) who bid me compare it with the nonsense words of Lewis Carroll[3] as the invention of a lunatic with those of a sane man. But surely it was *myself* (and myself in a perfectly clear-headed state) that kept me trying all night to get the word by heart, on the ground that it would afterwards be useful in literature if I wanted to deal with mad folk. It must have been myself, I say, because *the other fellow* believed (or pretended to believe) that he was reading the passage in a book where it could always be found again when wanted.

Experience C. The next night *the other fellow* had an explanation ready for my sufferings, of which I can only say that it had something to do with the navy, that it was sheer undiluted nonsense, had neither end nor beginning, and was insusceptible of being expressed in words. *Myself* knew this; yet I gave way, and my watcher was favoured with some references to the navy. Not only that: *the other fellow* was annoyed—or *I* was annoyed—on two inconsistent accounts; first, because he had failed to make his meaning comprehensible, and second, because the nurse displayed no interest. *The other fellow* would have liked to explain further; but *myself* was much hurt at having been got into this false position and would be led no further.

*   *   *

2. A biography of the British writer Jonathan Swift (1667–1745), who was called Dean Swift later in his life when he took on the deanship of St. Patrick's Cathedral, Dublin.
3. British writer known for his children's fiction and his nonsense verse.

I have called the one person *myself*, and the other *the other fellow*. It was myself who spoke and acted; the other fellow seemed to have no control of the body or the tongue; he could only act through myself, on whom he brought to bear a heavy strain, resisted in one case, triumphant in the two others. Yet I am tempted to think that I know the other fellow; I am tempted to think he is the dreamer described in my 'Chapter on Dreams'[4] to which you refer. * * *

* * *

4. Excerpted above, pp. 77–84.

Correspondence and Reception

Stevenson was known as a charming letter writer to his large circle of friends, many themselves writers. The letters in this section chronicle his conversations with them about the personal contexts, composition, and publication of *Strange Case of Dr. Jekyll and Mr. Hyde*. Both sides of an exchange with John Addington Symonds about the novella are included here. Symonds, a close friend and a fellow writer, would later become known for his struggles with homosexuality. His letter implies that the two selves of Jekyll and Hyde mirror his own dual life as a husband to his wife and as a lover of men. The novelist Henry James, another dear friend, comments on Stevenson's style in the final excerpt.

ROBERT LOUIS STEVENSON

To Sidney Colvin[†]

[*Late September/early October 1885*][1]   [*Skerryvore*][2]

Dear Colvin, So much the worse, and yet perhaps its better to wait till we can take you in to the Box. Do you remember a Mrs Montagu Blackett?[3] She introduced herself to us on your name; but has since confessed it was partly an imposture, as she only once met you for a week at Minto. She is very nice however; and her brother (or cousin) another Elliot, is supposed to know you well. She asked if you were married; I said you were not. I am however and my wife has a headache. The world is too much with us; and coin it grows so sparsely on the tree! (Scotch Ballad) I am pouring forth a penny (12

---

† This and the following four selections are from *The Letters of Robert Louis Stevenson*, ed. Bradford A. Booth and Ernest Mehew (New Haven: Yale UP, 1995), vol. 5, pp. 128–29, 150, 161–63, 168, 212–13. Copyright © 1995 Yale University. Reprinted by permission of the publisher. Notes are by Booth and Mehew except where indicated.
1. Brackets are used by the editors of the Yale UP edition when the date of the letter is estimated [*Editor*].
2. Stevenson and his wife, Fanny, named their house in Bournemouth, in the south of England, after a lighthouse in Scotland built by Stevenson's uncle, Alan Stevenson [*Editor*].
3. Emma Mary, daughter of the Very Revd Gilbert Elliot, Dean of Bristol (who was a nephew of the first Earl of Minto), married (1862) Montagu Blackett (1826–66).

penny) dreadful;[4] it is dam dreadful; they call it the Abbot George of
Shaw (beg pardon: Scottish poesie)—I mean, they call it Doctor
Jekyll, but they also call it Mr Hyde, Mr Hyde, but they also, also
call it Mr Hyde.[5] I seem to bloom by nature—oh, by nature, into
song; but for all my tale is silly it shall not be very long. So farewell,
my noble Colvin, and if ever to our door You shall guide your pacing
charger as repeatedly* before, You shall find the face of welcome in
the halls of Skerryvore. R.L.S.

*So on mere poetic grounds, for the fancy of the bard
Rather leaned to thinking metre and not reason was the card.

To Charles Longman[1]

[? 1 November 1885]   [Skerryvore]

It may interest you to know that the main incident occurred in a
nightmare: indigestion has its uses. I woke up, and before I went to
sleep again, the story was complete.[2]

To Will H. Low

26 December 1885[1]   Skerryvore

*   *   *

4. A "penny dreadful" was a tale that came out in weekly installments that cost a penny.
   Usually sensational or melodramatic and often featuring crime, violence, and/or supernatural elements, the stories were also sometimes published in paperback novel form and
   then cost a shilling (12 pence). These were often called "shilling shockers" [Editor].
5. Fanny wrote at this time to Colvin: 'Again Louis is better, and possessed by a story that
   he will try to work at. To stop him seems to annoy him to such a degree that I am letting
   him alone; as the better alternative; but I fear it will be only energy wasted, as all his late
   work has been. For the last few days he has, however, seemed much clearer in his mind
   about things, but has been suffering from dreadful nightmares, and headaches at night.'
   On 4 October Lloyd [Stevenson's stepson] wrote to MIS [Stevenson's mother, Margaret
   Isabella.] 'Louis is doing very well though still very weak. He has been writing a most
   terrible story which he said occurred to him in the night. It is certainly one of the most
   ghostly and unpleasant stories I have ever heard. He is still writing it.' (Extract in Balfour Biography Notebook, 177, NLS [National Library of Scotland, Edinburgh].)
1. RLS's letter sending the MS of Dr Jekyll and Mr Hyde to Longmans does not appear to
   have survived but Charles Longman acknowledged it on 31 October 1885 (recorded by
   [Andrew] Lang in the Athenaeum when quoting this extract from RLS's reply). The
   contract for book-publication was signed on 3 November and proofs were available by
   mid-November.
2. In an earlier letter to the Athenaeum of 12 January 1895, Lang noted that the dream
   occurred after RLS had had 'a copious supper of bread and jam'.
1. Written in reply to a letter from Low dated 11 December 1885.

* * * I send you herewith a gothic gnome for your Greek nymph; but the gnome is interesting I think and he came out of a deep mine, where he guards the fountain of tears. It is not always the time to rejoice. Yours ever   R.L.S.

The gnome's name is *Jekyll and Hyde*; I believe you will find he is likewise quite willing to answer to the name of Low or Stevenson.

2 January

I have copied out on the other sheet some bad verses, which somehow your pictures suggested: as a kind of image of things that I pursue and cannot reach, and that you seem—no, not to have reached—but to have come a thought nearer to than I. This is the life we have chosen: well, the choice was mad, but I should make it again.

* * *

To Katharine de Mattos

1 January 1886   [*Skerryvore*]

Dearest Katharine, Here, on a very little book and accompanied with your lame verses, I have put your name.[1] Our kindness is now getting well on in years; it must be nearly of age; and it gets more valuable to me with every time I see you. It is not possible to express any sentiment, and it is not necessary to try at least between us. You know very well that I love you dearly, and that I always will. I only wish the verses were better, but at least you like the story; and it is sent to you by the one that loves you—Jekyll and not Hyde.

                                        R.L.S.

1. *Strange Case of Dr Jekyll and Mr Hyde*, dedicated to Katharine de Mattos [Stevenson's cousin], was published on 9 January 1886. Colvin prints as part of this letter the following poem:

KATHARINE DE MATTOS
AVE!

Bells upon the city are ringing in the night;
High above the gardens are the houses full of light;
On the heathy Pentlands is the curlew flying free;
And the broom is blowing bonnie in the north countrie.

We cannae break the bonds that God decreed to bind,
Still we'll be the children of the heather and the wind;
Far away from home, O, it's still for you and me
That the broom is blowing bonnie in the north countrie!
                                        R.L.S.

In his Galleys (Silverado), the poem is dated 19 May 1885 and was evidently written for the wedding anniversary dinner [celebrating Stevenson's marriage to Fanny] on that date * * * and not, as previously supposed, sent with the letter. The second verse was printed in *Dr Jekyll* as part of the dedication, with the opening words amended to 'It's ill to loose the bands'.

To Edward Purcell[1]

* * *

* * * What you say about the confusion of my ethics, I own to be all too true.[2] It is, as you say, where I fall, and fall almost consciously. I have the old Scotch Presbyterian preoccupation about these problems; itself morbid; I have alongside of that a second, perhaps more—possibly less—morbid element—the dazzled incapacity to choose, of an age of transition.[3] The categorical imperative[4] is ever with me, but utters dark oracles. This is a ground almost of pity. The Scotch side came out plain in *Dr Jekyll*; the XIXth century side probably baffled me even there, and in most other places baffles me entirely. Ethics are my veiled mistress; I love them, but I know not what they are. Is this my fault? Partly, of course, it is; because I love my sins like other people. Partly my merit, because I do not take, and rest contented in, the first subterfuge.

* * *

JOHN ADDINGTON SYMONDS

To Robert Louis Stevenson†

Am Hof, Davos Platz, Switzerland. March 3 1886

My dear Louis

At last I have read Dr Jekyll. It makes me wonder whether a man has the right so to scrutinize "the abysmal deeps of personality." It is indeed a dreadful book, most dreadful because of a certain moral

---

1. Purcell wrote a review in *The Academy* (February 27, 1886) of *Strange Case of Dr. Jekyll and Mr. Hyde* and other works by Stevenson [*Editor*].
2. 'We have no right to demand his scheme of human life; but this is certain, that his puzzling enigmatic ethics, whether they be individual, or whether they are a true reflection of a present transitional state of society, are the real hindrance to his aim of producing a great romance worthy of his genius.'
3. A reference to a religious preoccupation with sin, punishment, and hell, and a wavering about his beliefs, brought on in part by the growing religious doubt of his era, one of transition [*Editor*].
4. Binding moral obligations, from the philosophical ideas of Immanuel Kant (1724–1804) [*Editor*].
† From *The Letters of John Addington Symonds*, ed. Herbert M. Schueller and Robert L. Peters (Detroit: Wayne State UP, 1969), vol. 3, pp. 120–21. Copyright © 1969 Herbert M. Schueller and Robert L. Peters. Reprinted by permission of the Literary Executive of Robert L. Peters. Notes are by the editor of this Norton Critical Edition.

callousness, a want of sympathy, a shutting out of hope. The art is burning and intense. The Peau de Chagrin disappears; Poe is as water.[1] As a piece of literary work, this seems to me the finest you have done—in all that regards style, invention, psychological analysis, exquisite fitting of parts, and admirable employment of motives to realize the abnormal. But it has left such a deeply painful impression on my heart that I do not know how I am ever to turn to it again.

The fact is that, viewed as an allegory, it touches one too closely. Most of us at some epoch of our lives have been upon the verge of developing a Mr Hyde.

Physical and biological Science on a hundred lines is reducing individual freedom to zero, and weakening the sense of responsibility. I doubt whether the artist should lend his genius to this grim argument. Your Dr Jekyll seems to me capable of loosening the last threads of self-control in one who should read it while wavering between his better and worse self. It is like the Cave of Despair in the Faery Queen.[2]

I had the great biologist Lauder Brunton[3] with me a fortnight back. He was talking about Dr Jekyll and a book by W. O. Holmes,[4] in wh atavism is played with. I could see that, though a Christian, he held very feebly to the theory of human liberty; and these two works of fiction interested him, as Dr Jekyll does me, upon that point at issue.

I understand now thoroughly how much a sprite you are. Really there is something not quite human in your genius!

The denouement would have been finer, I think, if Dr Jekyll by a last supreme effort of his lucid self had given Mr Hyde up to justice—wh might have been arranged after the scene in Lanyon's study. Did you ever read Raskolnikow?[5] How fine is that ending! Had you made your hero act thus, you would at least have saved the sense of human dignity. The doors of Broadmoor[6] would have closed on Mr Hyde.

1. The American author Edgar Allan Poe (1809–1849), who wrote macabre stories of crime, horror, and the supernatural. The 1831 novel La Peau de chagrin by the French author Honoré de Balzac (1799–1850) concerns a man who finds a magical pelt that grants his every wish, but shrinks with each fulfillment, taking away some of his physical health.
2. Referring to thoughts of despair potentially leading to suicide, from Faerie Queene, by the English poet Edmund Spenser (c. 1552–1599).
3. Sir Thomas Lauder Brunton, a Scottish doctor, known for his discoveries of new medicines.
4. Oliver Wendell Holmes, Sr. (1809–1894), American doctor and author. (Symonds inadvertently inverts his initials.) The book may be Elsie Venner (1861), about a girl with reptilian characteristics caused when her mother was bitten by a snake while pregnant with her, or The Guardian Angel (1867), in which a young woman inherits "primitive" qualities from her Native American ancestors.
5. The main character of the novel Crime and Punishment (1866) by the Russian author Fyodor Dostoevsky (1821–1881), who commits murder, then later confesses, admits his responsibility, and begins a path toward Christian redemption.
6. An insane asylum.

Goodbye. I seem quite to have lost you. But if I come to England I shall try to see you.

Love to your wife.

Everyrs

J A Symonds

ROBERT LOUIS STEVENSON

To John Addington Symonds†

[Early March 1886]   *Skerryvore*

My dear Symonds, If we have lost touch it is (I think) only in a material sense; a question of letters not hearts. You will find a warm welcome at Skerryvore from both the light keepers; and indeed we never tell ourselves one of our financial fairy tales, but a run to Davos is a prime feature. I am not changeable in friendship; and I think I can promise you you have a pair of trusty well-wishers and friends in Bournemouth; whether they write or not is but a small thing; the flag may not be waved, but it is there.

Jekyll is a dreadful thing, I own; but the only thing I feel dreadful about is that damned old business of the war in the members.[1] This time it came out; I hope it will stay in, in future.

Raskolnikoff[2] is the greatest book I have read easily in ten years; I am glad you took to it. Many find it dull; Henry James could not finish it: all I can say is, it nearly finished me. It was like having an illness. James did not care for it because the character of Raskolnikoff was not objective; and at that I divined a great gulf between us and, on further reflection, the existence of a certain impotence in many minds of today, which prevents them from living *in* a book or a character, and keeps them standing afar off, spectators of a puppet show. To such I suppose the book may seem empty in the centre; to the others it is a room, a house of life, into which they themselves enter, and are tortured and purified. * * *

God knows where I am driving to. But here comes my lunch.

Which interruption happily for you seems to have stayed the issue. I have now nothing to say, that had formerly such a pressure of twaddle. Pray don't fail to come this summer. It will be a great disappointment now it has been spoken of, if you do.

Yours ever   Robert Louis Stevenson

† From *The Letters of Robert Louis Stevenson*, ed. Bradford A. Booth and Ernest Mehew (New Haven: Yale UP, 1995), vol. 5, pp. 220–22. Copyright © 1995 Yale University. Reprinted by permission of the publisher. Notes are by Booth and Mehew except where indicated.

1. Cf. 'Your lusts that war in your members'—James 4:1.

2. Dostoevsky's *Crime and Punishment*. Cf. n. 5 on p. 91 above [*Editor*].

To John Paul Bocock[†]

[*? Mid-November 1887*]   *Saranac Lake*[1]

Private
Dear Mr Bocock, * * *

* * *

* * * Your prominent dramatic critic,[2] writing like a journalist, has
written like a braying ass; what he meant is probably quite different
and true enough—that the book is ugly and the allegory too like
the usual pulpit fudge and not just enough to the modesty of facts.
You are right as to Mansfield.[3] Hyde was the younger of the two. He
was not good looking however; and not, Great Gods! a mere voluptuary. There is no harm in a voluptuary; and none, with my hand
on my heart and in the sight of God, none—no harm whatever—in
what prurient fools call 'immorality'. The harm was in Jekyll,
because he was a hypocrite—not because he was fond of women;
he says so himself; but people are so filled full of folly and inverted
lust, that they can think of nothing but sexuality. The Hypocrite let
out the beast Hyde—who is no more sexual than another, but who
is the essence of cruelty and malice, and selfishness and cowardice:
and these are the diabolic in man—not this poor wish to have a
woman, that they make such a cry about. I know, and I dare to say,
you know as well as I, that bad and good, even to our human eyes,
has no more connection with what is called dissipation than it has
with flying kites. But the sexual field and the business field are perhaps the two best fitted for the display of cruelty and cowardice and
selfishness. That is what people see; and these they confound.

* * *

Yours truly   Robert Louis Stevenson

---

† From *The Letters of Robert Louis Stevenson*, ed. Bradford A. Booth and Ernest Mehew
(New Haven: Yale UP, 1995), vol. 6, pp. 56–57. Copyright © 1995 Yale University.
Reprinted by permission of the publisher. Notes are by the editor of this Norton Critical Edition.
1. Stevenson writes from upper New York State, where he was living with his family.
2. He is responding to a report on the reception of a stage version of *Strange Case of
Dr. Jekyll and Mr. Hyde,* which played at the Madison Square Theater in New York City
from September 12 to October 1, 1887.
3. Richard Mansfield, the actor playing Jekyll and Hyde.

"I am, Yours, RLS": A Stevenson Signature

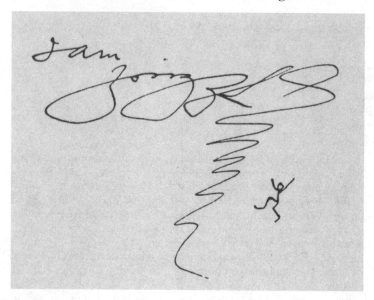

This signature, with its agitated—or exhilarated—falling man, is one of a number of cartoonish doodles found in Stevenson's letters which are enjoyably reproduced in the Booth and Mehew edition of his letters. It appears at the end of a brief note Stevenson wrote to his literary friend Edmund Gosse on March 26, 1886, accepting an invitation to dine in London several months after the publication of *Strange Case of Dr. Jekyll and Mr. Hyde*. Reprinted in *The Letters of Robert Louis Stevenson*, ed. Bradford A. Booth and Ernest Mehew (New Haven: Yale UP, 1995), vol. 5, p. 239, from a facsimile in the Sotheby's catalogue for The Gosse Library Part III sale, Lot 306 (February 25, 1929). Photograph courtesy of Sotheby's, Inc. © 1929.

HENRY JAMES

[A Wide Margin for the Wonderful]†

Mr. Stevenson leaves so wide a margin for the wonderful—it impinges with easy assurance upon the text—that he escapes the danger of being brought up by cases he has not allowed for. When he allows for Mr. Hyde he allows for everything, and one feels

† From "Robert Louis Stevenson" (1887) in *Partial Portraits* (Macmillan, 1888); rpt. in *Partial Portraits* (Westport, CT: Greenwood P, 1970), pp. 165–66, 169–71.

moreover that even if he did not wave so gallantly the flag of the imaginative and contend that the improbable is what has most character, he would still insist that we ought to make believe. He would say we ought to make believe that the extraordinary is the best part of life even if it were not, and to do so because the finest feelings—suspense, daring, decision, passion, curiosity, gallantry, eloquence, friendship—are involved in it, and it is of infinite importance that the tradition of these precious things should not perish.
* * *

*   *   *

Is *Doctor Jekyll and Mr. Hyde* a work of high philosophic intention, or simply the most ingenious and irresponsible of fictions? It has the stamp of a really imaginative production, that we may take it in different ways; but I suppose it would generally be called the most serious of the author's tales. It deals with the relation of the baser parts of man to his nobler, of the capacity for evil that exists in the most generous natures; and it expresses these things in a fable which is a wonderfully happy invention. The subject is endlessly interesting, and rich in all sorts of provocation, and Mr. Stevenson is to be congratulated on having touched the core of it. I may do him injustice, but it is, however, here, not the profundity of the idea which strikes me so much as the art of the presentation—the extremely successful form. There is a genuine feeling for the perpetual moral question, a fresh sense of the difficulty of being good and the brutishness of being bad; but what there is above all is a singular ability in holding the interest. I confess that that, to my sense, is the most edifying thing in the short, rapid, concentrated story, which is really a masterpiece of concision. There is something almost impertinent in the way, as I have noticed, in which Mr. Stevenson achieves his best effects without the aid of the ladies, and *Doctor Jekyll* is a capital example of his heartless independence. It is usually supposed that a truly poignant impression cannot be made without them, but in the drama of Mr. Hyde's fatal ascendency they remain altogether in the wing. It is very obvious—I do not say it cynically—that they must have played an important part in his development. The gruesome tone of the tale is, no doubt, deepened by their absence: it is like the late afternoon light of a foggy winter Sunday, when even inanimate objects have a kind of wicked look. I remember few situations in the pages of mystifying fiction more to the purpose than the episode of Mr. Utterson's going to Doctor Jekyll's to confer with the butler when the Doctor is locked up in his laboratory, and the old servant, whose sagacity has hitherto encountered successfully the problems of the sideboard and the pantry, confesses that this time he is utterly baffled. The way the two men, at the door of the laboratory, discuss the identity of the mysterious personage inside, who has revealed himself in two or three inhuman glimpses to Poole, has those touches of which irresistible shudders are made. The butler's theory is that his master has been murdered, and that the murderer is in the room, personating him with a sort of clumsy diabolism. "Well, when that masked thing like a monkey jumped from among the chemicals and whipped into the cabinet, it went down my spine like ice." That is the effect upon the reader of most of the story. I say of most rather than of all, because the ice rather melts in the sequel, and I have some difficulty in accepting the business of the powders, which seems to me too explicit and explanatory. The powders constitute the machinery of the transformation, and it will probably have struck many readers that this uncanny process would be more con-ceivable (so far as one may speak of the conceivable in such a case), if the author had not made it so definite.

Historical and Cultural Contexts

Stevenson's novella brings alive 1880s London at night, which he based in part on Edinburgh, the city of his youth. In this section, the historian Judith Walkowitz explores perceptions of London during this time as a place of delights and dangers. Some Victorians found sexual freedoms here, including same-sex encounters, and a number of Stevenson's contemporaries read Hyde's illicit experiences as homosexual. Such activities became increasingly visible and criminal with the passing in 1885 of the amendment to the Criminal Law Act that made "acts of gross indecency" between men punishable by up to two years of hard labor. The excerpt from the memoirs of Stevenson's friend John Addington Symonds describes Symonds's torments as a man committing the "sin"—as it was considered by most at this time—of desiring other men, and his nighttime encounters on the London streets with other such "sinners."

JUDITH R. WALKOWITZ

["Dreadfully Delightful City"]†

When Henry James arrived in London in 1876, he found the city "not a pleasant place" nor "agreeable, or cheerful, or easy, or exempt from reproach." He found it "only magnificent . . . the biggest aggregation of human life, the most complete compendium in the world." It was also the "largest chapter of human accidents," scarred by "thousands of acres covered by low black houses of the cheapest construction" as well as by "unlimited vagueness as to the line of division between centre and circumference." "London is so clumsy and brutal, and has gathered together so many of the darkest sides of life," that it would be "frivolous to ignore her deformities." The city itself had become a "strangely mingled monster," the principal

† From "Urban Spectatorship" in *City of Dreadful Delight: Narratives of Sexual Danger in Late-Victorian London* (Chicago: U of Chicago P, 1992), pp. 15–39. © 1992 by Judith R. Walkowitz. Reprinted by permission of the publisher. Notes are by the author except where indicated.

character in its own drama: an "ogress who devours human flesh to keep herself alive to do her tremendous work."[1]

Despite its brutalities, London offered James an oasis of personal freedom, a place of floating possibilities as well as dangers. Alone in lodgings, James first experienced himself in London as "an impersonal black hole in the huge general blackness." But the streets of London offered him freedom and imaginative delights. "I had complete liberty, and the prospect of profitable work; I used to take long walks in the rain. I took possession of London; I felt it to be the right place." As an artist, bachelor and outsider, James aestheticized this "world city," the "center of the race," into a grand operatic panorama of movement, atmosphere, labyrinthine secrets and mysteries. London's "immeasurable circumference," argued James, gave him a "sense of social and intellectual elbow room"; its "friendly fogs," which made "everything brown, rich, dim, vague," protected and enriched "adventure." For the "sympathetic resident," such as James, the social ease of anonymity was matched by an ease of access to and imaginative command of the whole: one may live in one "quarter" or "plot" but in "imagination and by a constant mental act of reference . . . [inhabit] the whole."[2]

James celebrated the traditional prerogatives of the privileged urban spectator to act, in Baudelaire's[3] phrase, as *flaneur,* to stroll across the divided spaces of the metropolis, whether it was London, Paris, or New York, to experience the city as a whole. The fact and fantasy of urban exploration had long been an informing feature of nineteenth-century bourgeois male subjectivity. * * *

✳   ✳   ✳

James's affectionate portrait of London, that "dreadfully delightful city," is dominated by the flaneur's attention to the viewer's subjectivity and by the capacity of the city to stimulate. In James's "strangely mingled monster," activities of manufacture, trade, and exchange were overshadowed by rituals of consumption and display. Extremes of wealth and poverty aroused the senses, for "the impression of suffering was part of the general vibration," while London's status as repository of continuous culture and national heritage—its "great towers, great names, great memories"—served as a further stimulant to his own consciousness and memory: "All

---

1. Henry James, "London," in *Essays in London and Elsewhere* (Freeport, N.Y.: Books for Libraries, 1922 [first pub. 1893]) pp. 27, 32. ° ° °
2. Henry James, *The Complete Notebooks of Henry James*, ed. Leon Edel (New York: Oxford University Press, 1987), pp. 215–18; James, "London," pp. 7, 14.
3. Charles Baudelaire (1821–1867), French poet and essayist who wrote about the modern city [*Editor*].

history appeared to live again and the continuity of things to vibrate through my mind."[4]

The literary construct of the metropolis as a dark, powerful, and seductive labyrinth held a powerful sway over the social imagination of educated readers. It remained the dominant representation of London in the 1880s, conveyed to many reading publics through high and low literary forms, from Charles Booth's surveys of London poverty, to the fictional stories of Stevenson, Gissing, and James, to the sensational newspaper exposés by W. T. Stead and G. R. Sims. These late-Victorian writers built on an earlier tradition of Victorian urban exploration, adding some new perspectives of their own. Some rigidified the hierarchical divisions of London into a geographic separation, organized around the opposition of East and West. Others stressed the growing complexity and differentiation of the world of London, moving beyond the opposition of rich and poor, palace and hovels, to investigate the many class cultures in between. Still others among them repudiated a fixed, totalistic interpretive image altogether, and emphasized instead a fragmented, disunified, atomistic social universe that was not easily decipherable.

Historians and cultural critics have linked this contest over and "crisis" in representation to a range of psychological and social crises troubling literary men and their social peers in the 1880s: religious self-doubt, social unrest, radical challenges to liberalism and science, anxiety over imperial and national decline, as well as an imaginative confrontation with the defamiliarized world of consumer culture "where values and perception seem in constant flux."[5] Equally crucial may have been the psychic difficulties produced by the imperatives of a "hard" physical manliness, first developed in the mid- and late-nineteenth century public schools and then diffused among the propertied classes of the Anglo-Saxon world. The hallmarks of this "virile" ethos were self-control, self-discipline, and the absence of emotional expression. Whatever the precipitating causes, the public landscape of the privileged urban flaneur of the period had become an unstable construct: threatened internally by contradictions and tensions and constantly challenged

4. James, "London," p. 27.
5. Gareth Stedman Jones, *Outcast London: A Study in the Relationship Between Classes in Victorian Society* (Oxford: Clarendon Press, 1971); Frank Miller Turner, *Between Science and Religion: The Reaction to Scientific Naturalism in Late-Victorian England* (New Haven: Yale University Press, 1974); Colin Ford and Brian Harrison, *A Hundred Years Ago: Britain in the 1880s in Words and Photographs* (Cambridge: Harvard University Press, 1983); Norman MacKenzie and Jeanne MacKenzie, *The Fabians* (New York: Simon and Schuster, 1977); T. J. Jackson Lears, *No Place of Grace: Anti-modernism and the Transformation of American Culture, 1880–1920* (New York: Pantheon, 1981); Richard Wightman Fox and T. J. Jackson Lears, eds., *The Culture of Consumption: Critical Essays in American History, 1880–1980* (New York: Pantheon, 1983).

from without by social forces that pressed these dominant representations to be reworked, shorn up, reconstructed.

Middle-class men were not the sole explorers and interpreters of
the city in the volatile decade of the 1880s. On the contrary, as the
end of the century approached, this "dreadfully delightful city"
became a contested terrain, where new commercial spaces, new
journalistic practices, and a range of public spectacles and reform
activities inspired a different set of social actors to assert their own
claims to self-creation in the public domain. Thanks to the material
changes and cultural contests of the late-Victorian city, protesting
workers and "gents" of marginal class position, female philanthro-
pists and "platform women," Salvation Army lasses and match girls,
as well as glamorized "girls in business," made their public appearances and established places and viewpoints in relation to the urban
panorama. These new entrants to the urban scene produced new
stories of the city that competed, intersected with, appropriated,
and revised the dominant imaginative mappings of London.

*   *   *

By the 1880s, most of the salient features of London's imaginary
landscape, which writers like Dickens, Mayhew, and Greenwood[6]
had helped to construct, had formalized into a conception of London as an immense world-city, culturally and economically important, yet socially and geographically divided and politically
incoherent. Social and political developments of the mid- and late-
Victorian period materially reinforced this complex image. London
was the largest city in the world, totalling four million inhabitants
in the 1880s. Since the first half of the nineteenth century, it had
reclaimed its status as the cultural and nerve center of the nation
and empire, overshadowing Manchester and Liverpool as the
embodiment of the "modern city."[7]

In the second half of the century, the West End of Mayfair and
St. James had undergone considerable renovation; from a wealthy
residential area it had been transformed and diversified into the
bureaucratic center of empire, the hub of communications, trans-
portation, commercial display, entertainment, and finance. In the
process, a modern landscape had been constructed—of office
buildings, shops, department stores, museums, opera, concert

6. Charles Dickens (1812–1870), Victorian novelist and essayist whose work often
   described London. Henry Mayhew (1812–1887), journalist and social researcher who
   wrote about the poor in London and published the influential three-volume work *London Labour and the London Poor* (1851). James Greenwood (1832–1929), journalist
   who wrote a series of articles about poverty in London [*Editor*].
7. Asa Briggs, *Victorian Cities* (New York and Evanston: Harper and Row, 1963), chap. 8.

halls, music halls, restaurants, and hotels—to service not only the traditional rich of Mayfair but a new middle class of civil servants and clerks, living in such areas as Bayswater and the nearby suburbs.[8] New figures appeared in this urban landscape, most significantly "girls in business," neither ladies nor prostitutes, but working women employed in the tertiary sector of the economy, there to assist the large numbers of "shopping ladies," attracted to the new feminized world of department stores that had been created for them in the center. In late-Victorian London, the West End was not just the home and fixed reference of the urban flaneur; it had become a new commercial landscape, used by men and women of different classes.

Yet, in the 1880s, these commercial and institutional developments were imaginatively overshadowed by representations of urban pathology and decline. As the capital city, London epitomized the power of the empire but also its vulnerability. The disquieting effects of the Great Depression,[9] the erosion of mid-Victorian prosperity, the decline of London's traditional industries, and international competition from the United States and Germany for industrial and military supremacy, all contributed to a sense of malaise and decline. This anxious mood was communicated through representations of London itself, particularly those involving political disorder, urban pathology, and physical degeneration.[1]

✻ ✻ ✻

Other writers on the city in the 1880s were far less sanguine about unlocking its mysteries and sustaining a fixed, unified gaze on its denizens. Instead, George Gissing, R. L. Stevenson, and Henry James produced meditations on London that emphasized fragmentation and introspection. All three articulated an epistemological crisis that precipitated changes in the visual image of the city and that produced new representations of the self and the Other.

✻ ✻ ✻

Other male writers of the period invented somewhat different strategies to represent what Poole characterizes as a growing "imbalance between an expanding world of consciousness" and a "narrowing and rigidifying world of peremptory self-assertion."[2]

---

8. Gavin Weightman and Steve Humphries, *The Making of Modern London, 1815–1914* (London: Sidgwick and Jackson, 1983).
9. A lengthy economic depression (1872–96) that made many luxury goods unaffordable for the middle class [*Editor*].
1. Jones, *Outcast London*, pp. 12–16; chaps. 6, 16.
2. See Adrian Poole, *Gissing in Context* (Rowman and Littlefield, 1975), p. 42 [*Editor*].

Aesthete-decadents like Whistler, Symons, and Wilde[3] accepted the disconnection between appearance and reality, fashioning an aristo-cratic, dandified aesthetic of surface impressions, of detached cos-mopolitan observation. For many writers of the fin de siècle, the epistemological crisis intersected with and manifested itself as a cri-sis of gender and class identity. In Stevenson's *Strange Case of Dr. Jekyll and Mr. Hyde* (1886), the fragmentation of the social world seems to have precipitated a division of the self. The London streets of *Dr. Jekyll and Mr. Hyde* appear as a vast, empty wasteland; here the integrity of the inner self is threatened less by social disorder or external constraint than by a failure to reach expression. Part of the problem of self-definition resulted from the marginalization of women in this professional bachelordom: as Stephen Heath observes, women exist on the margins of the text, as observers and incidental victims of Jekyll's crime, or as threatening, ephemeral manifesta-tions of the commercial city itself, but they have no effective embodi-ment as central characters.[4] This virtual absence itself presents a problem in male self-definition: as critics like Eve Sedgwick have argued, to sustain the fiction of a unified heterosexual male subject, Western sexual narratives have traditionally required a female figure to serve as a contrasting sexual Other and mediator among men.[5] The perils of excluding women from the picture are fully revealed in Jekyll's "closet" world: men rapidly disintegrate into split personali-ties when they turn their gaze on themselves.

As a novelist, Henry James also retreated from a totalizing vision into a more constrained introspection, without necessarily invoking the same kind of psychic splitting suffered by the male persona in Stevenson's "shilling shocker." In his fiction of the eighties, Henry James was able to spare some of his female protagonists the "hor-ror" of disintegration, when, as in the case of Isabel Archer,[6] they remained relatively untouched by the disorienting effects of the market. Their gender, however, made them different spectators of the city. Although Isabel Archer learns "a great many things" from her few walks around London, in the end she is driven into intro-spection and relinquishes all claims to the urban pleasures of anonymity, movement, and imaginative command of the whole enjoyed by James and his alter ego, the "sympathetic resident."

3. Followers of a *fin de siècle* movement in art and literature that promoted beauty for its own sake, not for didactic or political purposes. James McNeill Whistler (1834–1903), American painter who spent much of his time in London. Arthur Symons (1865–1945), British poet and critic. Oscar Wilde (1854–1900), Irish novelist and playwright known for the novella *The Picture of Dorian Gray* (1890) [*Editor*].
4. ° ° ° Stephen Heath, "Psychopathia Sexualis: Stevenson's *Strange Case*," in Colin Mac-Cabe, ed., *Futures for English* (Manchester: Manchester University Press, 1988): 94. ° ° °
5. See Eve Kosofsky Sedgwick, *Between Men: English Literature and Male Homosocial Desire* (Columbia UP, 1985) [*Editor*].
6. Central character in the novel *The Portrait of a Lady* (1881).

Social investigation, serious fiction, and "shilling shockers" of the 1880s all bear witness to a growing skepticism among men of letters about their capacity to read the city and to sustain a coherent vision of a structured public landscape. They expressed this unease by constructing a mental map of London marked by fragmentation, complexity, and introspection, all of which imperiled the flaneur's ability to experience the city as a totalizing whole. Forces inside and outside of bourgeois culture provoked this epistemological crisis: for while it undoubtedly mirrored the self-doubts of professional and literary men, the crisis was also precipitated by the actions and energies of different social actors making claims on city space and impinging on the prerogatives of privileged men.

JOHN ADDINGTON SYMONDS

[Passion for the Male Sex]†

It was my primary object when I began these autobiographical notes to describe as accurately and candidly as I was able a type of character, which I do not at all believe to be exceptional, but which for various intelligible reasons has never yet been properly analysed. I wanted to supply material for the ethical psychologist and the student of mental pathology, by portraying a man of no mean talents, of no abnormal depravity, whose life has been perplexed from first to last by passion—natural, instinctive, healthy in his own particular case—but morbid and abominable from the point of view of the society in which he lives—persistent passion for the male sex.

(December 1891: This was written by me at Venice in May 1889. I had not then studied the cases of sexual inversion recorded by Casper-Liman, Ulrichs and Krafft-Ebing.[1] Had I done so, I should not perhaps have dealt with my personal experience so diffusely as I have done in this chapter. What I wrote, I now leave as it stands. It forms a more direct contribution to the psychology of sexual

---

† From "Emotional Development," Chapter 12 in Symonds's *Memoirs* manuscript held by the London Library. Reprinted by permission of the London Library. Notes are by the editor of this Norton Critical Edition.

1. Johann Ludwig Casper and Carl Liman were German physicians who wrote about homosexuality ("sexual inversion") in the *Handbuch der Gerichtlichen Medicin* (*Manual of Forensic Medicine*, first published in 1856). Karl Heinrich Ulrichs, a German lawyer, published essays in the 1860s and '70s in support of the legal rights of homosexuals, whom he called "Uranians." Richard von Krafft-Ebing, a German psychiatrist, wrote the influential *Psychopathia Sexualis* (1886), which details the "pathology" of homosexuality.

abnormality than if I were to mix it up with the discussion of theories unknown to me at the time of writing.)[2]

This was my primary object. It seemed to me, being a man of letters, possessing the pen of a ready writer and the practised impartiality of a critic accustomed to weigh evidence, that it was my duty to put on record the facts and phases of this aberrant inclination in myself—so that fellow-sufferers from the like malady, men innocent as I have been, yet haunted as I have been by a sense of guilt and dread of punishment, men injured in their character and health by the debasing influences of a furtive and lawless love, men deprived of the best pleasures which reciprocated passion yields to mortals, men driven in upon ungratified desires and degraded by humiliating outbursts of ungovernable appetite, should feel that they are not alone, and should discover at the same time how a career of some distinction, of considerable energy and perseverance, may be pursued by one who bends and sweats beneath a burden heavy enough to drag him down to pariahdom. Nor this only. I hoped that the unflinching revelation of my moral nature, connected with the history of my intellectual development and the details of my physical disorders, might render the scientific handling of similar cases more enlightened than it is at present, and might arouse some sympathy even in the breast of Themis[3] for not ignoble victims of a natural instinct reputed vicious in the modern age. No one who shall have read these memoirs, and shall possess even a remote conception of my literary labours, will be able to assert that the author was a vulgar and depraved sensualist. He may be revolted; he may turn with loathing from the spectacle. But he must acknowledge that it possesses the dignity of tragic suffering.

As a secondary object, I had in view the possibility of madness supervening on the long continued strain, the lifelong struggle of this tyrannous desire. Should the worst come to the worst, I wanted to leave an *apologia pro vita mea*—no excuse, no palliation of my acts, but an explanation of them; from the perusal of which it should appear that my ἁμαρτία [*hamartia*, flaw], my deviation from the paths of order, my stumbling up against the altar of Justinian's edict,[4] has been, like that of Ajax or of Phaedra,[5] something which the old Greek instinct recognized as fraught with fate or sent by God.

2. Phyllis Grosskurth explains, in an edition of Symonds's memoirs, that he added this paragraph in the margin of his manuscript. See *The Memoirs of John Addington Symonds: The Secret Homosexual Life of a Leading Nineteenth-Century Man of Letters*, ed. Grosskurth (U of Chicago P, 1984), p. 182.
3. Greek titan representing natural law and justice.
4. The Byzantine emperor's laws against homosexuality passed in the 6th century.
5. Heroes in Greek mythology who commit suicide when they dishonor themselves or the laws of nature.

This being the case, I shall not shrink from continuing the analysis which I have undertaken, painful as it is to do so, and extraordinary as the needful confessions will have to be.

I have sufficiently described the character of my emotions during the period of adolescence.[6] Up to the time of my marriage they were sentimental, romantic, without a touch of avowed sensuality. Even in daydreams about the boys I loved, no thought of anything obscene formed itself distinctly in my mind. I experienced, indeed, the strongest physical disturbance when I came into close contact with them. The touch of their hands, the laughter of their eyes, and the silkiness of their hair provoked the same agreeable sexual sensations as young men ordinarily obtain from the company of girls. And at night, when I dreamed of them, the visions were erotic. But my wildest flights of fancy did not soar definitely beyond a kiss, a clasp, the virginal embrace which Daphnis gave to Chloe before Lycaenion taught him what the way of a man with a maid should be.[7] There was, of course, an indefinite background, made sufficiently apparent by the tumult of my blood, the quickening of my heartbeats, and the rising of my flesh. But these symptoms annoyed me; I strove to put them aside, and evaded the attempt to formulate their significance. I only twice kissed a male friend in those years—as I have already related in what I wrote about Willie. Good heavens! what an uproar in the city of my soul those kisses wrought, as we lay together couched in ivy and white wood anemones upon the verge of the red rocks which dominate the Avon!

I came to marriage then fatigued and fretted by intense desires, the worse for being still unconscious of their sensuality. Marriage, I thought, would satisfy the side of my nature which thrilled so strangely when I touched a boy. It did not, however; and the difficulties of my married life—difficulties connected with my wife's repugnance to childbearing and her constitutional indifference to sexual intercourse—whereby I spent many successive months as a bachelor beside the woman I had wedded, and with whom I strangely bedded—these difficulties prepared me for the three phases I have now to describe. * * *

Being what I am, the great mistake—perhaps the great crime of my life, was my marriage. I ought not to have married when I did and whom I did. I ought not to have married at all. Yet I am able after nearly twenty-five years of matrimony to record my conviction that this marriage has not been a failure for either my wife or myself.

---

6. In previous chapters of these memoirs, not included here.
7. In Longus's ancient Greek prose romance *Daphnis and Chloe*, the two lovers know nothing about sexual acts until Lycaenion, a married woman, initiates the boy Daphnis.

I called it a mistake in the first place, because I was urged to marry by my father, by my own earnest desire to overcome abnormal inclinations, by the belief that I should regain health, and by the confidence that I should not make a bad husband. I did not overcome abnormal passions. I did not regain health. In so far I mistook my path. I think, however, that I have been upon the whole a good husband; my wife emphatically says so now.

I called it a crime in the second place, because none of these reasons for marrying justify the step, because I married without passion or the feeling that this particular woman was the only woman in the world for me. Thus I deceived her practically, if not intentionally or deliberately. And I deceived myself, in so far as her temperament was incapable of sharpening the sexual appetites which in me had hardly any edge where woman was concerned.

Some sorts of self-deceit are crimes. They are the sign of a soul's willingness to accept the second best and to give the second best, instead of waiting through all suffering and all privation for the best in life.

There is no word of blame for my wife here. She has been at every point a good, true, honest, loving and devoted wife to me. She is a woman whom better and happier men than I am might have worshipped with sex-penetrated passion. No: if anyone in our marriage has been the injured party, it is she. The imperfections of our life in common are due far less to her temperament than to the fact that I could not love her in the way which makes a man enamoured of his wife's peculiarities. I married her without giving my whole self; and the best things which marriage has brought us both are friendship and our children. I do not believe that she has ever been acutely sensible of what we both missed—that supreme joy which made Romeo and Juliet[8] happy in the jaws of death. But I shall go to the grave with an unsatisfied desire. Here am I fashioned in every fibre for passionate pleasure, and married to a woman who has borne me four children. Yet we have never had any really passionate moments together. And for the last eleven years, after shillyshallying with an ill-participated nuptial bed, we have found it best to live as male and female quite apart.

In spite of all this, my marriage has not to be regretted. So far as I am concerned, it probably saved my life from wreckage and prolonged my power of moral resistance. On the other hand I feel tolerably sure that she has not suffered as other women might from the imperfection of our sexual relations. She married late—at twenty-seven—and carried into matrimony the instincts of a virgin, for

---

8. Lovers in Shakespeare's play of this name, who kill themselves because they can't be together.

whom there is something ignoble in physical appetite and nauseous
in childbirth. Any touch in literature upon the pleasures of the
senses gives her pain. She shrinks from what men and women are,
and what they must be, as from something common and unclean.
'That vulgar and trivial way of coition,' as Sir Thomas Browne puts
it, has for her no attraction.[9] Having realized by a life in common of
twenty-six years how much better it is to be married than to remain
single, having found satisfaction in my society and a sphere of activity in her domestic cares, she is satisfied. She could not have enjoyed
the society of her daughters, whom she deeply loves, except through
the troublesome process by which alone the human race is propa-
gated. On the whole then, I estimate that our marriage, so far as it
has gone, may be reckoned among the successful experiments of
this nature—at any rate not among the more unsuccessful.

How far can anything in our mental and moral evolution be considered accidental? Nothing, I believe. And yet some of the most decisive turning points in life seem to depend on casual circumstance.
I well remember three apparently trivial occurrences during the
first fifteen months after my marriage, which aroused the latent
trouble of my nature, and opened a new phase of conflict with
incurable desire.

In the spring of 1865 we were living in lodgings in Albion Street,
Hyde Park. I had been one evening to the Century Club, which
then met near St Martin le Grand in rooms, I think, of the Alpine
Club. Walking home before midnight, I took a little passage which
led from Trafalgar into Leicester Square, passing some barracks.
This passage has since then been suppressed. I was in evening
dress. At the entrance of the alley a young grenadier came up and
spoke to me. I was too innocent, strange as this may seem, to guess
what he meant. But I liked the man's looks, felt drawn toward him,
and did not refuse his company. So there I was, the slight nervous
man of fashion in my dress clothes, walking side by side with a
strapping fellow in scarlet uniform, strongly attracted by his physical magnetism. From a few commonplace remarks he broke abruptly
into proposals, mentioned a house we could go to, and made it quite
plain for what purpose. I quickened my pace, and hurrying through
the passage broke away from him with a passionate mixture of
repulsion and fascination.

What he offered was not what I wanted at the moment, but the
thought of it stirred me deeply. The thrill of contact with the man
taught me something new about myself. I can well recall the linger-
ing regret, and the quick sense of deliverance from danger, with

9. From *Religio Medici* (1643), part 2, section 9, referring to sex for procreation.

which I saw him fall back, after following and pleading with me for about a hundred yards. The longing left was partly a fresh seeking after comradeship and partly an animal desire the like of which I had not before experienced.

The memory of this incident abode with me, and often rose to haunt my fancy. Yet it did not disturb my tranquillity during the ensuing summer, which we spent at Clifton and Sutton Court. Toward autumn we settled into our London house, 47 Norfolk Square, Hyde Park. Here it happened that a second seemingly fortuitous occurrence intensified the recrudescence of my trouble. I went out for a solitary walk on one of those warm moist unhealthy afternoons when the weather oppresses and yet irritates our nervous sensibilities. Since the date of my marriage I had ceased to be assailed by what I called 'the wolf'—that undefined craving coloured with a vague but poignant hankering after males. I lulled myself with the belief that it would not leap on me again to wreck my happiness and disturb my studious habits. However, wandering that day for exercise through the sordid streets between my home and Regent's Park, I felt the burden of a ponderous malaise. To shake it off was impossible. I did not recognize it as a symptom of the moral malady from which I had resolutely striven to free myself. Was I not protected by my troth-pledge to a noble woman, by my recent entrance upon the natural career of married life? While returning from this fateful constitutional, at a certain corner, which I well remember, my eyes were caught by a rude *graffito* scrawled with slate-pencil upon slate. It was of so concentrated, so stimulative, so penetrative a character—so thoroughly the voice of vice and passion in the proletariat—that it pierced the very marrow of my soul.[1] I must have seen a score such *graffiti* in my time. But they had not hitherto appealed to me. Now the wolf leapt out: my malaise of the moment was converted into a clairvoyant and tyrannical appetite for the thing which I had rejected five months earlier in the alley by the barracks. The vague and morbid craving of the previous years defined itself as a precise hunger after sensual pleasure, whereof I had not dreamed before save in repulsive visions of the night.

It is difficult to say how far the exercise of sex in marriage helped to determine this new phase of the old instinct. I am inclined to think that it had much to do with the acuteness of the attack. Inborn instincts, warped by my will and forced to take a bias contrary to my peculiar nature, reasserted themselves with violence. I did not recognize the phenomenon as a temptation. It appeared to

---

1. 'Prick to prick, so sweet'; with an emphatic diagram of phallic meeting, glued together, gushing [*Symonds's note*].

me, just what it was, the resurrection of a chronic torment which had been some months in abeyance. Looking back upon the incident now, I know that obscene *graffito* was the sign and symbol of a paramount and permanent craving of my physical and psychical nature. It connected my childish reveries with the mixed passions and audacious comradeship of my maturity. Not only my flesh, but my heart also, was involved in the emotion which it stirred.

The awakening spasm of desire had as little to do with either fancy or will as the return of neuralgia in a sudden throb of agony. God help me! I cried. I felt humiliated, frightened, gripped in the clutch of doom. Nothing remained but to parry, palliate, procrastinate. There was no hope of escape. And all the while the demon ravished my imagination with 'the love of the impossible'. Hallucinations of the senses crowded in upon my brain together with the pangs of shame and the prevision of inevitable woes. From this decisive moment forward to the end, my life had to fly on a broken wing, and my main ambition has been to constitute a working compromise. This afternoon walk to which I attach so great an importance must have taken place a few weeks before my eldest daughter Janet's birth. Soon after my wife was fit to move, we went down to Clifton, and there my father discovered that my left lung was seriously affected. During this visit I read Seeley's *Ecce Homo*,[2] which interested me by reason of its style and its philanthropy. And it so happened that I also read Greenwood's article 'The Amateur Casual' in an early number of the *Pall Mall Gazette*.[3] This brought the emotional tumour which was gathering within me to maturity. Almost without premeditation or plan I wrote the first part of the poem called 'John Mordan'. Since then I have suffered incessantly from my moral trouble, which I have beguiled by sundry feeble devices, and which has assumed forms of bewildering and often painfully distressing variety.

A distinct stage in what I may call the palliative treatment I adopted was marked by the composition of 'John Mordan'. I began to make verse the vehicle and safety valve for my tormenting preoccupations. A cycle of poems gradually got written, illustrating the love of man for man in all periods of civilization. Of these the two best are perhaps 'A Cretan Idyll' and 'Eudiades'. The composition of the cycle lasted over the period between January 1866 and some time after 1875.

2. Sir John Robert Seeley's *Ecce Homo: A Survey in the Life and Work of Jesus Christ* (1865), a controversial biography of Jesus focusing on the historical man who founded a religious order, rather than on the divine figure.
3. James Greenwood published a series of articles in January 1866 using the name "The Amateur Casual," exposing the horrific conditions of workhouses for the poor.

Nothing could, I think, have been much worse for my condition than this sustained utterance through verse of passions which I dared not indulge. It kept me in a continual state of *orexis*, or irritable longing. And for my literary career it was at least unprofitable. I knew that all those thousands of lines, into which I poured my red hot soul, would never see the light of publication. Consequently I gave way to the besetting foibles of my literary temperament—facility, fluency, or carelessness of execution. The writing of these poems was a kind of mental masturbation.

While thus engaged, and very early after the commencement of my cycle, I came across W. Whitman's *Leaves of Grass*. I was sitting with F. M. Myers in his rooms at Trinity, Cambridge, when he stood up, seized a book and shouted out in his nasal intonation with those brazen lungs of his, 'Long I thought that knowledge alone would content me.' This fine poem, omitted from later editions of *Leaves of Grass*, formed part of 'Calamus'.[4] The book became for me a sort of Bible. Inspired by 'Calamus' I adopted another method of palliative treatment, and tried to invigorate the emotion I could not shake off by absorbing Whitman's conception of comradeship. The process of assimilation was not without its bracing benefit. My desires grew manlier, more defined, more direct, more daring by contact with Calamus. I imbibed a strong democratic enthusiasm, a sense of the dignity and beauty and glory of simple healthy men. This has been of great service to me during the eleven years I have passed at Davos. I can now declare with sincerity that my abnormal inclinations, modified by Whitman's idealism and penetrated with his democratic enthusiasm, have brought me into close and profitable sympathy with human beings even while I sinned against law and conventional morality.

The immediate result of this study of Walt Whitman was the determination to write the history of paiderastia[5] in Greece and to attempt a theoretical demonstration of the chivalrous enthusiasm which seemed to me implicit in comradeship. Both of these literary tasks I accomplished. The former has been privately printed under the title of *A Problem in Greek Ethics*. The latter exists in manuscript; and though I do not regard its conclusions as wholly worthless or its ideal as quite incapable of realization, I cannot take a favourable view of my achievement. My own thwarted and perplexed instincts rendered me incapable of sound or absolutely sincere treatment.

Such was the expenditure of time and intellectual energy demanded by this inexorable and incurable disease.

---

4. Homoerotic poem appearing in the 1860 edition of *Leaves of Grass* in section 8, but excised by Whitman in later editions.
5. The love of boys.

L'amour de l'impossible est la maladie de l'âme.[6] It cannot be doubted that the congenital aberration of the passions which I have described has been the poison of my life. In the first place I shall die without realizing what constitutes the highest happiness of mortals, an ardent love reciprocated with ardour. This I could never enjoy, for the simple reason that I have never felt the sexual attraction of women. The following paragraph from a diary dated 23 March 1889 shows what I mean:

> I have been sitting opposite a young man in the *diligence*[7] all day—a peasant about nineteen, with a well-knit frame and a good healthy face, exhibiting no special beauty but radiating intelligence and the magnetic force of the male adolescent. I looked at his hands—great powerful palms and fingers, fashioned to mould and clasp, yet finely shaped, and attached to sinewy wrists, where the skin had smoother texture, showing veins and the salience of sinews. Enough of his throat and forearms was visible to make one divine how white and wholesome was the flesh of the young man's body. I felt I could have kissed these hands hardened with labour, bruised here and there, brown in complexion—have kissed them and have begged of them to touch me. Then it flashed across my mind that no woman's hands—whether of duchess or milkmaid, maiden or married—had ever possessed for me such sexual attraction as these of the young peasant had.

A man who feels like that has failed as certainly in finding life's chief boon as a repulsive hunchback has. For no young man will return his passion. Then again what hours and days and weeks and months of weariness I have endured by the alternate indulgence and repression of my craving imagination. What time and energy I have wasted on expressing it. How it has interfered with the pursuit of study. How marriage has been spoiled by it. What have I suffered in violent and brutal pleasures of the senses, snatched furtively with shame on my part, with frigid toleration on the part of my comrades, and repented of with terror.

Nature is a hard and cruel stepmother. Nothing that I could have done would have availed to alter my disposition by a hair's breadth—unless perhaps I had been forced to fornicate by my father at the age of puberty. I doubt even then whether I could have been rendered normal. These sexual aberrations cannot of course be rare. The more frequent they are, the more grim is human destiny.

* * *

6. "To desire the impossible is a disease of the soul." Generally attributed to the Greek sage Bias of Priene. Symonds, a scholar of ancient Greek literature and culture, probably translated the phrase himself from Greek into French.
7. Horse-drawn passenger coach.

CRITICISM

ELAINE SHOWALTER

Dr. Jekyll's Closet[†]

In January 1886, the same month that Robert Louis Stevenson published *The Strange Case of Dr. Jekyll and Mr. Hyde,* another strange case of "multiple personality" was introduced to English readers in the pages of *The Journal of Mental Science.* It involved a male hysteric named "Louis V.," a patient at Rochefort Asylum in France whose case of "morbid disintegration" had fascinated French doctors. Louis V.'s hysterical attacks had begun in adolescence, when he underwent a startling metamorphosis. Having been a "quiet, well-behaved, and obedient" street urchin, he abruptly became "violent, greedy, and quarrelsome," a heavy drinker, a political radical, and an atheist. So far his "symptoms" might be those of any teenage boy; but what seems to have upset his doctors particularly was that he tried to caress them. The French physicians attributed his condition to a shock he received from being frightened by a viper, and they cured him through hypnosis so effectively that he could not even remember what he had done.[1]

Stevenson (called "Louis" by his friends), may well have read the case of Louis V.; it had been written up earlier in the *Archives de Neurologie,* and his wife recalled that he had been "deeply impressed" by a "paper he read in French journal on sub-consciousness" while he was writing *Jekyll and Hyde.*[2] He was also a friend of Frederic W. H. Myers, who discussed the case for English specialists. But male hysteria was a topic of considerable scientific interest in 1886. Berjon in France published his book, *La grande hystérie chez l'homme;* and in Austria Freud made his debut at the Vienna Medical Society with a controversial paper about male hysteria. While it was recognized in men, hysteria carried the stigma of being a humiliatingly female affliction. Another scholar of male hysteria, Charcot's[3] disciple Emile Batault, observed that hysterical men in the Sâlpetrière's special ward were "timid and fearful men, whose gaze is neither

† From *Sexual Anarchy: Gender and Culture at the Fin de Siècle* (New York: Viking Penguin, 1990), pp. 105–16. Copyright © Elaine Showalter, 1990. Reprinted by permission of Writers House LLC acting as agent for the author. The author's notes have been expanded to include full bibliographic information. Additional notes by the editor are so indicated.

1. Frederic W. H. Myers, "Multiplex Personality," *The Nineteenth Century* (November 1886): 648–66.
2. Mrs. R. L. Stevenson, "Note," in *Works of Robert Louis Stevenson: Skerryvore Edition* (London: Heinemann, 1924), 4: xvii–xvii.
3. Jean-Martin Charcot (1825–1893), French neurologist and professor known for his study of hysteria and hypnosis. He worked and taught at the Salpêtrière Hospital in Paris and was Sigmund Freud's teacher [*Editor*].

lively nor piercing, but rather, soft, poetic, and languorous. Coquettish and eccentric, they prefer ribbons and scarves to hard manual labor."[4] Later this view of the hysterical man as effeminate would be carried into psychoanalytic theory, where the male hysteric is seen as expressing his bisexuality or homosexuality through the language of the body.

Homosexuality was also a topic of considerable scientific and legal interest in 1886. In January, just as Stevenson published his novel, the Labouchère Amendment criminalizing homosexual acts went into effect, and Krafft-Ebing's Psychopathia Sexualis offered some of the first case studies of homosexual men.[5] By the 1880s, such scholars as Jeffrey Weeks and Richard Dellamora have shown, the Victorian homosexual world had evolved into a secret but active subculture, with its own language, styles, practices, and meeting places. For most middle-class inhabitants of this world, homosexuality represented a double life, in which a respectable daytime world often involving marriage and family, existed alongside a night world of homoeroticism. Indeed, the fin de siècle was the golden age of literary and sexual doubles. "Late Victorian duality," writes Karl Miller in Doubles, "may be identified with the dilemmas, for màles, of a choice between male and female roles, or of a possible union of such opposites. The Nineties School of Duality framed a dialect and a dialectic, for the love that dared not speak its name—for the vexed question of homosexuality and bisexuality."[6] J. A. Symonds wrote poignantly in his journals of "the dual life . . . which had been habitual."[7] In Oscar Wilde's The Importance of Being Earnest, leading a double life is called "Bunburying" and represents, as one critic notes, "the 'posing' and 'double lives' to which homosexuals were accustomed."[8]

Stevenson was the fin-de-siècle laureate of the double life. In an essay on dreams, he described his passionate aim to "find a body, a vehicle for that strong sense of man's double being" which he had felt as a student in Edinburgh when he dreamed of leading "a double life—one of the day, one of the night."[9] The double life of the day and the night is also the double life of the writer, the split

---

4. Emile Batault, Contribution à l'étude de l'hystérie chez l'homme, (Paris, 1885), author's translation.
5. See Wayne Koestenbaum, "The Shadow Under the Bed: Dr. Jekyll, Mr. Hyde, and the Labouchère Amendment," Critical Matrix 1 (Spring 1988): 31–55.
6. Karl Miller, Doubles: Studies in Literary History (Oxford: Oxford UP, 1985), p. 216.
7. Phyllis Grosskurth, ed. The Memoirs of John Addington Symonds: The Secret Homosexual Life of a Leading Nineteenth-Century Man of Letters (Chicago: University of Chicago Press, 1984), p. 122. [See extract above, pp. 103–11—Editor.]
8. Regenia Gagnier, Idylls of the Marketplace: Oscar Wilde and the Victorian Public (Stanford: Stanford UP, 1986), p. 158.
9. "A Chapter on Dreams," in The Works of Robert Louis Stevenson (London, 1922), p. 247. [See extract above, pp. 77–84—Editor.]

between reality and the imagination. Nonetheless, biographers have long hinted that Stevenson's own double life was more than the standard round of brothels and nighttime bohemia, and have rattled such skeletons in Stevenson's closet as "homosexuality, impotence, a passionate feeling for his stepson, submission to a wilful and predatory wife."[1] In particular, Stevenson was the object of extraordinary passion on the part of other men. According to Andrew Lang, he "possessed, more than any man I ever met, the power of making other men fall in love with him."[2] Among the group of friends, both homosexual and heterosexual, in Stevenson's large literary and bohemian circle, "male appreciation of Stevenson was often intensely physical."[3]

Some of this appreciation and sexual ambiguity is vividly conveyed in the portrait, *Robert Louis Stevenson and His Wife* (1885), by one of the artists in Stevenson's circle who led his own double life, John Singer Sargent [see p. xvii]. In the foreground, a slender and anxious-looking Stevenson stares out at the painter, elongated fingers nervously stroking his droopy mustache. On the right, on the very margins of the painting, her body cut off by the picture frame, is the shadowy figure of his wife Fanny reclining on a velvet sofa, wrapped from head to toe in a gilded veil. Between the two is a door in the background wall, opening into a dark closet. For Stevenson himself, the painting was "too eccentric to be exhibited. I am at one extreme corner; my wife, in this wild dress, and looking like a ghost, is at the extreme other end . . . All this is touched in lovely, with that witty touch of Sargent's; but of course, it looks dam queer as a whole." For Sargent, the painting showed Stevenson trapped by domesticity and femininity; it is, he said, "the caged animal lecturing about the foreign specimen in the corner."[4] In his marriage to Fanny, Stevenson wrote to W. E. Henley, he had come out "as limp as a lady's novel. . . . the embers of the once gay R.L.S."[5]

Stevenson's real sexuality is much less the issue in *Jekyll and Hyde,* however, than his sense of the fantasies beneath the surface of daylight decorum, the shadow of homosexuality that surrounded

1. Miller, *Doubles,* p. 213. For discussions of Stevenson's homosociality/homosexuality, see William Veeder's brilliant essay, "Children of the Night: Stevenson and Patriarchy," in *Dr. Jekyll and Mr. Hyde after One Hundred Years,* (Chicago: University of Chicago Press, 1988), William Veeder and Gordon Hirsch, eds., especially pp. 159–60; and Wayne Koestenbaum, *Double Talk: The Erotics of Male Literary Collaboration* (New York and London: Routledge, 1989), pp. 145–51.
2. Andrew Lang, "Recollections of Robert Louis Stevenson," *Adventures Among Books* (London: Longmans, Green, and Co., 1903), p. 51.
3. Jenni Calder, *Robert Louis Stevenson: A Life Study* (New York: Oxford University Press, 1980), p. 65.
4. Quoted in Stanley Olson, *John Singer Sargent* (New York: St. Martin's Press, 1986), pp. 115, 114.
5. Malcolm Elwin, *The Strange Case of Robert Louis Stevenson* (London: Macdonald, 1950), p. 198; quoted in Koestenbaum, *Double Talk,* p. 150.

Clubland and the nearly hysterical terror of revealing forbidden emotions between men that constituted the dark side of patriarchy. In many respects, *The Strange Case of Dr. Jekyll and Mr. Hyde* is a case study of male hysteria, not only that of Henry J., but also of the men in the community around him. It can most persuasively be read as a fable of fin-de-siècle homosexual panic, the discovery and resistance of the homosexual self.[6] In contrast to the way it has been represented in film and popular culture, *Jekyll and Hyde* is a story about communities of men. From the moment of its publication, many critics have remarked on the "maleness," even the monasticism, of the story.[7] The characters are all middle-aged bachelors who have no relationships with women except as servants. Furthermore, they are celibates whose major emotional contacts are with each other and with Henry Jekyll. A female reviewer of the book expressed her surprise that "no woman's name occurs in the book, no romance is even suggested in it." Mr. Stevenson, wrote the critic Alice Brown, "is a boy who has no mind to play with girls."[8] The romance of Jekyll and Hyde is conveyed instead through men's names, men's bodies, and men's psyches.

Henry Jekyll is in a sense the odd man of fin-de-siècle literature. Unable to pair off with either a woman or another man, Jekyll divides himself, and finds his only mate in his double, Edward Hyde. Jekyll is thus both odd and even, both single and double. "Man is not truly one, but truly two," he observes, and his need to pursue illicit sexual pleasure and yet to live up to the exacting moral standards of his bleak professional community have committed him to "a profound duplicity of life," accompanied by "an almost morbid sense of shame." Coming to acknowledge his unutterable desires, Jekyll longs to separate his mind and his body: "If each, I told myself, could be housed in separable identities, life would be relieved of all that was unbearable."

Not only the personality of Jekyll, but everything else about the book seems divided and split; Stevenson wrote two drafts of the novel, the Notebook Draft and the Printer's Copy; the fragments or "fractions" of the manuscript are scattered among four libraries

---

6. Eve Kosofsky Sedgwick has called the genre to which Stevenson's novel belongs "the paranoid Gothic." According to Sedgwick, "the Gothic novel crystallized for English audiences the terms of a dialectic between male homosexuality and homophobia, in which homophobia appeared thematically in paranoid plots," (*Between Men: English Literature and Male Homosocial Desire* [New York: Columbia UP, 1985], 92). Such texts involved doubled male figures, one of whom feels obsessed by or persecuted by the other; and the central image of the unspeakable secret. ° ° °

7. See, for example, the excellent essay by Stephen Heath, "Psychopathia sexualis: Stevenson's *Strange Case*," *Critical Quarterly* 28 (1986), p. 28.

8. Julia Wedgwood, *Contemporary Review* 49 (April 1886): 594–95; and Alice Brown, *Study of Stevenson* (Boston: Copeland and Day, 1895); quoted in Koestenbaum, *Double Talk*, p. 145.

(two would obviously be more poetically just, but I cannot tell a lie); and Longmans published two Jekyll-and-Hyde-like simultaneous editions, a paperback shilling shocker and a more respectable cloth-bound volume.[9] Stevenson alludes obliquely to the composition process in the novel itself when Dr. Lanyon discovers the notebook in which Jekyll has recorded his experiments: "Here and there a brief remark was appended to a date, usually no more than a single word: 'double' occurring perhaps six times in a total of several hundred entries; and once very early in the list and followed by several marks of exclamation, 'total failure!'" Just as Jekyll searches for the proper dose to fight decomposition, Stevenson hints at his own frustration in composing the narrative of doubles.

Like the stories hysterical women told Freud, full of gaps, inconsistencies, and contradictions, Dr. Jekyll's story is composed of fragments and fractions, told through a series of narratives that the reader must organize into a coherent case history. The central narrator of the story is Gabriel John Utterson, who utters the tale, and eventually inherits Jekyll's estate. More than the others in their social circle, Utterson is a "Jekyll manqué."[1] Like many narrators in late-Victorian fiction, he is a lawyer, a spokesman for the Law of the Father and the social order, and "a lover of the sane and customary sides of life." His demeanor is muted and sober; "scanty and embarrassed in discourse"; "undemonstrative" and "backward in sentiment," austere and self-denying, he spends evenings alone drinking gin "to mortify a taste for vintages," or reading "a volume of some dry divinity"; although he likes the theater, he has not "crossed the doors of one for twenty years." He has almost a dread of the fanciful, a fear of the realm of the anarchic imagination.

Yet like Jekyll, Utterson also has an unconventional side to keep down; indeed, his self-mortification seems like an effort to stay within the boundaries of masculine propriety. Utterson's fantasies take the form of vicarious identification with the high spirits and bad fortune of "down-going men," for whom he is often the last respectable friend. "I incline to Cain's heresy," he is wont to say; "I let my brother go to the devil in his own way." Utterson, too, has a particular male friend, the younger "man about town" Richard Enfield, whom he sees every Sunday for an excursion that is the "chief jewel of every week," although "it was a nut to crack for many, what these two could see in each other." In another scene, he shares an intimate evening with his clerk Mr. Guest, his own confidant; at least "there was no man from whom he kept fewer secrets." Perhaps because his

---

9. See "Notes on the Manuscript," pp. 61–72 above [Editor].
1. James Twitchell, Dreadful Pleasures: An Anatomy of Modern Horror (New York: Oxford University Press, 1985), p. 236.

own life is so involved with repression and fantasy, Utterson becomes "enslaved" to the mystery of Hyde: "If he be Mr. Hyde . . . I shall be Mr. Seek." He begins to haunt the "by street" near Jekyll's house and to have rape fantasies of a faceless figure who opens the door to the room where Jekyll lies sleeping, pulls back the curtains of the bed, and forces Jekyll to rise and do his bidding.

Fin-de-siècle images of forced penetration through locked doors into private cabinets, rooms and closets permeate Utterson's narrative; as Stephen Heath notes, "the organising image for this narrative is the breaking down of doors, learning the secret behind them."[2] The narrators of Jekyll's secret attempt to open up the mystery of another man, not by understanding or secret sharing, but by force. "Make a clean breast of this [to me] in confidence," Utterson pleads with Jekyll, who rebuffs him: "it isn't what you fancy; it is not so bad as that." Jekyll cannot open his heart or his breast even to his dearest male friends. Thus they must spy on him to enter his mind, to get to the bottom of his secrets. The first chapter is called "The Story of the Door," and while Hyde, as the text repeatedly draws to our attention, has a key to Jekyll's house, Utterson makes violent entries, finally breaking down the door to Jekyll's private closet with an axe, as if into what Jekyll calls "the very fortress of identity."

One of the secrets behind these doors is that Jekyll has a mirror in his cabinet, a discovery almost as shocking to Utterson and the butler Poole as the existence of Hyde. "This glass has seen some queer doings," Poole exclaims in the manuscript (changed to "strange things" in the text).[3] The mirror testifies not only to Jekyll's scandalously unmanly narcissism, but also to the sense of the mask and the Other that has made the mirror an obsessive symbol in homosexual literature. Behind Jekyll's red baize door, Utterson sees his own mirrored face, the image of the painfully repressed desires that the cane and the axe cannot wholly shatter and destroy.

The agitation and anxiety felt by the bachelor friends of Jekyll's circle reflects their mutual, if tacit and unspoken, understanding of Jekyll's "strange preference" for Edward Hyde. Utterson, Enfield, and Lanyon initially think that Jekyll is keeping Hyde. What they see is that their rich friend Harry Jekyll has willed his very considerable estate to a loutish younger man, who comes and goes as he pleases, has expensive paintings and other gifts from Jekyll in his Soho apartment, gives orders to the servants, and cashes large checks Jekyll has signed. However unsuitable, this young man is Jekyll's "favorite," a term that, as Vladimir Nabokov noted in his

2. Heath, "Psychopathia sexualis," p. 95.
3. Veeder and Hirsch, Dr. Jekyll and Mr. Hyde, p. 55.

lecture on the novel, "sounds almost like *minion*."[4] Even when Hyde is suspected of a crime, Jekyll attempts to shield him, and begs Utterson to protect him: "I do sincerely take a great, a very great interest in that young man."

Jekyll's apparent infatuation with Hyde reflects the late-nineteenth-century upper-middle-class eroticization of working-class men as the ideal homosexual objects. "The moving across the class barrier," Weeks points out, "on the one hand the search for 'rough trade,' and on the other the reconciling effect of sex across class lines, was an important and recurrent theme in the homosexual world."[5] Edward Carpenter dreamed of being loved by "the thick-thighed hot coarse-fleshed young bricklayer with the strap round his waist," while E. M. Forster fantasized about "a strong young man of the working-class."[6] Furthermore, prostitution was "an indispensable part of the male homosexual life . . . with participants beginning usually in their mid-teens and generally leaving the trade by their mid-twenties." The "kept boy" was as common as the rough trade picked up on the streets; when he is "accosted" by the "aged and beautiful" M. P., Sir Danvers Carew, late at night in the dark streets by the river and beats him to death, Hyde both strikes at a father figure and suggests a male prostitute mugging a client on the docks.

Furthermore, Enfield calls Jekyll's abode "Blackmail House" on "Queer Street" and speculates that Jekyll is "an honest man paying through the nose for some of the capers of his youth." While Enfield explicitly does not want to pursue these implications—"the more it looks like Queer Street, the less I ask"—the butler Poole has also noted "something queer" about Hyde. As a number of scholars have noted, the homosexual significance of "queer" had entered English slang by 1900.[7] "'Odd,' 'queer,' 'dark,' 'fit,' 'nervous,'" notes Karl Miller, "these are the bricks which had built the house of the double."[8] For contemporary readers of Stevenson's novel, moreover, the term "blackmail" would have immediately suggested homosexual liaisons. Originating in sixteenth-century Scotland, it was generally associated with accusations of buggery.[9] Furthermore, the vision of blackmail as the penalty for homosexual sin was intensified by the Labouchère Amendment. While homosexual men had long been vulnerable to blackmail, the new law, as Edward Carpenter noted,

4. Vladimir Nabokov, "The Strange Case of Dr. Jekyll and Mr. Hyde," in *Lectures on Literature*, ed. Fredson Bowers (New York: Harcourt Brace Jovanovich, 1980), p. 194.
5. Jeffrey Weeks, *Sex, Politics, and Society: The Regulation of Sexuality Since 1800.* (Essex: Longman, 1989), p. 113.
6. Weeks, *Sex, Politics, and Society*, p. 113.
7. See Veeder, "Children of the Night," in *Dr. Jekyll and Mr. Hyde*, p. 159.
8. Miller, *Doubles*, p. 241.
9. Alexander Welsh, *George Eliot and Blackmail* (Cambridge: Harvard University Press, 1985), p. 9.

"opened wider than ever before the door to a real, most serious
social evil and crime—that of blackmailing."[1] Popularly known as
the "Blackmailer's Charter," the Labouchère Amendment put clos-
eted homosexual men like Wilde and J. A. Symonds at particular
risk. It made a major contribution to that "blackmailability" that
Sedgwick sees as a crucial component of the "leverage of
homophobia."[2]

In his original draft of the manuscript, Stevenson was more
explicit about the sexual practices that had driven Jekyll to a double life. Jekyll has become "from an early age . . . the slave of certain appetites," vices which are "at once criminal in the sight of the
law and abhorrent in themselves. They cut me off from the sympathy of those whom I otherwise respected."[3] While these passages
were omitted in the published version, Stevenson retained the
sense of abhorrence and dread that surrounds Hyde. The meta-
phors associated with Hyde are those of abnormality, criminality,
disease, contagion, and death. The reaction of the male characters
to Hyde is uniformly that of "disgust, loathing, and fear," suggestive of the almost hysterical homophobia of the late nineteenth
century. In the most famous code word of Victorian homosexuality,
they find something *unspeakable* about Hyde "that gave a man a turn,"
something "surprising and revolting." Indeed, the language surround-
ing Hyde is almost uniformly negative, although when Jekyll first
takes the drug, he feels "younger, lighter, happier in body." Hyde is
represented as apelike, pale, and inexpressibly deformed, echoing the
imagery of syphilitic afflictions in nineteenth-century medical texts,
and Utterson speculates that Jekyll may have contracted a disease
from Hyde, "one of those maladies that both torture and deform
the sufferer," for which he is seeking the drug as an antidote.
Meditating on Jekyll's possible youthful crime, Utterson fears
"the cancer of some concealed disgrace; punishment coming,
pede claudo." Along with the imagery of disease and retribution,
the Latin phrase (literally "on halting foot") suggests a bilingual
pun on "pederasty."

The male homosexual body is also represented in the narrative in
a series of images suggestive of anality and anal intercourse. Hyde
travels in the "chocolate-brown fog" that beats about the "back-end
of the evening"; while the streets he traverses are invariably
"muddy" and "dark," Jekyll's house, with its two entrances, is the
most vivid representation of the male body. Hyde always enters it

1. Edward Carpenter, *The Intermediate Sex,* p. 79; quoted in Jeffrey Weeks, *Coming Out:
    Homosexual Politics in Britain from the Nineteenth Century to the Present* (London:
    Quartet, 1979). p. 21.
2. Sedgwick, *Between Men,* p. 88.
3. Veeder, "Collated Fragments," pp. 34–35.

through the blistered back door, which, in Stevenson's words, is "equipped with neither bell nor knocker" and which bears the "marks of prolonged and sordid negligence."

Finally, the suicide which ends Jekyll's narrative is the only form of narrative closure thought appropriate to the Gay Gothic, where the protagonist's death is both martyrdom and retribution. To learn Jekyll-Hyde's secret leads to death; it destroys Dr. Lanyon, for example, as later, Dorian Gray also causes the suicides of a number of young men and then kills himself. While Jekyll tries to convince himself that his desire is merely an addiction, a bad habit that he can overcome whenever he wants, he gradually comes to understand that Hyde is indeed part of him. In a final spasm of homophobic guilt, Jekyll slays his other "hated personality." Death is the only solution to the "illness" of homosexuality. As A. E. Housman would write in *A Shropshire Lad:*

> Shot? so quick, so clean an ending?
> Oh that was right, lad, that was brave:
> Yours was not an ill for mending,
> 'Twas best to take it to the grave.

Jekyll is a "self-destroyer," Utterson concludes, not only because he has killed himself, but because it is self-destructive to violate the sexual codes of one's society.

In the multiplication of narrative viewpoints that makes up the story, however, one voice is missing: that of Hyde himself. We never hear his account of the events, his memories of his strange birth, his pleasure and fear. Hyde's story would disturb the sexual economy of the text, the sense of panic at having liberated an uncontrollable desire. Hyde's hysterical narrative comes to us in two ways: in the representation of his feminine behavior, and in the body language of hysterical discourse. As William Veeder points out, "despite all his 'masculine' traits of preternatural strength and animal agility, Hyde is prey to what the nineteenth century associated primarily with women."[4] He is seen "wrestling against the approaches of hysteria," and heard "weeping like a woman." Hyde's reality breaks through Jekyll's body in the shape of his hand, the timbre of his voice, and the quality of his gait.

In representing the effects of splitting upon the male body, Stevenson drew upon the advanced medical science of his day. In the 1860s, the French neuroanatomist Paul Broca had first established the concept of the double brain and of left cerebral dominance. Observing that language disorders resulted from

4. Veeder, "Children of the Night," p. 149.

left-brain injuries, he hypothesized that the left frontal brain lobes, which controlled the right side of the body, were the seat of the intellectual and motor skills. Thus the left brain was more important than the right and virtually defined the distinction between the animal and the human. The right frontal brain lobes, which controlled the left side of the body, were subordinate; they were the seat of lesser, non-verbal traits. Individuals in whom the right hemisphere predominated had to be low on the human evolutionary scale. In describing or imagining the operations of the double brain, European scientists were influenced by their cultural assumptions about duality, including gender, race and class. They characterized one side of the brain and body as masculine, rational, civilized, European, and highly evolved, and the other as feminine, irrational, primitive, and backward. Many scientists argued that the intellectual inferiority and social subordination of women and blacks could be attributed to their weak left brains. Furthermore, when mental disturbances occurred, as one physician noted in 1887, there must be a terrible struggle "between the left personality and the right personality, or in other more familiar terms, between the good and the bad side."[5]

These ideas about the brain were strongly related to late-nineteenth-century ideas about handedness, since handedness was usually inversely related to brain dominance; and considerable effort was made to get left-handed children to change. Freud's close friend Wilhelm Fliess, however, argued that all human beings were bisexual, with the dominant side of the brain representing the dominant gender, and the other the repressed gender. Thus Fliess believed that normal, heterosexual people would be right-handed, while "effeminate men and masculine women are entirely or partly left-handed."[6]

The imagery of hands is conspicuous in the text of *Jekyll and Hyde* and has also been dramatically put to use in the various film versions, where Hyde's hands seem almost to have a life of their own. It draws upon ideas of the double brain and hand, as well as upon other social and sexual meanings. As a child, Jekyll recalls, he had "walked with my father's hand," suggesting that he had taken on the bodily symbols of the "right"—or proper—hand of patriarchal respectability and constraint. Hyde seems to be the sinister left hand of Jekyll, the hand of the rebellious and immoral son. Suddenly Jekyll discovers that he cannot control

5. Anne Harrington, *Medicine, Mind, and the Double Brain* (Princeton: Princeton University Press, 1987), p. 170.
6. Harrington, *Medicine, Mind, and the Double Brain*, p. 94.

the metamorphosis; he wakes up to find that his own hand, the hand of the father, the "large, firm, white and comely" hand of the successful professional, has turned into the "lean, corded, knuckly," and hairy hand of Hyde. The implied phallic image here also suggests the difference between the properly socialized sexual desires of the dominant society and the twisted, sadistic, and animal desires of the other side. Jekyll's "hand" also means his handwriting and signature, which Hyde can forge, although his own writing looks like Jekyll's with a different slant. As Frederic W. H. Myers wrote to Stevenson, "Hyde's writing might look like Jekyll's, done *with the left hand*."[7] Finally, the image draws upon the Victorian homosexual trope of the left hand of illicit sexuality. Jekyll tells Lanyon that in the days of their Damon and Pythias friendship, he would have sacrificed "my left hand to help you." In his secret memoirs, Symonds, too, uses the figure of the useless hand "clenched in the grip of an unconquerable love" to express his double life and the sublimation of his homosexual desires.[8]

Some men, like Symonds and Wilde, may have read the book as a signing to the male community. "Viewed as an allegory," Symonds wrote to Stevenson, "it touches upon one too closely. Most of us at some epoch of our lives have been upon the verge of developing a Mr. Hyde."[9] Wilde included an anecdote in "The Decay of Lying" about "a friend of mine, called Mr. Hyde" who finds himself eerily reliving the events in Stevenson's story. But most Victorian and modern readers ignored such messages or evaded them. While there have been over seventy films and television versions of *Dr. Jekyll and Mr. Hyde*, for example, not one tells the story as Stevenson wrote it—that is, as a story about men. All of the versions add women to the story and either eliminate the homoerotic elements or suggest them indirectly through imagery and structural elements. * * *

* * *

7. Paul Maixner, *Robert Louis Stevenson: The Critical Heritage* (London: Routledge Kegan Paul, 1981), p. 215.
8. See Christopher Craft, "'Descend and Touch and Enter': Tennyson's Strange Manner of Address," *Genders* 1 (Spring 1988): 91–92.
9. J. A. Symonds to Stevenson, 3 March 1886, in *Letters of J. A. Symonds*, eds. Herbert M. Schueller and Robert L. Peters (Detroit: Wayne State University Press, 1969), pp. 120–21. [The letter is reproduced above, pp. 90–91—*Editor.*]

JACK HALBERSTAM

Parasites and Perverts: An Introduction to Gothic Monstrosity[†]

* * *

Victorian monsters produced and were produced by an emergent conception of the self as a body which enveloped a soul, as a body, indeed, enthralled to its soul. Michel Foucault writes in *Discipline and Punish* that "the soul is the prison of the body" and he proposes a genealogy of the soul that will show it to be born out of "methods of punishment, supervision and constraint."[1] Foucault also claims that, as modern forms of discipline shifted their gaze from the body to the soul, crime literature moved from confession or gallows speeches or the cataloguing of famous criminals to the detective fiction obsessed with identifying criminality and investigating crime. The hero of such literature was now the middle- or upper-class schemer whose crime became a virtuoso performance of skill and enterprise.

There are many congruities between Gothic fiction and detective fiction but in the Gothic, crime is embodied within a specifically deviant form—the monster—that announces itself (de-monstrates) as the place of corruption. Furthermore, just as the detective character appears across genres in many different kinds of fiction (in the sensation novel, in Dickens),[2] so Gothic infiltrates the Victorian novel as a symptomatic moment in which boundaries between good and evil, health and perversity, crime and punishment, truth and deception, inside and outside dissolve and threaten the integrity of the narrative itself. While many literary histories, therefore, have relegated Gothic to a subordinate status in relation to realism, I will be arguing that nineteenth-century literary tradition *is* a Gothic tradition and that this has everything to do with the changing technologies of subjectivity that Foucault describes.

Gothic fiction is a technology of subjectivity, one which produces the deviant subjectivities opposite which the normal, the healthy, and the pure can be known. Gothic, within my analysis,

---

[†] From *Skin Shows: Gothic Horror and the Technology of Monsters* (Durham and London: Duke UP, 1995), pp. 2–4, 6–7, 11–17, 19–22. © 1995 Duke University Press. All rights reserved. Republished by permission of the copyright holder. Notes are by the author except where indicated. Section titles have been omitted.

1. Michel Foucault, *Discipline and Punish: The Birth of the Prison*, trans. Alan Sheridan (New York: Vintage, 1979), 30, 29.

2. Charles Dickens (1812–1870), Victorian novelist who sometimes wrote about detectives, as in *Bleak House* (1853). *Sensation novel*: sensationalistic stories popular during the Victorian period, often dealing with crimes and sleuthing characters. Wilkie Collins and Mary Elizabeth Braddon were celebrated writers of this type of fiction [*Editor*].

may be loosely defined as the rhetorical style and narrative structure designed to produce fear and desire within the reader. The production of fear in a literary text (as opposed to a cinematic text) emanates from a vertiginous excess of meaning. Gothic, in a way, refers to an ornamental excess (think of Gothic architecture—gargoyles and crazy loops and spirals), a rhetorical extravagance that produces, quite simply, too much. Within Gothic novels, I argue, multiple interpretations are embedded in the text and part of the experience of horror comes from the realization that meaning itself runs riot. Gothic novels produce a symbol for this interpretive mayhem in the body of the monster. The monster always becomes a primary focus of interpretation and its monstrosity seems available for any number of meanings. While I will examine closely the implications of embodied horror (monstrosity) in nineteenth-century Gothic, I will also be paying careful attention to the rhetorical system which produces it (Gothic).

* * *

Within the nineteenth-century Gothic, authors mixed and matched a wide variety of signifiers of difference to fabricate the deviant body—Dracula, Jekyll/Hyde, and even Frankenstein's monster before them are lumpen bodies, bodies pieced together out of the fabric of race, class, gender, and sexuality. In the modern period and with the advent of cinematic body horror, the shift from the literary Gothic to the visual Gothic was accompanied by a narrowing rather than a broadening of the scope of horror. One might expect to find that cinema multiplies the possibilities for monstrosity but in fact, the visual register quickly reaches a limit of visibility. In *Frankenstein* the reader can only imagine the dreadful spectacle of the monster and so its monstrosity is limited only by the reader's imagination; in the horror film, the monster must always fail to be monstrous enough and horror therefore depends upon the explicit violation of female bodies as opposed to simply the sight of the monster.

Furthermore, as I noted, while nineteenth-century Gothic monstrosity was a combination of the features of deviant race, class, and gender, within contemporary horror, the monster, for various reasons, tends to show clearly the markings of deviant sexualities and gendering but less clearly the signs of class or race. * * *

* * *

Skin, I will argue with reference to certain nineteenth-century monsters, becomes a kind of metonym for the human; and its color, its pallor, its shape mean everything within a semiotic of monstrosity. Skin might be too tight (Frankenstein's creature), too dark (Hyde), too pale (Dracula), too superficial (Dorian Gray's canvas).[3] *** Skin houses the body and it is figured in Gothic as the ultimate boundary, the material that divides the inside from the outside. The vampire will puncture and mark the skin with his fangs, Mr. Hyde will covet white skin, Dorian Gray will desire his own canvas. *** Slowly but surely the outside becomes the inside and the hide no longer conceals or contains, it offers itself up as text, as body, as monster. The Gothic text, whether novel or film, plays out an elaborate skin show.

* * *

In her 1832 introduction to *Frankenstein,* Shelley writes, "I bid my hideous progeny go forth and prosper."[4] Shelley's "hideous progeny" was not merely her novel but the nineteenth-century Gothic novel itself. The Gothic, of course, did indeed prosper and thrive through the century. It grew in popularity until, by the turn of the century, its readership was massive enough that a writer could actually make a living from the sale of his Gothic works. In 1891, for example, Robert Louis Stevenson loosed his "shilling shocker," *Dr. Jekyll and Mr. Hyde,* upon the reading public hoping for commercial returns. Stevenson described his novella as a "Gothic gnome" and worried that he had produced a gross distortion of literature.[5] Such an anxiety marked Gothic itself as a monstrous form in relation to its popularity and its improper subject matter. The appellation "Gothic gnome" labeled the genre as a mutation or hybrid form of true art and genteel literature.

* * *

Producing and consuming monsters and monstrous fictions, we might say, adds up to what Eve Sedgwick has called, in her study of Gothic conventions, "an aesthetic of pleasurable fear."[6] The Gothic, in other words, inspires fear and desire at the same time—fear of and desire for the other, fear of and desire for the possibly latent perversity lurking within the reader herself. But fear and desire within the same body produce a disciplinary effect. In other words,

3. Main character in the novella *The Picture of Dorian Gray* (1890) by Irish author Oscar Wilde (1854–1900). Dorian Gray, a beautiful young man, commits crimes over many years, but his face never ages or shows his evil. A portrait painted of him when he was innocent takes on these changes instead, showing his corruption and degradation [*Editor*].
4. Mary Shelley, *Frankenstein or The Modern Prometheus* (1831; reprint, ed. M. K. Joseph, New York and Oxford: Oxford University Press, 1980), 10.
5. See Stevenson's letter to Will H. Low of December 26, 1885, reproduced on pp. 88–89 above [*Editor*].
6. Eve Kosofsky Sedgwick, *The Coherence of Gothic Conventions* (New York and London: Methuen, 1986), vi.

a Victorian public could consume Gothic novels in vast quantities without regarding such a material as debased because Gothic gave readers the thrill of reading about so-called perverse activities while identifying aberrant sexuality as a condition of otherness and as an essential trait of foreign bodies. The monster, of course, marks the distance between the perverse and the supposedly disciplined sexuality of a reader. Also, the signifiers of "normal" sexuality maintain a kind of hegemonic power by remaining invisible.

So, the aesthetic of pleasurable fear that Sedgwick refers to makes pleasure possible only by fixing horror elsewhere, in an obviously and literally foreign body, and by then articulating the need to expel the foreign body. Thus, both Dracula and Hyde are characters with markedly foreign physiognomies; they are dark and venal, foreign in both aspect and behavior. Dracula, for example, is described by Harker as an angular figure with a strong face notable for "peculiarly arched nostrils . . . a lofty domed forehead," bushy hair and eyebrows, "sharp white teeth," and ears pointed at the tops.[7] Hyde is described as small and deformed, "pale and dwarfish . . . troglodytic."[8] By making monstrosity so obviously a physical condition and by linking it to sexual corruption, such fictions bind foreign aspects to perverse activities.

* * *

Benedict Anderson has written about the cultural roots of the nation in terms of "imagined communities" which are "conceived in language, not in blood."[9] By linking the development of a print industry, particularly the popularization of novels and newspapers, to the spread of nationalism, Anderson pays close attention to the ways in which a shared conception of what constitutes "nation-ness" is written and read across certain communities. If the nation, therefore, is a textual production which creates national community in terms of an inside and an outside and then makes those categories indispensable, Gothic becomes one place to look for a fiction of the foreign, a narrative of who and what is not-English and not-native. The racism that becomes a mark of nineteenth-century Gothic arises out of the attempt within horror fiction to give form to what terrifies the national community. Gothic monsters are defined both as other than the imagined community and as the being that cannot be imagined as community.

7. Bram Stoker, *Dracula* (1897; reprint, New York: Bantam, 1981), 18.
8. Robert Louis Stevenson, *Strange Case of Dr. Jekyll and Mr. Hyde* (1886; reprint, New York; Bantam, 1981), 18.
9. Benedict Anderson, *Imagined Communities: Reflections on the Origin and Spread of Nationalism* (London and New York: Verso, 1983), 133.

"Racism and anti-Semitism," Anderson writes, "manifest themselves, not across national boundaries, but within them. In other
words, they justify not so much foreign wars as domestic oppression
and domination" (136). The racism and anti-Semitism that I have
identified as a hallmark of nineteenth-century Gothic literature
certainly direct themselves towards a domestic rather than a foreign scene. Gothic in the 1890s, as represented by the works of
Robert Louis Stevenson, Bram Stoker, and Oscar Wilde, takes
place in the backstreets of London in laboratories and asylums, in
old abandoned houses and decaying city streets, in hospitals and
bedrooms, in homes and gardens. The monster, such a narrative
suggests, will find you in the intimacy of your own home; indeed, it
will make your home its home (or you its home) and alter forever
the comfort of domestic privacy. The monster peeps through the
window, enters through the back door, and sits beside you in the par-
lor; the monster is always invited in but never asked to stay. The
racism that seems to inhere to the nineteenth-century Gothic monster, then, may be drawn from imperialistic or colonialist fantasies
of other lands and peoples, but it concentrates its imaginative force
upon the other peoples in "our" lands, the monsters at home. The
figure of the parasite becomes paramount within Gothic precisely
because it is an internal not an external danger that Gothic identifies and attempts to dispel.

In *The Origins of Totalitarianism,* Hannah Arendt has argued
convincingly that the modern category of anti-Semitism emerges
from both nineteenth-century attempts to make race the "key to
history" and the particular history of the Jews as "a people without
a government, without a country, and without a language."[1] As such,
the Jew, with regards to nation and, for our purposes, to English
nationality, might be said to represent the not-English, the not-
middle-class, the parasitical tribe that drains but never restores or
produces. Arendt shows how the decline of the aristocracy and of
nationalism by the mid-nineteenth century made people seek new
ground for both commonality and superiority. She writes, "For if
race doctrines finally served more sinister and immediately political purposes, it is still true that much of their plausibility and per-
suasiveness lay in the fact that they helped anybody feel himself an
aristocrat who had been selected by birth on the strength of 'racial'
qualification." Arendt's point is of central importance to an understanding of the history of Gothic. We might note in passing that,
from the late eighteenth century to the nineteenth century, the terrain of Gothic horror shifted from the fear of corrupted aristocracy

1. Hannah Arendt, *The Origins of Totalitarianism* (New York and London: Harcourt Brace
   Jovanovich, 1979), 8.

or clergy, represented by the haunted castle or abbey, to the fear embodied by monstrous bodies. Reading Gothic with nineteenth-century ideologies of race suggests why this shift occurs. If, then, with the rise of bourgeois culture, aristocratic heritage became less and less of an index of essential national identity, the construction of national unity increasingly depended upon the category of race and class. Therefore, the blood of nobility now became the blood of the native and both were identified in contradistinction to so-called "impure" races such as Jews and Gypsies. The nobility, further-more, gave way to a middle class identified by both their relation to capital as producers and consumers and a normal sexuality that leads to reproduction.

The Gothic novel, I have been arguing, establishes the terms of monstrosity that were to be, and indeed were in the process of being, projected onto all who threatened the interests of a dwin-dling English nationalism. As the English empire stretched over oceans and continents, the need to define an essential English character became more and more pressing. Non-nationals, like Jews, for example, but also like the Irish or Gypsies, came to be increasingly identified by their alien natures and the concept of "foreign" became ever more closely associated with a kind of para-sitical monstrosity, a non-reproductive sexuality, and an anti-English character. Gothic monsters in the 1880s and 1890s made parasitism—vampirism—the defining characteristic of horror. The parasitical nature of the beast might be quite literal, as in Stoker's vampire, or it might be a more indirect trait, as suggested by the creeping and homeless Hyde; it might be defined by a homoerotic influence, as exerted by Dorian Gray. Parasitism, especially with regards to the vampire, represents a bad or pathological sexuality, non-reproductive sexuality, a sexuality that exhausts and wastes and exists prior to and outside of the marriage contract.

The ability of race ideology and sexology to create a new elite to replace the aristocracy also allows for the staging of historical battles within the body. This suggests how Gothic monstrosity may intersect with, participate in, and resist the production of a theory of racial superiority. The Gothic monster—Frankenstein's crea-ture, Hyde, Dorian Gray, and Dracula—represents the dramatiza-tion of the race question and of sexology in their many different incarnations. If Frankenstein's monster articulates the injustice of demonizing one's own productions, Hyde suggests that the most respectable bodies may be contaminated by bad blood; and if Dorian Gray's portrait makes an essential connection between the homosexual and the uncanny, Dracula embodies once and for all the danger of the hybrid race and the perverse sexuality within the form of the vampire.

In Gothic, as in many areas of Victorian culture, sexual material was not repressed but produced on a massive scale, as Michel Foucault has argued.[2] The narrative, then, that professed outrage at acts of sexual perversion (the nightly wanderings of Hyde, for example, or Dracula's midnight feasts) in fact produced a catalogue of perverse sexuality by first showcasing the temptations of the flesh in glorious technicolor and then by depicting so-called normal sex as a sickly enterprise devoid of all passion. One has only to think of the contrast between Mina Harker's encounter with Count Dracula—she is found lapping at blood from his breast—and her sexually neutral, maternal relations with her husband.

* * *

In an introduction to *Studies on Hysteria* written in 1893, Freud identifies the repressed itself as a foreign body. Noting that hysterical symptoms replay some original trauma in response to an accident, Freud explains that the memory of trauma "acts like a foreign body which, long after its entry, must continue to be regarded as an agent that is still at work."[3] In other words, until an original site of trauma reveals itself in therapy, it remains foreign to body and mind but active in both. The repressed, then, figures as a sexual secret that the body keeps from itself and it figures as foreign because what disturbs the body goes unrecognized by the mind.

The fiction that Freud tells about the foreign body as the repressed connects remarkably with the fiction Gothic tells about monsters as foreigners. Texts, like bodies, store up memories of past fears, of distant traumas. "Hysterics," writes Freud, "suffer mainly from reminiscences" (7). History, personal and social, haunts hysterics and the repressed always takes on an uncanny life of its own. Freud here has described the landscape of his own science—foreignness is repressed into the depths of an unconscious, a kind of cesspool of forgotten memories, and it rises to the surface as a sexual disturbance. Psychoanalysis gothicizes sexuality; that is to say, it creates a body haunted by a monstrous sexuality and forced into repressing its Gothic secrets. Psychoanalysis, in the Freudian scenario, is a sexual science able to account for and perhaps cure Gothic sexualities. Gothicization in this formula, then, is the identification of bodies in terms of what they are not. A Gothic other stabilizes sameness, a gothicized body is one that disrupts the

2. Michel Foucault, *The History of Sexuality*, vol. 1, *An Introduction*, trans. Robert Hurley (New York: Vintage, 1980).
3. Sigmund Freud and Josef Brauer, *Studies on Hysteria* (1893; reprint, trans. and ed. James Strachey, New York: Basic, 1987), 6.

surface-depth relationship between the body and the mind. It is the body that must be spoken, identified, or eliminated.

Eve Sedgwick has advanced a reading of Gothic as the return of the repressed. She reads fear in the Gothic in terms of the trope of "live burial" and finds in Gothic "a carceral sublime of representation, of the body, and potentially of politics and history as well" (*Coherence*, vi). Live burial as a trope is, of course, standard fare in the Gothic, particularly in eighteenth-century Gothic like Matthew Lewis's *The Monk* and Ann Radcliffe's *The Mysteries of Udolpho*. Live burial also works nicely as a metaphor for a repressed thing that threatens to return. Sedgwick's example of the repressed in Gothic is homosexuality. She characterizes the "paranoid Gothic novel" in terms of its thematization of homophobia and thus, she describes *Frankenstein*'s plot in terms of "a tableau of two men chasing each other across the landscape" (*Coherence*, ix).

But Sedgwick's reading tells only half the story. The sexual outsider in Gothic, I am suggesting, is always also a racial pariah, a national outcast, a class outlaw. The "carceral sublime of representation" that, for Sedgwick, marks the role of textuality or language in the production of fear does not only symbolize that Gothic language buries fear alive. Live burial is certainly a major and standard trope of Gothic but I want to read it alongside the trope of parasitism. Parasitism, I think, adds an economic dimension to live burial that reveals the entanglement of capital, nation, and the body in the fictions of otherness sanctified and popularized by any given culture. If live burial, for Sedgwick, reveals a "queerness of meaning," an essential doubleness within language that plays itself out through homoerotic doubles within the text, the carceral in my reading hinges upon a more clearly metonymic structure. Live burial as parasitism, then, becomes a tooth buried in an exposed neck for the explicit purpose of blood sucking or a monstrous Hyde hidden within the very flesh of a respectable Jekyll. Live burial is the entanglement of self and other within monstrosity and the parasitical relationship between the two. The one is always buried in the other.

The form of the Gothic novel, again as Sedgwick remarks, reflects further upon the parasitical monstrosity it creates. The story buried within a story buried within a story that Shelley's *Frankenstein* popularizes evolves into the narrative with one story but many different tellers. This form is really established by Wilkie Collins's *The Woman in White* (1860). In this novel, Collins uses a series of narrators so that almost every character in the novel tells his or her side of the story. Such a narrative device gives the effect of completion and operates according to a kind of judicial model of narration where all witnesses step forward to give an account. Within this narrative system, the author professes to be no more than a collector of documents, a compiler of the facts of the case. The reader, of course, is the judge and jury, the courtroom audience, and often, a land of prosecuting presence expected to know truth, recognize guilt, and penalize monstrosity.

In *Dracula* Bram Stoker directly copies Collins's style. Stevenson also uses Collins's narrative technique in *Dr. Jekyll and Mr. Hyde* but he frames his story in a more overtly legal setting so that our main narrator is a lawyer, the central document is the last will and testament of Dr. Jekyll, and all other accounts contribute to the "strange case." All Gothic novels employing this narrative device share an almost obsessive concern with documentation and they all exhibit a sinister mistrust of the not-said, the unspoken, the hidden, and the silent. Furthermore, most Gothic novels lack the point of view of the monster. Collins does include in his novel a chapter by the notorious Count Fosco but Fosco's account is written as a forced confession that confirms his guilt and reveals his machinations. Neither Dracula nor Dorian Gray ever directly give their versions of events and Jekyll stands in at all times for his monstrous double, Hyde.

*   *   *

Novels in a Gothic mode transform class and race, sexual and national relations into supernatural or monstrous features. The threat posed by the Gothic monster is a combination of money, science, perversion, and imperialism but by reducing it to solely sexual aberrance, we fail to historicize Gothic embodiments.

* * * Gothic novels are technologies that produce the monster as a remarkably mobile, permeable, and infinitely interpretable body. The monster's body, indeed, is a machine that, in its Gothic mode, produces meaning and can represent any horrible trait that the reader feeds into the narrative. The monster functions as monster, in other words, when it is able to condense as many fear-producing traits as possible into one body. Hence the sense that Frankenstein's monster is bursting out of his skin—he is indeed filled to bursting point with flesh and meaning both. Dracula, at the other end of the nineteenth century, is a body that consumes to excess—the vampiric body in its ideal state is a bloated body, sated with the blood of its victims.

Monsters are meaning machines. They can represent gender, race, nationality, class, and sexuality in one body. And even within these divisions of identity, the monster can still be broken down. Dracula, for example, can be read as aristocrat, a symbol of the masses; he is predator and yet feminine, he is consumer and producer, he is parasite and host, he is homosexual and heterosexual, he is even a lesbian. Monsters and the Gothic fiction that creates them are therefore technologies, narrative technologies that produce the perfect figure for negative identity. Monsters have to be everything the human is not and, in producing the negative of human, these novels make way for the invention of human as white, male, middle class, and heterosexual.

* * *

MARTIN DANAHAY

Dr. Jekyll's Two Bodies†

I argue in this article that Robert Louis Stevenson's *Strange Case of Dr. Jekyll and Mr. Hyde* (1886) is a cautionary tale about the increasing emphasis on the appetites of the masculine body in late Victorian culture. The narrative represents Stevenson's rearguard action against such indulgence of bodily appetites, which in *Jekyll and Hyde* leads to the complete loss of manly self-control. Dr. Jekyll loses his social standing as a result of his indulgence of his desires and inhabits a working-class body to seek gratification of unseemly appetites. * * * Dr. Jekyll wears a working-class body as if it were a suit of clothing. In a telling phrase Dr. Jekyll talks of being "accustomed to sleep in the body of Edward Hyde" while in Soho (*Jekyll* 84), as if Mr. Hyde were a pair of pajamas that he would wear while sleeping in one location, but not in the other. The different bodies encode at the corporeal level the geographical, class-based division of London into East and West.

Dr. Jekyll therefore has two bodies in Robert Louis Stevenson's *Strange Case of Dr. Jekyll and Mr. Hyde* (1886); when he becomes Mr. Hyde he switches from a "decent" and respectable body into the "indecent" body of a working-class man. In keeping with the class-based stereotypes of the period, the respectable, self-denying body is that of a gentleman, while the hedonistic body is marked both as "degenerate" and of a lower social class. This corporeal duality registers the conflict between competing versions of manliness. Dr. Jekyll tries to adhere to a self-regulated and pious discipline, like that of his friend Utterson, but fails when he discovers a way to

† From *Nineteenth-Century Contexts* 35.1 (2013): 23–37. © 2013 Taylor & Francis. Reprinted by permission of the publisher, Taylor & Francis Ltd. Notes have been omitted. Parenthetical references are to the list of works cited at the end of the essay, to which Stevenson's works have been added.

switch into another body, that of Mr. Hyde. Dr. Jekyll suffers a double loss of status, losing both self-discipline, which was essential to the status of a gentleman, and the title "Dr." as he becomes a mere "Mr." However, Mr. Hyde is still dressed as a gentleman, which leads to cognitive dissonance for all those who look at him as they register the contrast between the working-class, muscular body and the rich fabrics in which he is dressed.

Stevenson said of writing *Jekyll and Hyde* that "I had long been trying to write a story on this subject, to find a body, a vehicle, for this strong sense of man's double being." (*Jekyll* 104) Stevenson finds in *Jekyll and Hyde* not one body, but two bodies to convey this duality and uses them as vehicles of horror. One of the earliest commentators on the story noted that the double in the tale "does not take the form of a personified conscience" (which is the plot of "Markheim") but a "separable self," a different entity more horrifying than "a spectre, a ghoul, or even a vampire." (Maixner 200) It is this splitting of Dr. Jekyll into "separable selves" and even separable bodies that gives the tale its power and makes it such an unsettling story.

Class status and the body were intimately connected in Stevenson's mind. This comes across most clearly in his essay on "The Character of Dogs." Stevenson characterizes a dog as a "gentleman of leisure" and says that "to follow for ten minutes in the street some swaggering, canine cavalier, is to receive a lesson in the dramatic art and the cultured conduct of the body." ("Character" 296–7) "Every dog aspires to be a high-mannered and high-minded gentleman" according to this essay, and this canine social pretension is visible in the movements of the dog's body. ("Character" 297) For Stevenson bodily disposition is therefore linked directly to class status. Being a gentleman, then, is a matter of "the conduct of the body," and although dog's bodies are in question here, the terms clearly apply to human gentlemen too. Victorian class distinctions are once again inscribed on the animal kingdom in this essay. Stevenson's comments on dogs allow him to discuss the male body and its connection to class frankly because troubling issues are safely transposed onto animals.

Stevenson's term for the importance of the physical in defining the gentleman is "the commentary of the body," a phrase that he uses in his essay "Truth of Intercourse." ("Truth" 44) In this essay Stevenson discusses how to "read" the body for signs of class status as if it were a text. In an extended passage on the relationship between language and the body, he begins by contrasting "life" and "literature," and how we all have "legible countenances, like an open book." ("Truth" 44) Stevenson's terms initially blur the distinction between body and text, making both into legible surfaces that give off "appealing signals" that can easily be decoded.

("Truth" 44) However, the body ultimately takes precedence because "to explain in words takes time . . . but the look or the gesture explains in a breath." ("Truth" 44) The body speaks louder than words, which would seem to suggest that it can be a guarantor of class distinctions because it can be "read" so easily and unambiguously.

The narrative of *Jekyll and Hyde,* however, belies this faith in the "commentary of the body" because Mr. Hyde is referred to consistently as a "gentleman." Enfield calls him "my gentleman" (*Jekyll* 33) and Mr. Hyde says that "no gentleman but wishes to avoid a scene" when blackmailed, for instance. (*Jekyll* 34) Mr. Hyde looks like a gentleman thanks to his "decent" clothing but his behavior, the conduct of his body, contradicts his appearance. Dr. Jekyll's body language changes dramatically when he becomes Mr. Hyde. As Katz emphasizes, Stevenson and his contemporaries faced great difficulty in defining appropriate behavior and class status because of social changes, and this is true in Mr. Hyde's case. (51–3) He should not really be referred to as a "gentleman," both because of his conduct and because of the disposition of his body.

Stevenson represents Dr. Jekyll as "plunging into the sea of liberty" when he becomes Mr. Hyde in the transformation scene. (*Jekyll* 82) In his essay on "Gentlemen" Stevenson asserts that advances in civilization are "paid for by the loss of liberty" ("Gentlemen" 346) so that the "liberty" that Dr. Jekyll gains in becoming Mr. Hyde leads directly to his loss of the social status of a gentleman. For Stevenson, being a "gentleman" is to "behave with decency" ("Gentlemen" 350) and restraint (like Mr. Utterson), so that even a servant can behave like a gentleman in Stevenson's terms when he is socially dexterous. Later in his essay, Stevenson claims that "for all this ambiguity . . . we know clearly what we mean by the word" and even if the word "gentleman" can't be defined, it can be explained by a story ("Gentlemen" 352), a confident claim that is undermined by his use of "gentleman" in *Jekyll and Hyde.*

The problem is that, as Stevenson says elsewhere in "Talk and Talkers," clothes can utter "voices to corroborate the story in the face," ("Talk" 269) but they can also contradict the signs of the body. Clothes can be used to disguise the true class status of the wearer, so that clothes can indeed make the man. In a comic vein in his essay on umbrellas, Stevenson makes just this point; after characterizing umbrellas as "the stamp of Respectability" ("Umbrellas" 46) and true indicators of character, he goes on to lament, that it is possible to carry a "mendacious umbrella" that is a sign of hypocrisy, particularly in the case of bearers of "inappropriate umbrellas," that contradict the true class of the owner. ("Umbrellas" 49) Identity and rank are not stable, especially in a consumer society where goods like umbrellas are increasingly becoming affordable for those lower on the social scale.

Furthermore, Dr. Jekyll's experiment turns his body into a piece of clothing that he believes he can put on or taken off at will, so that bodily identity itself is unstable. Both clothing and the body in *Jekyll and Hyde* can be used to conceal the class status of the wearer, and thus belie a faith in exterior class markers. It is possible in the terms of the narrative to masquerade as somebody from a different class not just by wearing inappropriate clothing but also by assuming the body of a working-class man; Dr. Jekyll, therefore, is a gentleman who inhabits the body of a working-class man whilst wearing clothing that is "above" Mr. Hyde's bodily status.

The ideal of the "gentleman" was under particular pressure in the late Victorian period because * * * it was redefined from a category based on inherited status to one linked to newly acquired capital and thus made an elevated social status theoretically available to anybody with enough money to buy the right clothes. As clothes became cheaper thanks to new production techniques, they were more accessible to the lower classes so that even footmen could aspire to dress as a "gentleman." Ying S. Lee gives the example of William Tayler who purchased a one guinea suit and attempted a "gentlemanly masquerade" (Lee 57) which ultimately did not succeed because he was taken for a land surveyor, tailor and a grocer, but not a gentleman.

In a nonfiction text such as *The Gentleman's Art of Dressing with Economy* (1876), the status of "gentleman" is treated solely as a matter of using the right tailor and buying the correct accessories, so that class status is a matter of attire and economics rather than inherited rank. As the anonymous author of the text says:

> The cheap tailor of the day, aided by the sewing machine, has been a great reformer and leveller of class, breaking down the social distinction which formerly separated men in dress. At present it is impossible to distinguish a gentleman by his raiment only; and whatever gradations of rank may exist in this country, I consider it an advantage that *prima facie* all should appear equal, and entitled to class themselves as a gentleman, so far as outward and visible signs may go. Even to be mistaken for a gentleman may often give noble aspirations and induce a man to try to "behave as such." (*Gentleman's* ix)

On the face of it, *The Gentleman's Art of Dressing with Economy* seems a subversive text in that it claims that cheap clothing has eradicated class distinctions in dress. However, the author recoups the rank of "gentleman" later in the book by asserting that knowing how to dress well is "innate" and that "simply wearing good clothes will not constitute dressing as a gentleman." (*Gentleman's* 5) The appeal to innate knowledge of how to wear the correct clothing, not simply purchase it, restores the class distinctions so airily dismissed in the Preface.

In the *Gentleman's Art of Dressing with Economy* the author is aware that "for a man to devote his heart and soul to the art of bedizening is to write himself down an ass" (*Gentleman's* x), making the wearer an object of ridicule. Nonetheless, the text also shows awareness of the importance of appearance for class status and creates a taxonomy of masculine appearance, from "the cad," to the "snob," to "the swell" and finally the "gentleman" as the ultimate goal in terms of dress. While men were conventionally not supposed to be concerned with their dress, the text shows an acute awareness of male display on the streets of London and the importance of clothing in establishing status in terms of age, profession and wealth. All these "types" are described as visible in the West End of London and are associated with different men's clubs. *The Gentleman's Art of Dressing with Economy* focuses on the world of London fashion, and the city itself was seen as a particularly dangerous "sensual trap" leaching away manliness and "moral fibre" because of the rampant commercialism and the enticements for play and frivolity. (Breward, 152) In *Jekyll and Hyde* Utterson and Enfield walk down a London street in which the shops laid out "the surplus of their gains in coquetry," (*Jekyll* 32) but these two upstanding gentlemen are immune to their charms. Mr. Hyde, however, is not and in fact revels in the "sensual trap" that is London, allowing Dr. Jekyll to enjoy activities incompatible with his status as a respectable gentleman.

London, however, was simply the most extreme example of a burgeoning culture of consumption in the Victorian period. Brent Shannon in *The Cut of His Coat: Men, Dress and Consumer Culture, 1860–1914* argues that the late nineteenth century witnessed the "development of a massive and sophisticated consumer culture machine" (Shannon 14) in which "the male body became a decorated and eroticized medium of the public display of masculinity." (Shannon 17) In a striking passage Shannon describes the way in which:

> In the increasingly visual culture of late-nineteenth-century Britain, men were publicly acknowledged to possess a physical, visible self, in ways that had formerly been suppressed. This public visibility often manifested itself in a more open acknowledgment of the sexuality and sexualization of men's clothing. (Shannon 81)

This statement must be tempered in the light of Stevenson's *Jekyll and Hyde*. While the forces of capitalism were indeed fostering a desire for consumer goods and commodifying men's bodies, the process was initially uneven in its internalization. As Christopher Breward has argued in *The Hidden Consumer,* men had an uneasy relationship with the emerging consumer culture of the late Victorian period given models of masculinity that stressed an indifference to appearance. This uneasiness is evident in the conflict in *Jekyll and Hyde* between desire and restraint. Stevenson's tale records a contest between the "Great Masculine Renunciation" of the early nineteenth century, that stressed sober clothing and the strict regulation of desire, and the *fin de siècle* eroticized body. Partly, as has been observed by several commentators, this eroticization was fostered by the creation of the category of the "homosexual" that both gave an identity to and made accessible to legal and medical discourse homoerotic desires between men.

*   *   *

Mr. Utterson in *Jekyll and Hyde* is the epitome of the respectable, self-controlled gentleman who eschews overindulgence of any senses and the antithesis to Mr. Hyde and his sensual self-indulgence. The opening of the narrative relentlessly underscores his self control and the severe restraint that he places upon all his desires:

> He was austere with himself; drank gin when he was alone, to mortify a taste for vintages; and though he enjoyed the theatre, had not crossed the doors of one for twenty years. But he had an approved tolerance for others; sometimes wondering, almost with envy, at the high pressure of spirits involved in their misdeeds; and in any extremity inclined to help rather than to reprove. (*Jekyll* 31)

There are a number of clues in this passage that mark Mr. Utterson as the antithesis of Mr. Hyde, and as an epitome of the Great Masculine Renunciation. The emphasis on not drinking wine underscores his difference from Dr. Jekyll, who drinks a potion that makes him lose all self-control; as Thomas Reed has argued, the story can be read as a cautionary tale about the evils of drinking and Dr. Jekyll could be viewed as an alcoholic. Utterson's self-control is a class marker in that his restraint makes him a gentleman, in contrast to Mr. Hyde.

In the context of Newman's definition of the "gentleman" in *The Idea of a University*, Mr. Utterson is a model gentleman in both his restraint and his lack of expression, being "cold, scanty and embarrassed in discourse." (*Jekyll* 31) Newman says that "the true gentleman . . . carefully avoids whatever may cause a jar or a jolt in the minds of those with whom he is cast" and melts into the background like an "easy chair or a good fire." (Newman 179–80) A gentleman is a space, an absence, not a physical presence and more like a piece of domestic furniture than an active, desiring body. Similarly in *The Gentleman's Art of Dressing with Economy* the author says that the mark of a gentleman's dress is that "no one could remember nor describe any article of dress he wore" so that not being noticed becomes the hallmark of status. (*Gentleman's* 8) However, while Mr. Utterson may appear to be the antithesis of Mr. Hyde, a "Mr. Seek" to his "Mr. Hide," the need to be "austere with himself" in private betrays a fear about what might happen if he indulged his desires in the privacy of his own home, rather than in public and in the company of other men (he drinks at social occasions "when the wine was to his taste"). (*Jekyll* 31) It would be trite to say he has a Mr. Hyde of his own; rather, what is at stake here is a generalized fear of an unrestrained masculine desire. Stevenson's use of "mortify" in this context suggests a religious practice of self-denial of desire, and of a severe bodily discipline that is the antithesis of Mr. Hyde's unrestrained self-indulgence. The religious aspect of the double motif is more evident in "Markheim" where the memory of a religious education plays a pivotal role in the redemption of the main character. "Markheim" shows the strength of Stevenson's early religious training, despite his later atheism, in that a divine presence in the story leads the protagonist to confess his crime and implicitly find redemption. While Mr. Hyde is referred to as a "devil" and as "hellish" the religious aspects of the duality are overshadowed by the emphasis on the results of masculine desire that is not "mortified" under a severe bodily self discipline.

In conduct manuals like *Manliness and Culture* (1877) "manliness" involves an "absolute guidance of a man's physical, intellectual and moral being" that "must regulate his life" (Brookes 14). The terms "guidance" and "regulate" invoke the kind of stern self-denial ascribed to Mr. Utterson and the "pastoral care" described by Michel Foucault in which "governing" the self is a form of self-discipline modeled on a religious hierarchy. Submission to a higher power is used as a model for self-government, which regulates both the "social body" and the private body. The mark of a gentleman is control over his body and to lose this control is to lose one's class status and to sink from a "Dr." to a "Mr."

Perhaps nowhere is the importance of religion and self-regulation more obvious than in Mr. Utterson's Sunday routine, which was "to sit close by the fire, a volume of some dry divinity on his reading-desk, until the clock of the neighbouring church rang out the hour of twelve, when he would go soberly and gratefully to bed." (*Jekyll* 37) It is not clear whether the gratitude here is based on his appreciation for a blameless life or relief that Sunday is over, but the portrait here is of a "sober" man in whom spirituality and self-control are combined. Mr. Hyde, by contrast, annotates pious works with "startling blasphemies." (*Jekyll* 68)

The description of Utterson makes it clear that he was not completely immune to such desires since he watched the "misdeeds" of others "almost with envy." (*Jekyll* 31) While this envy is qualified, it sets up within Utterson a fissure that mirrors the conflicted desires of Dr. Jekyll. Utterson's envy is one of the few suggestions in the text that he is troubled by the same desires as his friend Jekyll and that he must maintain severe self-repression to keep his bodily desires under control. In the final analysis, however, Mr. Utterson perseveres in a pious bodily self-discipline and "regulates" his life in the manner extolled by *Manliness and Culture* where Dr. Jekyll quite spectacularly does not.

Even though outwardly Mr. Hyde is a gentleman like Mr. Utterson, he betrays his class status through his body. This becomes clear in one of the most remarkable passages in the novel, so over-determined with markers of class and gender status that it could be the subject of an entire article alone:

> I smiled to myself, and, in my psychological way began lazily to inquire into the elements of this illusion, occasionally, even as I did so, dropping back into a comfortable morning doze. I was still so engaged when, in one of my more wakeful moments, my eyes fell upon my hand. Now the hand of Henry Jekyll (as you have often remarked) was professional in shape and size: it was large, firm, white, and comely. But the hand which I now saw, clearly enough, in the yellow light of a mid-London morning, lying half shut on the bed-clothes, was lean, corded, knuckly, of a dusky pallor and thickly shaded with a swart growth of hair. It was the hand of Edward Hyde. (*Jekyll* 84)

Others have noted the markers of degeneration in this passage, particularly the "swart growth of hair." The term "comely" introduces some gender confusion, because it places Dr. Jekyll closer to the feminine than masculine, but the majority of adjectives here point to Mr. Hyde's hand being working class: it is muscled, tanned from being outside and shows signs of inadequate nutrition. What has not been noted is that this hand, representing Mr. Hyde's body, appears in the context of a moment of sensual indulgence in which Dr. Jekyll is "lazy" and engaged in an inquiry into his own body. Simply being lazy rather than industrious is scandalous enough, but the indecency of this moment is compounded by Dr. Jekyll's frank focus on his own body.

I use the term "indecency" deliberately because the body that Dr. Jekyll is wearing is a direct threat to the "decent" furniture and proportions of his bedroom. Mr. Hyde is working class partly because his hand is muscular (the result of manual labor) and betrays the effects of malnutrition, but also because he expresses overtly desires that are repressed in respectable society. Stevenson is drawing upon images here of the working classes as closer to the "animal" and as lower down the social scale, and thus able to express desires that were off limits to the respectable man. Mr. Hyde is masculine desire made visible and erupting indecently into the "light of a mid-London morning." (*Jekyll* 84)

The three most charged moments in the text then occur when Dr. Jekyll is focusing on his body. The first is during the moment when he experiences "a current of disordered sensual images" (*Jekyll* 80) when he initially assumes the identity of Mr. Hyde, the second when he sees Mr. Hyde's hand while lying in his bed, quoted above, and the third when he is relaxing on a park bench enjoying the sunshine and indulging "the animal within." (*Jekyll* 88) All three are moments of sensual self-indulgence and awareness of the masculine body. As Grace Moore says of Dr. Jekyll, "the only body in which he shows any interest is his own" (Moore 155) and it is in these moments of bodily self-awareness that he becomes Hyde. Mr. Hyde is described as more sensual, more aware of his body than Dr. Jekyll; he notes that "my faculties seemed sharpened to a point and my spirits more tensely elastic" (*Jekyll* 89) as Mr. Hyde. Dr. Jekyll assumes an eroticized male body whose desires are not "hidden" but can be read visibly on his face when he becomes Mr. Hyde.

Mr. Hyde enacts the violence commonly associated with the working classes. Mr. Hyde registers as a "social body" the class divisions of London, which Simon Joyce has so ably mapped in his analysis of the symbolism of Soho in his chapter on *Jekyll and Hyde* and Jack the Ripper. (Joyce 164–78) As the antithesis of the gentleman, Mr. Hyde overturns Newman's definition of the gentleman as "one who never inflicts pain." He also contradicts the image of the gentleman as one who is never cruel to women and children, as cited by Girouard. (260) Mr. Hyde inflicts pain on a small child early in the text, and as further evidence of his status as an anti-gentleman makes a doctor "turn sick and white with the desire to kill him." (*Jekyll* 33) He is quite literally a mirror image of the professional men he meets, drawing out of them a repressed violence that is inappropriate for a gentleman, thus dragging them down the social hierarchy with him. * * *

* * *

Those who look at Mr. Hyde cite something wrong with him that they cannot pinpoint, using terms like "deformity." Enfield says of him, for example, that "he must be deformed somewhere; he gives a

Figure 1. August Sander, *Country Band, 1913.* Museum of Modern Art, object no. 472.2015.73. Acquired through the generosity of the family of August Sander. © 2020 Die Photographische Sammlung / SK Stiftung Kultur–August Sander Archiv, Cologne / ARS, NY. Reproduced as "Village Band, Westerwald, 1913" in Berger's "The Suit and the Photograph."

strong feeling of deformity" (*Jekyll* 35) although Enfield cannot say precisely why he has this impression. Mr. Utterson experiences "the haunting sense of unexpressed deformity with which the fugitive impressed his beholders" when he encounters Hyde for the first time. (*Jekyll* 49) The adjective "unexpressed" indicates that Mr. Hyde's body betrays his true character and class status, but not his speech or clothing. * * *

The contrast between the working-class body and clothing has been analyzed by John Berger in his classic essay on "The Suit and the Photograph." Berger gives an important clue as to what is at stake here in the sense of Mr. Hyde's deformity. Analyzing a photograph of peasants wearing suits, Berger asks why it is obvious that their class position does not match their clothes. (Figure 1) The answer, Berger concludes, is that the muscled peasant body is not appropriate for the suits that they are wearing, which were created for English gentlemen and inhibited vigorous action. The suit values sedentary occupations over manual labor, as is obvious for instance in the fashion plate from 1880 reproduced in *The Hidden*

Consumer where the suit emphasizes a slender figure with a narrow waist exemplifying a "simple, lean shape." (Breward 32) Berger says in a striking formulation that "their suits *deform* them" (italics Berger's 35) and that the bodies inside make them appear "abnormal" because the muscled peasant body does not fit a lean, tapered suit. Applying Berger's striking analysis to the descriptions of Mr. Hyde * * * we can see that Stevenson is describing a class conflict between the gentleman's clothing and the body inside the clothes. Like the peasants, Mr. Hyde appears "deformed" because he has a working-class body that is not suited to his attire and people who look at him react to the contradiction between his clothing and body. Like the peasants in the photograph that Berger analyzes, there is a contradiction between body and clothing that signals visually a discrepancy in class markers.

The most extended commentary on the contradiction between Mr. Hyde and his clothing comes from Dr. Lanyon. On meeting Hyde he is immediately struck by the contrast between the "shocking expression on his face," his small body, and the tasteful attire that does not fit the wearer:

> This person (who had thus, from the first moment of his entrance, struck in me what I can only describe as a disgustful curiosity) was dressed in a fashion that would have made an ordinary person laughable; his clothes, that is to say, although they were of rich and sober fabric, were enormously too large for him in every measurement—the trousers hanging on his legs and rolled up to keep them from the ground, the waist of the coat below his haunches, and the collar sprawling wide upon his shoulders. Strange to relate, this ludicrous accoutrement was far from moving me to laughter. Rather, as there was something abnormal and misbegotten in the very essence of the creature that now faced me—something seizing, surprising, and revolting—this fresh disparity seemed but to fit in with and to reinforce it; so that to my interest in the man's nature and character, there was added a curiosity as to his origin, his life, his fortune and status in the world. (*Jekyll* 74)

Mr. Hyde is represented as small in stature to underline the mismatch between his body and his clothes, which mark him as a gentleman of means. Mr. Hyde's clothes of a "rich and sober" fabric bespeak wealth and restraint in their subdued colors, but what Lanyon terms his "great muscular activity" and "shocking expression" (*Jekyll* 74) contradict the message of his clothes. Mr. Hyde's expression is "shocking" because his desires are legible on his body which, along with his muscles and size, contradict the class status implied by his attire. Lanyon describes Hyde as "abnormal" and "misbegotten"

as he tries to reconcile his own mixed reactions to the figure before
him and he tries to make sense of the profoundly contradictory messages that the body and the clothing represent.

Lanyon also develops a "disgustful curiosity" about Hyde because
of this cognitive dissonance and like Utterson feels compelled to try
to solve the mystery of Mr. Hyde's contradictory appearance. His curiosity is specifically about Mr. Hyde's "fortune and status in the world,"
that is to say his exact class status, because of Mr. Hyde's mixed messages, and the fact that he is not only unable to fill Dr. Jekyll's shoes,
but his jacket too. Mr. Hyde is a class anomaly so shocking and abnormal that curiosity about him is "disgustful," leading Lanyon to specu-
late about matters that should remain private; Enfield earlier in the
text warns against such curiosity about the behavior of others because
of the unsavory matters it might reveal. (*Jekyll* 35)

*   *   *

In order to encompass the fall from gentleman to working-class
man Dr. Jekyll had to change not just consciousness, but bodies as
well. It is for this reason that Stevenson's *Jekyll and Hyde* is a tale
about two bodies and not just two identities. To become Mr. Hyde,
Dr. Jekyll had to enter a different body and suffer a fall in social
status in order to indulge his "indecent" physical desires. This
aspect of the story is lost in adaptations of *Jekyll and Hyde* which
approach it as a psychological drama of conflicted desires. For Stevenson, class was intimately connected with the body, as his commentary on dogs' bodies shows, so that when he wrote *Jekyll and
Hyde* he dramatized a conflict not just within the psyche of one
person, but between two different bodies.

Works Cited

Anon. *The Gentleman's Art of Dressing with Economy.* "by a Lounger
    at the Clubs." London: Frederick Warne & Co, 1876.
Berger, John. "The Suit and the Photograph." *About Looking.* New
    York: Vintage, 1992. 31–40.
Breward, Christopher. *The Hidden Consumer: Masculinities, Fash-
    ion and City Life 1860–1914.* Manchester: Manchester UP, 1999.
Brookes, John. *Manliness and Culture.* London: Blackwood, 1878.
Foucault, Michel. *Security, Territory, Population: Lectures at the
    Collège de France, 1977–1978.* Trans. Graham Burchell. New
    York: Palgrave Macmillan, 2007.
Gilmour, Robin. *The Idea of the Gentleman in the Victorian Novel.*
    London: George Allen & Unwin, 1981.
Girouard, Mark. *The Return to Camelot: Chivalry and the English
    Gentleman.* New Haven: Yale UP, 1981.

Joyce, Simon. *Capital Offenses: Geographies of Class and Crime in Victorian London.* Charlottesville: U of Virginia P, 2003.

Katz, Wendy R. "Stevenson, Conrad and the Idea of the Gentleman: Long John Silver and Gentleman Brown." *Journal of Stevenson Studies* 3(2006): 51–68.

Lee, Ying S. *Masculinity and the English Working Class.* New York: Routledge, 2007.

Maixner, Paul. *Robert Louis Stevenson: The Critical Heritage.* New York: Routledge, 1996.

Moore, Grace. "Something to Hyde: The 'Strange Preference' of Henry Jekyll." *Victorian Crime, Madness and Sensation.* Ed. Andrew Maunder and Grace Moore. Aldershot: Ashgate Publishing, 2004.

Newman, J. H. *The Idea of a University.* Ed. I. T. Kerr. Oxford: Clarendon P, 1976.

Shannon, Brent. *The Cut of his Coat: Men, Dress, and Consumer Culture in Britain, 1860–1914.* Athens, OH: Ohio UP, 2006.

Stevenson, Robert Louis. "The Character of Dogs." *The Travels and Essays of Robert Louis Stevenson.* Vol. 13. New York: Scribner's, 1918. 293–305.

———. "Gentlemen." *The Travels and Essays of Robert Louis Stevenson.* Vol. 14. New York: Scribner's, 1918. 346–60.

———. "The Philosophy of Umbrellas." *Letters and Miscellanies of Robert Louis Stevenson.* Vol. 22. New York: Scribner's, 1918. 46–51.

———. *Strange Case of Dr. Jekyll and Mr. Hyde.* Edinburgh: Edinburgh UP, 2004.

———. "Talk and Talkers." *The Travels and Essays of Robert Louis Stevenson.* Vol. 13. New York: Scribner's, 1918. 265–79.

———. "Truth of Intercourse." *The Travels and Essays of Robert Louis Stevenson.* Vol. 13. New York: Scribner's, 1918. 40–50.

STEPHEN D. ARATA

The Sedulous Ape: Atavism, Professionalism, and Stevenson's *Jekyll and Hyde*†

In an early review of *The Strange Case of Dr. Jekyll and Mr. Hyde* (1886), Andrew Lang noted the most striking feature of Robert Louis Stevenson's tale. "His heroes (surely *this* is original) are all

† From *Criticism* 37.2 (1995): 233–244. Reprinted in *Fictions of Loss in the Victorian Fin de Siècle: Identity and Empire* (Cambridge: Cambridge UP, 1996), pp. 33–43. Copyright © 1995 Wayne State University Press. Reprinted by permission of the publisher. Notes are by the author except where indicated. Some notes have been omitted or expanded to include full bibliographic information.

successful middle-aged professional men," he wrote.[1] Indeed, one could hardly miss the novel's foregrounding of the stature enjoyed by "Henry Jekyll, M.D., D.C.L., LL.D., F.R.S., etc."[2] In Lang's view this interest in professional men defined Stevenson's novel at least as much as its portrayal of the grotesque Edward Hyde. If *Jekyll and Hyde* articulates in Gothic fiction's exaggerated tones late-Victorian anxieties concerning degeneration, devolution, and "criminal man," it invariably situates those concerns in relation to the practices and discourses of lawyers like Gabriel Utterson, doctors like Henry Jekyll and Hastie Lanyon, or even "well-known men about town" (29) like Richard Enfield. The novel in fact asks us to do more than simply register the all-too-apparent marks of Edward Hyde's "degeneracy." It compels us also to examine how those marks come to signify in the first place. As Stevenson understood, one thing professional men tend to be good at is close reading. Another is seeing to it that their interpretations have consequences in the real world. *Jekyll and Hyde* proves to be an uncannily self-conscious exploration of the relation between professional interpretation and the construction of criminal deviance. * * *

In Edward Hyde, Stevenson's first readers could easily discern the lineaments of Cesare Lombroso's[3] atavistic criminal. Lombroso, in one of degeneration theory's defining moments, had "discovered" that criminals were throwbacks to humanity's savage past. While contemplating the skull of the notorious Italian bandit Vilella, Lombroso suddenly saw history open up before him, illumined as if by lightning.

> This was not merely an idea [he wrote later], but a revelation. At the sight of that skull, I seemed to see all of a sudden, lighted up as a vast plain under a flaming sky, the problem of the nature of the criminal—an atavistic being who reproduces in his person the ferocious instincts of primitive humanity and the inferior animals.[4]

"Thus were explained anatomically," Lombroso continues, such diverse attributes as the "enormous jaws, high cheek bones, prominent

---

1. See Paul Maixner, ed., *Robert Louis Stevenson: The Critical Heritage* (London: Routledge & Kegan Paul, 1981), 200–201.
2. Robert Louis Stevenson, *The Strange Case of Dr. Jekyll and Mr. Hyde* (1886; reprint, Harmondsworth: Penguin, 1979), 35. Further references to this novel are given parenthetically in the text.
3. Italian criminologist and physician who believed that criminality was inherited and could be detected in the features of the individual [*Editor*].
4. *Criminal Man According to the Classification of Cesare Lombroso*, briefly summarized by his daughter Gina Lombroso Ferrero, with an introduction by Cesare Lombroso (New York and London: G. P. Putnam's Sons, 1911), xiv. The quotations in the next paragraph can be found on xiv–xv.

superciliary arches, solitary lines in the palms, extreme size of the orbits, [and] handle-shaped ears" of the criminal, as well as various moral deformities like the propensity for "excessive idleness, love of orgies, and the irresponsible craving of evil for its own sake." These features were all signs of a form of primitive existence which normal men and women had transcended but which the criminal was condemned to relive. In his physiognomy as in his psyche, the criminal bore the traces of humanity's history and development.

From the first publication of Stevenson's novel, readers have noted the similarities between Lombroso's criminal and the atavistic Mr. Hyde. Less often noted is how snugly descriptions of criminal deviance fit with longstanding discourses of class in Great Britain. Lombroso's work first reached a wide audience in England thanks to Havelock Ellis's *The Criminal* (1891); the combined influence of Ellis and Lombroso was in part due to the ease with which the new "scientific" categories mapped onto older, more familiar accounts of the urban poor from Mayhew[5] onward. Lombroso's theory was in part a discourse on class, and much of its "legitimacy" derived from the way it reproduced the class ideologies of the bourgeoisie. Equating the criminal with atavism, and both with the lower classes, was a familiar gesture by the 1880s, as was the claim that deviance expressed itself most markedly through physical deformity. Stevenson's middle-class readers would have had as little trouble deciphering the features of the "abnormal and misbegotten" Hyde, his "body an imprint of deformity and decay," as Stevenson's middle-class characters do (78, 84). "God bless me," exclaims Utterson, "the man seems hardly human. Something troglodytic, shall we say? . . . or is it the mere radiance of a foul soul that thus transpires through, and transfigures, its clay continent?" (40). Utterson's remark, moreover, nicely demonstrates how old and new paradigms can overlap. He at once draws on familiar Christian imagery—Hyde's foul soul transfiguring its clay continent—and a Lombrosan vocabulary of atavism, with Hyde-as-troglodyte reproducing in his person the infancy of the human species.

In considering degenerationism as a class discourse, however, we need to look up as well as down. Late-Victorian pathologists routinely argued that degeneration was as endemic to a decadent aristocracy as to a troglodytic proletariat. And, indeed, Hyde can be read as a figure of leisured dissipation. While his impulsiveness and savagery, his violent temper, and his appearance all mark Hyde as lower-class and atavistic, his vices are clearly those of a monied gentleman.

---

5. Henry Mayhew (1812–1887), journalist and social researcher who wrote about the poor in London and published the influential three-volume work *London Labour and the London Poor* (1851) [*Editor*].

This aspect of Hyde's portrayal has gone largely unnoticed by later critics, but for Stevenson's contemporaries the conflation of upper and lower classes into a single figure of degeneracy would not have seemed unusual. Lombroso's criminal may have been primitive in appearance, but his moral shortcomings—"excessive idleness, love of orgies, the irresponsible craving of evil"—make him a companion of Jean Floressas des Esseintes and Dorian Gray,[6] not Vilella. In his highly influential *Degeneration* (1895), Max Nordau took pains to insist that the degenerate population "consists chiefly of rich educated people" who, with too much time and means at their disposal, succumb to decadence and depravity.[7]

Lombroso and Nordau have in mind not only the titled aristocracy but also a stratum of cultured aesthetes considered dangerously subversive of conventional morality. That Stevenson meant us to place Hyde among their number is suggested by the description of his surprisingly well-appointed Soho rooms, "furnished with luxury and good taste" (49). Hyde's palate for wine is discriminating, his plate is of silver, his "napery elegant." Art adorns his walls, while carpets "of many plies and aggreeable in colour" cover his floors. This is not a savage's den but the retreat of a cultivated gentleman. Utterson supposes that Jekyll bought the art for Hyde (49), but Stevenson in a letter went out of his way to say that the lawyer is mistaken. The purchases were Hyde's alone.[8]

In Edward Hyde, then, Stevenson created a figure who embodies a bourgeois readership's worst fears about both a marauding and immoral underclass and a dissipated and immoral leisure class. Yet Stevenson also shows how such figures are not so much "recognized" as created by middle-class discourse. He does this by foregrounding the interpretive acts by means of which his characters situate and define Hyde. Despite the confident assertions of the novel's professional men that Hyde is "degenerate," his "stigmata" turn out to be troublingly difficult to specify. In fact, no one can accurately describe him. "He must be deformed somewhere," asserts Enfield. "He gives a strong feeling of deformity, though I couldn't specify the point. He's an extraordinary-looking man, and yet I really can name nothing out of the way. No, sir . . . I can't describe him" (34). Enfield's puzzled response finds its counterparts

6. Jean Floressas des Esseintes, main character in French writer Joris-Karl Huysmans's *À rebours* (1884), a wealthy, noble art collector who lives a decadent lifestyle. Dorian Gray, principal character in Oscar Wilde's novella *The Picture of Dorian Gray* (1890), a rich young man, also a collector of rare objects, who commits crimes [*Editor*].

7. Max Nordau, *Degeneration* (New York: D. Appleton, 1895), 7.

8. See Stevenson's letter of 1 March 1886 to F. W. H. Myers in *The Letters of Robert Louis Stevenson*, 4 vols., ed. Sidney Colvin (New York: Charles Scribner's Sons, 1911), 3:326: "About the picture, I rather meant that Hyde had bought it himself; and Utterson's hypothesis of the gift an error."

in the nearly identical statements of Utterson (40), Poole (68), and Lanyon (77–78). In Utterson's dream Hyde "had no face, or one that baffled him and melted before his eyes" (36–37). "The few who could describe him differed widely," agreeing only that some "unexpressed deformity" lurked in his countenance (50). That last, nearly oxymoronic formulation—unexpressed deformity—nicely captures the troubled relation between the "text" of Hyde's body and the interpretive practices used to decipher it. Hyde's stigmata are everywhere asserted and nowhere named. In this way Stevenson underscores how the act of interpretation is grounded less in empirical data (the shape of Hyde's face, the hue of his skin) than in the categories brought to bear upon him. The novel continually turns the question of Hyde back on his interlocutors so that their interpretive procedures become the object of our attention. "There is my explanation," Utterson claims. "It is plain and natural, hangs well together and delivers us from all exorbitant alarms" (66). It is also, we are immediately given to understand, wrong, though its delusions differ only in degree from other "plain and natural" explanations brought forward in the tale.

Indeed, what makes *Jekyll and Hyde* compelling is the way it turns the class discourses of atavism and criminality back on the bourgeoisie itself. As Lang recognized, Stevenson's novel is finally more concerned with its middle-class professional "heroes" than it is with the figure of Edward Hyde. Among the story's first readers, F. W. H. Myers felt this aspect acutely, and it prompted him to protest in a remarkable series of letters to Stevenson. Since the letters suggest that Hyde can be read as a figure not of degenerate depravity but of bourgeois "virtue," they are worth pausing over.[9]

Shortly after its publication Myers wrote to Stevenson, whom he did not know, enthusiastically praising *Jekyll and Hyde* but suggesting that certain minor revisions would improve the novel. After noting some infelicities of phrasing and gaps in plotting, Myers came to what he considered the story's "weakest point," the murder of Sir Danvers Carew. Hyde's mauling of Carew's "unresisting body" offended the decorous Myers ("no, not an elderly MP's!"), but his primary objection was that such an act was untrue to Hyde's nature. Because "Jekyll was thoroughly civilized . . . his degeneration must needs take certain lines only." Hyde should be portrayed as "not a generalized but a specialized fiend," whose cruelty would never take the form Stevenson gave it. At most "Hyde would, I think, have brushed the baronet aside with a curse."

---

9. Myers wrote four letters to Stevenson on the subject of *Jekyll and Hyde* (21 February, 28 February, and 17 March 1886, and 17 April 1887), which are reprinted in *Critical Heritage*, 213–22. [See also Stevenson's letter to Myers of July 14, 1892, excerpted on pp. 84–86 above—*Editor.*]

Stevenson's reply was polite, passing over the bulk of Myers's suggestions in silence. He did pause to correct him on one subject,
though, that of a painting in Hyde's lodgings. Myers had questioned
whether the doctor would have acquired artwork for his alter ego.
Stevenson answered that Hyde purchased the painting, not Jekyll.
Myers's response was disproportionately vehement. "Would Hyde
have bought a picture? I think—and friends of weight support my
view—that such an act would have been altogether unworthy of
him." Unworthy? Myers and his weighty friends appear to feel that
Hyde's character is being impugned, that his good name must be
defended against some implied insult. Asking "what are the motives
which would prompt a person in [Hyde's] situation" to buy artwork,
Myers suggests three, none of which, he argues, applies to Hyde's
case.

> 1. There are jaded voluptuaries who seek in a special class
> of art a substitute or reinforcement for the default of primary
> stimuli. Mr. Hyde's whole career forbids us to insult him by
> classing him with these men.
> 2. There are those who wish for elegant surroundings to
> allure or overawe the minds of certain persons unaccustomed to
> luxury or splendour. But does not all we know of Hyde teach us
> that he disdained those modes of adventitious attractions? . . .
> 3. There are those, again, who surround their more concen-
> trated enjoyments with a halo of mixed estheticism. . . . Such,
> no doubt, was Dr. Jekyll; such, no doubt, he *expected* that
> Mr. Hyde would be. But was he not deceived? Was there not
> something unlooked for, something Napoleonic, in Hyde's way
> of pushing aside the aesthetic as well as the moral superfluities
> of life? . . . We do not imagine the young Napoleon as going to
> concerts or taking a walk in a garden. . . . I cannot fancy Hyde
> looking in at picture shops. I cannot think he ever left his
> rooms, except on business.

This is a most unfamiliar Hyde! On the evidence of Myers's letter
we would have to pronounce him an upstanding citizen. Myers
clearly perceives how easily Stevenson's Hyde could be taken not
for a brute but for a dandy. At no point is Myers worried that Hyde
might be considered atavistic. Instead, he is concerned that Hyde's
reputation not be smeared by association with "jaded voluptuaries"
and aesthetes. In attempting to clear him of such charges, Myers
presents Jekyll's alter ego as the very image of bourgeois sobriety
and industry, manfully disdainful of the shop window, the art gal-
lery, the concert hall—of anything that might savor of the aesthetic
or the frivolous. Myers praises Hyde's simplicity of dress: he's not a
fop but a "man aiming only at simple convenience, direct sufficiency."

Unconcerned with personal adornment, he is "not anxious to present himself as personally attractive, but [relies] frankly on the cash nexus, and on that decision of character that would startle" those less forceful than himself.

We might dismiss Myers's reading as eccentric, especially given the absence of any irony in his references to Hyde's "business," freedom from personal vanity, or reliance on the cash nexus * * * Yet Myers's admittedly exaggerated response illuminates an important aspect of Stevenson's novel. Edward Hyde may not be an image of the *upright* bourgeois male, but he is decidedly an image of the bourgeois male. While Hyde can be read as the embodiment of the degenerate prole, the decadent aristocrat, or the dissipated aesthete, it is also the case that his violence is largely directed *at* those same classes. * * * That Hyde shares Myers's disdain for aesthetes is made plainer in Stevenson's manuscript draft of the novel. There, Hyde murders not Sir Danvers but a character who appears to be a caricature of the aesthetic stereotype, the "anoemically pale" Mr. Lemsome. Constantly "shielding a pair of suffering eyes under blue spectacles," Lemsome is considered by the respectable Utterson as both "a bad fellow" and "an incurable cad." The substitution of Carew for Lemsome suggests that the two characters were connected in Stevenson's mind, just as for Nordau aesthetes like Oscar Wilde are grouped with troubling aristocrats like Lord Byron[1] as disruptive of middle-class mores.

Mr. Hyde thus acts not just as a magnet for middle-class fears of various "Others" but also as an agent of vengeance. He is the scourge of (a bourgeois) God, punishing those who threaten patriarchal code and custom. Indeed, the noun used most often in the story to describe Hyde is not "monster" or "villain" but—"gentleman." This novel portrays a world peopled almost exclusively by middle-class professional men, yet instead of attacking Hyde, these gentlemen more often close ranks around him. Enfield's "Story of the Door," though it begins with Hyde trampling a little girl until she is left "screaming on the ground" (31), concludes with Enfield, the doctor, and the girl's father breakfasting with Hyde in his chambers (32). Recognizing him as one of their own, the men literally encircle Hyde to protect him from harm. "And all the time . . . we were keeping the women off him as best we could, for they were as wild as harpies. I never saw a circle of such hateful faces; and there was the man in the middle, . . . frightened too, I could see that" (32). The homosocial bonding that occurs in this scene is only intensified by its overt misogyny. Though both he and the doctor profess to feel a profound loathing for Hyde, Enfield refers to him with the

---

1. British Romantic poet who was known for his adulterous affairs [*Editor*].

politeness due a social equal, consistently calling him "my gentle-man" or "my man." Indeed, Enfield derives vicarious pleasure from watching Hyde maul the girl. Though he could easily have pre-vented their collision, Enfield allows them to run into one another "naturally enough" (31). Neglecting to intervene until Hyde has fin-ished his assault, Enfield describes the incident with some relish, nonchalantly admitting to Utterson that the beating "sounds noth-ing to hear" (31). (Though he goes on to say that it "was hellish to see," that does not unring the bell.) That Hyde acts out the aggres-sions of timid bourgeois gentlemen is emphasized once again in the beating of Sir Danvers. That gesture of "insensate cruelty" is per-formed with a cane "of some rare and very tough and heavy wood" (47), which was originally in the possession of Gabriel Utterson. The stick breaks in two, and Stevenson takes care to let us know that both halves make their way back into the lawyer's hands after the murder (47, 49).

It is Edward Hyde's covert affinities with professional men that prompted Myers to describe him as a kind of bourgeois Napoleon. Myers recognized that Stevenson had created a figure whose rage is the rage of a threatened patriarchy. It is only a seeming paradox to say that Hyde is most like himself when he behaves like a gentle-man. Yet to leave matters here would do an injustice to the com-plexity of Stevenson's vision, an injustice Myers himself is guilty of. While *Jekyll and Hyde* is a compelling expression of middle-class anger directed at various forms of the Other, the novel also turns that anger back on the burgesses themselves, Stevenson included.

It does this in part by taking as one of its themes the education of a gentleman, in this case Mr. Hyde. Most critical accounts of the novel have with good reason focussed on the social and psychologi-cal pressures that lead Jekyll to become Hyde. Yet Stevenson is also concerned with the reverse transformation. That is, the novel details the pressures which move Hyde closer to Jekyll. It is one thing to say that Hyde "acts out" the aggressive fantasies of repressed Victorian men, another altogether to say that he comes eventually to embody the very repressions Jekyll struggles to throw off. Yet this is in fact a prime source of horror in the tale: not that the professional man is transformed into an atavistic criminal, but that the atavist learns to pass as a gentleman. Hyde unquestionably develops over the course of the novel, which is to say he becomes more like the "respectable" Jekyll, which in turn is to say he "degenerates." Degeneration becomes a function not of lower-class depravity or aristocratic dis-sipation but of middle-class "virtue."

Needless to say, then, Mr. Hyde's education into gentlemanliness exacts a considerable cost. The Hyde who ends his life weeping and crying for mercy (69) is not the same man whose original "raging energies" and "love of life" Jekyll found "wonderful" (95–96). By the time he is confined to the doctor's laboratory, Hyde is no longer Jekyll's opposite but his mirror image. Where earlier the transitions between Jekyll and Hyde were clean and sharp (and painful), later the two personalities develop a mutual fluidity. By the end the doctor's body metamorphoses continually from Jekyll to Hyde and back again, as if to indicate that we need no longer distinguish between them.

How does one become a gentleman? If born into a good family, by imitating one's father. That Jekyll and Hyde stand in a father-son relationship is suggested by Jekyll himself (89) as well as by Utterson (37, 41–42), who suspects that Hyde is the doctor's illegitimate offspring. After "gentleman," the words used most often to describe Hyde are "little" and "young." As William Veeder notes, when Hyde appears at Lanyon's door ludicrously engulfed in Jekyll's oversized clothes we are likely to be reminded of a little boy dressing up as daddy.[2] The idea that Hyde is being groomed, as Utterson says, "to step into the said Henry Jekyll's shoes" (35) is reinforced by the doctor's will naming him sole heir, as well as by the lawyer's description of this "small gentleman" (46) as Jekyll's "*protege*" (37). Indeed, when Jekyll assures Utterson that "I do sincerely take a great, a very great interest in that young man" (44) he sounds like a mentor sheltering a promising disciple. "Bear with him," he urges the lawyer, "and get his rights for him. I think you would, if you knew all" (44).

If Hyde is to assume his mentor-father's position, he must be indoctrinated in the codes of his class. As Jekyll repeatedly insists, Hyde indulges no vices that Jekyll himself did not enjoy. What differs is the manner in which they enjoy them: Hyde openly and vulgarly, Jekyll discretely and with an eye to maintaining his good name. Gentlemen may sin so long as appearances are preserved. This is the lesson Hyde learns from his encounter with Enfield. Having collared Hyde after his trampling of the little girl, Enfield and the doctor are "sick . . . with the desire to kill him" (thus replicating Hyde's own homicidal rage), but "killing being out of the question" they do "the next best": they threaten to "make such a scandal . . . as should make his name stink" (31–32). They extort money as the price of their silence, in the process teaching Hyde the value of a good reputation. "No gentleman but wishes to avoid a scene," Hyde acknowledges. "Name your figure" (32). When Enfield winds up his narration of this incident by telling Utterson that "my man was a fellow that nobody could have to do with" (33) he seems

2. William Veeder, "Children of the Night: Stevenson and Patriarchy," *Dr. Jekyll and Mr. Hyde After One Hundred Years*, ed. William Veeder and Gordon Hirsch (Chicago: U of Chicago P, 1988), p. 126 [*Editor*].

to be describing not a violent criminal but a man who cannot be trusted to respect club rules. Enfield underscores this point when he says that, in contrast to Hyde, Jekyll "is the very pink of the proprieties" (33).

A commitment to protecting the good names of oneself and one's colleagues binds professional men together. Utterson, remarkably unconcerned with the fates of Hyde's victims, directs all his energies toward shielding Jekyll from "the cancer of some concealed disgrace" (41). Sir Danvers' death awakens fears that the doctor's "good name . . . [will] be sucked down in the eddy of the scandal" (53). After the murder Jekyll himself admits, "I was thinking of my own character, which this hateful business has rather exposed" (52). As Enfield's actions indicate, blackmail is an acceptable way to prevent such exposure. Utterson mistakenly believes that Hyde is blackmailing Jekyll, but rather than going to the police he hits on the happier and more gentlemanly idea of blackmailing Hyde in turn (42). By far the most potent weapon these men possess, however, is silence. Closing ranks, they protect their own by stifling the spread not of crime or sin but of indecorous talk. "Here is another lesson to say nothing" (34). "Let us make a bargain never to refer to this again" (34). "This is a private matter, and I beg of you to let it sleep" (44). "I wouldn't speak of this" (55). "I cannot tell you" (57). "You can do but one thing . . . and that is to respect my silence" (58). "I daren't say, sir" (63). "I would say nothing of this" (73). In turn, the commitment to silence ultimately extends to self-censorship, a pledge not to know. Respectable men like Utterson and Enfield invert the Biblical injunction to seek a truth that will set them free. For them, a careful ignorance works better. Utterson's motto—"I let my brother go to the devil in his own way" (29)—finds its counterpart in Enfield's unvarying rule of thumb: "The more it looks like Queer Street, the less I ask" (33). ("A very good rule, too," Utterson agrees.) Enfield explicitly equates knowledge with scandal when he says that asking a question is like rolling a stone down a hill: "presently some bland old bird . . . is knocked on the head . . . and the family have to change their name" (33). Knowledge's harm is suffered most acutely by Dr. Lanyon, whose Christian name of Hastie nicely indicates his fatal character flaw. Warned by Hyde that it is always wiser not to know, Lanyon nevertheless succumbs to that "greed of curiosity" (79) which leads directly deathward.

By means of Mr. Hyde, Jekyll seeks of course to slough off these same burdens of respectability, reticence, decorum, self-censorship— of gentlemanliness—and "spring headlong into the sea of liberty" (86). In tracing the arc of Hyde's brief career, however, Stevenson shows how quickly he becomes simply one of the boys. Over the last half of the novel Stevenson links Hyde, through a series of verbal echoes and structural rhymes, to various bourgeois "virtues" and practices. Not only do we discover Hyde beginning to exercise remarkable self-control—that most middle-class of virtues and seemingly the furthest from his nature—but we hear him speaking confidently in Jekyll's tones to Lanyon concerning the benefits of science and the sanctity of "the seal of *our* profession" (80; my emphasis).

The kind of structural rhyming I refer to is most noticeable during Hyde's death-scene, when Utterson and Poole, having violently burst in the door of the rooms above Jekyll's laboratory, are startled by what they find.

> The besiegers, appalled by their own riot and the stillness that had succeeded, stood back a little and peered in. There lay the cabinet before their eyes in the quiet lamplight, a good fire glowing and chattering on the hearth, the kettle singing its strain, a drawer or two open, papers neatly set forth on the business table, and nearer the fire, the things laid out for tea; the quietest room, you would have said, and except for the glazed presses full of chemicals, the most commonplace that night in London. (69–70)

We are apt to share their bewilderment at first, since this is the last tableau we might expect Stevenson to offer us at this juncture in the story. Yet it has been carefully prepared for. The novel is full of similar domestic tableaux, invariably occupied by solitary gentlemen. When they are not walking or dining, it seems, these men sit at their hearths, usually alone. It is Utterson's "custom of a Sunday . . . to sit close by the fire, a volume of some dry divinity on his reading-desk" (35). When the lawyer visits Lanyon, he finds the doctor sitting alone over his wine after dinner (36). Later he finds Jekyll in nearly the same position (51). Utterson shares a friendly fireside bottle of wine with Mr. Guest, though their conversation leaves him singularly unhappy (54–55). It is one of Stevenson's triumphs that he transforms the hearth—that too-familiar image of cozy Victorian domesticity—into a symbol of these men's isolation and repression. In turn, the most notable thing about the scene Utterson and Poole stumble upon is that it is empty of life. The lamplight soothes, the kettle sings, the chairs beckon—but no one is home. Recognizing this, we recognize too the stubtle irony of calling it "the most commonplace" sight to be seen in London. The outward forms remain in place, but the indwelling spirit has fled.

We next discover that the lifeless Hyde's "contorted and still twitching" body lay "right in the midst" of this scene (70). On the one hand, it is a fit setting for Hyde's last agony and suicide. The terrors suffered by Hyde during his final days arise in part from his surroundings: the very symbols of bourgeois respectability that he exists to repudiate do him in. On the other hand, he seems to feel bizarrely at home in these surroundings. If for instance we ask who set the table for tea on this final night, the answer has to be Hyde and not Jekyll, since Utterson and Poole, prior to breaking in the door, agree that they have heard only Hyde's voice and Hyde's "patient" footsteps from within the room that evening (69). (Poole insists that his master "was made away with eight days ago" [65].) Beside the tea things is "a copy of a pious work for which Jekyll had . . . expressed a great esteem, annotated, in his own hand, with startling blasphemies" (71). Generations of readers have assumed that Hyde is responsible for those annotations, but that is not what the sentence says. These are not fussy or pedantic quibbles, but rather indicate how carefully Stevenson has blurred the boundary between the two identities. It is Jekyll who is now blasphemous and who violently berates the man at Maw's (66) Hyde who sets a quiet tea table and cries to heaven for mercy. On adjacent tables Utterson and Poole discover two cups, one containing the white salt used in Jekyll's potion, the other containing the white sugar used in Hyde's tea (71). Both are magic elixirs: the first transforms a gentleman into a savage while the second performs the reverse operation. Having found his place by the hearth, Mr. Hyde also knows what posture to assume: "Thenceforward, he sat all day over the fire in the private room, gnawing his nails; there he dined, sitting alone with his fears" (94). If this sounds more like Utterson or Lanyon than the Hyde we first met, it is meant to. Bitter, lonely, frightened, nervous, chewing his nails (we recall that Utterson bites his finger when agitated [65]), and contemplating violence; Edward Hyde is now a gentleman.

The Strange Case of Dr. Jekyll and Mr. Hyde is an angry book, its venom directed against what Stevenson contemptuously referred to as that "fatuous rabble of burgesses called the public."[3] The novel turns the discourses centering on degeneration, atavism, and criminality back on the professional classes that produced them, linking gentlemanliness and bourgeois virtue to various forms of depravity. At the same time the novel plumbs deep pools of patriarchal anxiety about its continued viability. Indeed, *Jekyll and Hyde* can be read as a meditation on the pathology of late-Victorian masculinity. Jekyll's case is "strange," Stevenson suggests, only in the sense that it is so common among men of the doctor's standing and beliefs.

* * *

3. Letter to Edmund Gosse dated January 2, 1886, *The Letters of Robert Louis Stevenson*, ed. Bradford A. Booth and Ernest Mehew (New Haven: Yale UP, 1995), vol. 2, p. 313 [*Editor*].

Robert Louis Stevenson:
A Chronology

1850	Born November 13 in Edinburgh, Scotland, the only child of Thomas Stevenson, member of a famous family of lighthouse and civil engineers, and Margaret Isabella Balfour, daughter of a Church of Scotland (Presbyterian) minister.
1852–67	An imaginative, affectionate, high-strung child who suffers frequent illness. His parents engage as a nurse Alison Cunningham, to whom RLS will later dedicate *A Child's Garden of Verses*. RLS is educated at various private schools, Edinburgh Academy, and by private tutors.
1867	Enrolls at Edinburgh University to study engineering. Through what he later called "an extensive and highly rational system of truancy," RLS reads widely and pursues his chosen task of learning to write.
1871	In April tells his father that he has no interest in engineering and cares for nothing but literature. As a compromise agrees to study law. Builds a circle of close friends. His chief intimate and confidant is his cousin Bob Stevenson. A period of bohemianism in the pubs and brothels of Edinburgh. Continues to write, mostly essays, literary sketches, and stories.
1873	Bitter conflict with his father over religion. A turning point is his meeting with Sidney Colvin (then newly appointed Slade Professor of Fine Art at Cambridge and later Keeper of Prints and Drawings at the British Museum) and Colvin's friend Mrs. Frances Sitwell. Colvin becomes a mentor and lifelong friend. RLS falls in love with Mrs. Sitwell and for the next two years she becomes, through his long diary-letters, his adored confidante. Colvin and Mrs. Sitwell both encourage RLS's ambition to become a writer. Suffering from nervous exhaustion and threatened lung trouble RLS

spends the winter of 1873–74 at Menton in the south of France.

1874   Resumes legal studies. Through Colvin's influence his essays begin to be published in leading literary magazines.

1875   Becomes friends with William Ernest Henley, poet and journalist. Pays first visits to the artists' colonies in the Forest of Fontainebleau, France, frequented by his cousin Bob Stevenson, and for next three years spends much time at Barbizon and Grez, as well as in Paris. In July 1875 passes final examination and is admitted to the Scottish Bar. After four routine appearances in court, RLS abandons the pretense of law altogether and returns to writing.

1876   With friend Walter Simpson, takes a canoe trip in Belgium and France. In September at Grez meets and falls in love with his future wife, Fanny Osbourne, an American woman ten years his senior, estranged from her husband but not yet divorced. She is in France with her two surviving children to study art. Isobel (known as Belle) is eighteen; Samuel Lloyd (known then as Sam, later as Lloyd) is eight.

1877   In January joins Fanny in Paris and spends much of the next eighteen months with her and her children in Paris and Grez. Closely involved with Henley in short-lived magazine, *London*. RLS's first published short story appears there anonymously. Other stories soon follow, published in established journals and under his own name.

1878   Fanny and her children return to America in August. RLS goes to France for the walking tour described in *Travels with a Donkey in the Cévennes* (1879). Collaborates with W. E. Henley on a play RLS had first worked on at the age of fourteen about the eighteenth-century Edinburgh figure Deacon Brodie, master craftsman by day and burglar by night. (The play, printed in 1880 as *Deacon Brodie, or, The Double Life*, was produced several times during the 1880s but achieved no commercial success.) First book published: *An Inland Voyage*, an account of the 1876 canoe trip with Simpson. Publication in December (following serial publication earlier in the year) of *Edinburgh: Picturesque Notes*.

1879   In August, in response to a telegram from Fanny, without consulting his parents and in spite of efforts by friends to dissuade him, RLS travels by emigrant ship to New York and by train across America to join her in Monterey, California. Determined to live from his own resources, he badly strains his health as a result of the hardships of the journey and his dearth of funds. Fanny returns home to Oakland and in December obtains an uncontested divorce.

1880   In San Francisco, RLS has a complete physical breakdown and comes very near death following the first of the lung hemorrhages that were to plague him the rest of his life. Fanny nurses him devotedly and they are married in San Francisco in May. RLS and Fanny spend their honeymoon in a bunkhouse at an abandoned silver mining camp on Mount Saint Helena, overlooking the Napa Valley, California. In August, RLS returns to Scotland with his wife and twelve-year-old stepson Lloyd Osbourne. *The Amateur Emigrant,* describing his journey to America, is withdrawn from publication, RLS and his father agreeing that it is too personal and not his best work. (The first part, an account of the voyage, was posthumously published in 1895; the second part, the train journey, appeared in *Longman's Magazine* as "Across the Plains" in 1883.)

1880–82   With RLS suffering from chronic lung disease and at risk of hermorrhages, he and Fanny for two years alternate summers in the Highlands of Scotland with winters in Davos, Switzerland, then favored for treatment of respiratory complaints. RLS becomes friends at Davos with Renaissance historian and man of letters J. A. Symonds. *Treasure Island,* begun as an amusement for Stevenson's stepson, is published serially in *Young Folks* magazine starting in October 1881. (Its real fame was to begin with its publication in book form in 1883.) Publication in 1881 of *Virginibus Puerisque,* a collection of early essays most of which had appeared in the *Cornhill Magazine* and elsewhere from 1876 onwards. Publication in 1882 of *Familiar Studies of Men and Books* (previously published essays on such figures as Victor Hugo, Robert Burns, Walt Whitman, and John Knox) and *New Arabian Nights* (previously published tales, including "The Suicide Club," "The Rajah's Diamond," "Pavilion on the Links," and "Providence and the Guitar").

1882–84   In a further vain search for health RLS and Fanny spend nearly two years in the south of France, most of it at the winter health resort of Hyères, near Marseilles, later recalled by RLS as the happiest period of his life. He works on new essays, stories, and a novel to be titled *Prince Otto*. *The Silverado Squatters* (based on the journal kept during his honeymoon) is published serially in 1883 and in book form in January 1884. In early 1884, his health takes a particularly bad turn, culminating in a severe hemorrhage in May.

1884   RLS and Fanny move to Bournemouth, on the south coast of England. There over the next three years RLS was to live the life of an invalid, plagued by colds and hemorrhages and often confined to bed. Nevertheless he maintains productivity. Between July and December 1884, collaborates with W. E. Henley on several new plays, publishes "A Humble Remonstrance" in response to Henry James's "The Art of Fiction," and writes "Markheim" to fulfill a commission to the *Pall Mall Gazette* (though he ultimately submits "The Body Snatcher" instead).

1885   Publication in March of *A Child's Garden of Verses*. Publication in April of *More New Arabian Nights: The Dynamiter*, tales co-authored with Fanny. Also in April, RLS and Fanny move into the house in Bournemouth bought as a wedding present for Fanny by Stevenson's father; they give it the name "Skerryvore" in honor of the Scottish lighthouse built by an uncle of Stevenson's. Henry James becomes a frequent visitor and close friend. In August, John Singer Sargent paints the more famous of his two extant portraits of Stevenson: the thin, stalking figure by the open door at Skerryvore. In late September or early October, RLS has the dream that led to the writing of *Strange Case of Dr. Jekyll and Mr. Hyde*; by the end of October, he has submitted the manuscript for publication. In November *Prince Otto*, his first full-length adult novel, comes out in book form after serial publication earlier in the year.

1886   *Strange Case of Dr. Jekyll and Mr. Hyde* is published in January; by April, 16,000 copies have been sold in the United States alone; by July nearly 40,000 copies have been sold in Britain. *Kidnapped* is published that spring, first serially in *Young Folks* and then in book form.

1887   On May 8, RLS's father dies. In August, RLS travels to America with his mother, wife, and stepson. On arrival in New York City, finds himself sought after by reporters eager to interview the author of *Strange Case of*

Dr. Jekyll and Mr. Hyde. Spends the winter at Saranac Lake, New York (in the Adirondack Mountains), where Dr. J. L. Trudeau had recently established a sanitarium for tuberculosis. Over the course of this year three books are published: *The Merry Men and Other Tales* (previously published stories, including, besides the title piece, "Markheim," "Thrawn Janet," "Olalla," and "The Treasure of Franchard"); *Underwoods* (poetry); and *Memories and Portraits* (largely previously published essays, including "A Gossip on Romance" and "A Humble Remonstrance," RLS's closest approximations of an artistic credo).

1888   Works on various projects while at Saranac Lake, including twelve essays to be published monthly in *Scribner's Magazine*. They include "A Chapter on Dreams" (giving the genesis of *Strange Case of Dr. Jekyll and Mr. Hyde*) and "A Christmas Sermon" and "Pulvis et Umbra" (presenting his views on religion and ethics). In March, RLS and W. E. Henley quarrel irrevocably after Henley writes to suggest that Fanny has plagiarized a story called "The Nixie" that she has just published in *Scribner's Magazine*. RLS and Fanny decide upon a cruise in the South Seas, hoping that the tropical climate may benefit his health; they are also encouraged by a liberal offer of money from the publisher S. S. McClure for letters written during the voyage. In late June, the family party embarks from San Francisco in the chartered yacht *Casco* and visits the Marquesas and the Paumotu (or Tuamotu) Archipelago before reaching Tahiti at the end of September. RLS convalesces in Tahiti from a serious illness until the end of the year.

1889   The *Casco* cruise ends in Honolulu in January. Fanny's daughter Belle, her husband the painter Joe Strong, and young son Austin (who were living in Honolulu) join the family group. During his five months in Honolulu RLS completes his novel *The Master of Ballantrae* (begun at Saranac Lake) and it appears in book form in September, following serial publication. Also completed in Honolulu is *The Wrong Box*, a humorous story begun by Lloyd Osbourne at Saranac Lake, largely rewritten by Stevenson, and published under their joint authorship; it is the first of what is to be a series of literary collaborations between RLS and his stepson. In late June, RLS, Fanny, Lloyd, and Joe Strong (RLS's mother having returned to Scotland) set off on another cruise, on the trading schooner the *Equator*. After voyaging through the Gilbert Islands they reach Samoa in December.

1890   Because of the great improvement in his health RLS decides to settle in Samoa. In January buys an estate, which he calls Vailima, on the island of Upolu in the hills near the port town of Apia (good postal connections). Leaving the land to be cleared, he goes to Sydney. Here another serious illness forces him to abandon plans for a visit to Britain and he recuperates by a third Pacific voyage from April to August on a trading steamer, the *Janet Nicoll*. He returns to Samoa in September and he and Fanny live in a cottage while the "big house" is built.

1891   In April RLS and Fanny move into the new house. The household includes RLS's mother, his stepson Lloyd, his stepdaughter and her husband and son, and a number of Samoan servants. Stevenson is given the Samoan name "Tusitala" (Writer of Tales) and accomplishes a great deal of literary work as well as becoming interested in local politics. The collection of letters describing his voyages (copyrighted in November 1890 as *The South Seas*) is published serially in the New York *Sun*, in *Black and White* (London), and in Australian and New Zealand newspapers.

1892   Book publication of *The Wrecker*, a novel written in collaboration with Lloyd Osbourne. Publication of *A Footnote to History: Eight Years of Trouble in Samoa*.

1893   *David Balfour*, a continuation of *Kidnapped*, is published in book form in England and America; in England the title used is *Catriona*, the name of the heroine. Publication of *Island Nights' Entertainments*, consisting of three South Seas stories already published serially: "The Bottle Imp," "The Isle of Voices," and "The Beach of Falesá."

1894   On December 3, in the late afternoon, Stevenson suffers a cerebral hemorrhage. He dies that evening and the next day is buried, in keeping with his wishes, at the top of nearby Mt. Vaea. The last book published in his lifetime appeared earlier that year following serial publication: *The Ebb-Tide*, a novel sketched and partly drafted with Lloyd Osbourne, but written in final form entirely by RLS.

1895   Posthumous publication in *Longman's Magazine* of a group of fables written by RLS over a twenty-year period.

1896   Posthumous publication of the novel Stevenson was
              chiefly working on at the time of his death, under the
              title *Weir of Hermiston: An Unfinished Romance.*
              Another unfinished novel, *St. Ives,* begins serial publi-
              cation at the end of this year.

Selected Bibliography

• indicates works included or excerpted in this Norton Critical Edition.

Biography, Essays, Letters

• Balfour, Graham. *The Life of Robert Louis Stevenson*. 2 vols. Scribner's, 1901.
• Booth, Bradford A., and Ernest Mehew, eds. *The Letters of Robert Louis Stevenson*. 8 vols. Yale UP, 1994–95.
Calder, Jenni. *Robert Louis Stevenson: A Life Study*. Oxford UP, 1980.
Harman, Claire. *Myself and the Other Fellow: A Life of Robert Louis Stevenson*. Harper Collins, 2005.
McLynn, Frank. *Robert Louis Stevenson: A Biography*. Random House, 1993.
Norquay, Glenda, ed. *R. L. Stevenson on Fiction: An Anthology of Literary and Critical Essays*. Edinburgh UP, 1999.
Stevenson, Robert Louis. *The Travels and Essays of Robert Louis Stevenson*. Scribner's, 1918.
Swearingen, Roger. *The Prose Writings of Robert Louis Stevenson: A Guide*. Archon Books, 1980.

Criticism

• Arata, Stephen D. "The Sedulous Ape: Atavism, Professionalism, and Stevenson's *Jekyll and Hyde*." *Criticism* 37.2 (1995): 233–59.
Bratlinger, Patrick. *Reading Lesson: The Threat of Mass Literacy in Nineteenth-Century British Fiction*. Indiana UP, 1998.
Castricano, Jodey. "'Much Ado About Handwriting': Countersigning with the Other Hand in Stevenson's *The Strange Case of Dr. Jekyll and Mr. Hyde*." *Romanticism on the Net* 44 (2006).
Clunas, Alex. "Comely External Utterance: Reading Space in *The Strange Case of Dr. Jekyll and Mr. Hyde*." *The Journal of Narrative Technique* 24.3 (1994): 173–89.
• Danahay, Martin. "Dr. Jekyll's Two Bodies." *Nineteenth-Century Contexts* 35.1 (2013): 23–40.
Fernandez, Jean. *Victorian Servants, Class, and the Politics of Literacy*. Routledge, 2010.
Garrett, Peter K. "Cries and Voices: Reading Jekyll and Hyde." *Dr. Jekyll and Mr. Hyde After One Hundred Years*, ed. William Veeder and Gordon Hirsch. U of Chicago P, 1988. 59–72.
• Halberstam, Jack. *Skin Shows: Gothic Horror and the Technology of Monsters*. Duke UP, 1995.

Heath, Stephen. "Psychopathia Sexualis: Stevenson's Strange Case." *Critical Quarterly* 28.1–2 (1986): 93–108.

Hirsch, Gordon. "*Frankenstein,* Detective Fiction, and *Jekyll and Hyde.*" *Dr. Jekyll and Mr. Hyde After One Hundred Years.* 223–46.

Hogle, Jerrold E. "The Struggle for a Dichotomy: Abjection in Jekyll and His Interpreters." *Dr. Jekyll and Mr. Hyde After One Hundred Years.* 161–207.

Joyce, Simon. *Capital Offenses: Geographies of Class and Crime in Victorian London.* U of Virginia P, 2003.

Koestenbaum, Wayne. "The Shadow on the Bed: Dr. Jekyll, Mr. Hyde, and the Labouchère Amendment." *Critical Matrix* 4.1 (1988): 31–55.

Lawler, Donald. "Reframing *Jekyll and Hyde*: Robert Louis Stevenson and the Strange Case of Gothic Science Fiction." *Dr. Jekyll and Mr. Hyde After One Hundred Years.* 247–61.

McDonnell, Jenny. "Things at Once Spectral and Human: Robert Louis Stevenson's Ghosts." *The Ghost Story from the Middle Ages to the Twentieth Century: A Ghostly Genre,* ed. Helen Conrad O'Brian and Julie Anne Stevens. Four Courts Press, 2010. 155–71.

Mighall, Robert. *A Geography of Victorian Fiction: Mapping History's Nightmares.* Oxford UP, 1999.

Miller, Karl. *Doubles: Studies in Literary History.* Oxford UP, 1985.

Reed, Thomas L. *The Transforming Draught: Jekyll and Hyde, Robert Louis Stevenson and the Victorian Alcohol Debate.* McFarland & Co., 2006.

Reid, Julia. *Robert Louis Stevenson, Science, and the Fin de Siècle.* Palgrave, 2006.

Rosner, Mary. "'A Total Subversion of Character': Dr. Jekyll's Moral Insanity." *The Victorian Newsletter* 93 (1998): 27–31.

Sandison, Alan. *Robert Louis Stevenson and the Appearance of Modernism: A Future Feeling.* Macmillan, 1996.

• Showalter, Elaine. *Sexual Anarchy: Gender and Culture at the Fin de Siècle.* Viking, 1990.

Smith, Andrew. *Victorian Demons: Medicine, Masculinity, and the Gothic at the Fin-de-Siècle.* Manchester UP, 2004.

Stiles, Anne. *Popular Fiction and Brain Science in the Late Nineteenth Century.* Cambridge UP, 2012.

Veeder, William. "Children of the Night: Stevenson and Patriarchy." *Dr. Jekyll and Mr. Hyde After One Hundred Years.* 107–60.

———. "Collated Fractions of the Manuscript Drafts of *Strange Case of Dr. Jekyll and Mr. Hyde.*" *Dr. Jekyll and Mr. Hyde After One Hundred Years.* 14–15.

———. "The Texts in Question." *Dr. Jekyll and Mr. Hyde After One Hundred Years.* 3–13.

• Walkowitz, Judith. *City of Dreadful Delight: Narratives of Sexual Danger in Late-Victorian London.* U of Chicago P, 1992.

Wright, Daniel L. "'The Prisonhouse of My Disposition': A Study of the Psychology of Addiction in *Dr. Jekyll and Mr. Hyde.*" *Studies in the Novel* 26.3 (1994): 254–67.

Zieger, Susan. *Inventing the Addict: Drugs, Race, and Sexuality in Nineteenth-Century British and American Literature.* U of Massachusetts P, 2008.